Aiguo Lu and Manuel F. Montes (*editors*)
POVERTY, INCOME DISTRIBUTION AND WELL-BEING IN ASIA DURING THE TRANSITION

George Mavrotas and Anthony Shorrocks (*editors*)
ADVANCING DEVELOPMENT
Core Themes in Global Economics

George Mavrotas and Mark McGillivray (*editors*)
DEVELOPMENT AID
A Fresh Look

George Mavrotas (*editor*)
DOMESTIC RESOURCE MOBILIZATION AND FINANCIAL DEVELOPMENT

Mark McGillivray (*editor*)
ACHIEVING THE MILLENIUM DEVELOPMENT GOALS

Mark McGillivray (*editor*)
HUMAN WELL-BEING
Concept and Measurement

Mark McGillivray, Indranil Dutta and David Lawson (*editors*)
HEALTH INEQUALITY AND DEVELOPMENT

Mark McGillivray (*editor*)
INEQUALITY, POVERTY AND WELL-BEING

Robert J. McIntyre and Bruno Dallago (*editors*)
SMALL AND MEDIUM ENTERPRISES IN TRANSITIONAL ECONOMIES

Vladimir Mikhalev (*editor*)
INEQUALITY AND SOCIAL STRUCTURES DURING THE TRANSITION

Dennis Rodgers, Jo Beall and Ravi Kanbur (*editors*)
LATIN AMERICAN URBAN DEVELOPMENT INTO THE 21ST CENTURY
Towards a Renewed Perspective on the City

Gérard Roland (*editor*)
ECONOMICS IN TRANSITION
The Long-Run View

Studies in Development Economics and Policy
Series Standing Order ISBN 978–0333–96424–8 hardcover
Series Standing Order ISBN 978–0230–20041–8 paperback
(outside North America only)

Latin American Urban Development into the 21st Century

Towards a Renewed Perspective on the City

Edited by

Dennis Rodgers

Jo Beall

and

Ravi Kanbur

palgrave
macmillan

First published 2012 by
PALGRAVE MACMILLAN

Palgrave Macmillan in the UK is an imprint of Macmillan Publishers Limited, registered in England, company number 785998, of Houndmills, Basingstoke, Hampshire RG21 6XS.

Palgrave Macmillan in the US is a division of St Martin's Press LLC, 175 Fifth Avenue, New York, NY 10010.

Palgrave Macmillan is the global academic imprint of the above companies and has companies and representatives throughout the world.

Palgrave® and Macmillan® are registered trademarks in the United States, the United Kingdom, Europe and other countries

ISBN: 978–0–230–37154–5

This book is printed on paper suitable for recycling and made from fully managed and sustained forest sources. Logging, pulping and manufacturing processes are expected to conform to the environmental regulations of the country of origin.

A catalogue record for this book is available from the British Library.

A catalog record for this book is available from the Library of Congress.

10 9 8 7 6 5 4 3 2 1
21 20 19 18 17 16 15 14 13 12

Printed and bound in Great Britain by
CPI Antony Rowe, Chippenham and Eastbourne

Contents

List of Illustrations ix

Acknowledgements xi

Foreword by Finn Tarp xii

Notes on Contributors xiv

Part I Introduction

1 Re-thinking the Latin American City 3
Dennis Rodgers, Jo Beall, and Ravi Kanbur

Part II Reconceptualizing Urban Fragmentation

2 Urban Violence, Quality of Life, and the Future of Latin American Cities: The Dismal Record So Far and the Search for New Analytical Frameworks to Sustain the Bias towards Hope 37
Diane E. Davis

3 Cocaine Cities: Exploring the Relationship between Urban Dynamics and the Drug Trade in South America 60
Ignacio A. Navarro

4 Mobility Challenges in Santiago de Chile: Improving Diagnosis and the Need to Shift the Understanding of Urban Inequality from Fixed Enclaves to Mobile Gradients 80
Paola Jirón

5 The *Vecino* as Citizen: Neighbourhood Organizations in El Alto and the Transformation of Bolivian Citizenship 103
Helene Risør

6 Separate but Equal Democratization? Participation, Politics, and Urban Segregation in Latin America 123
Dennis Rodgers

Part III Reconnecting the City

7 Irregular Urbanization as a Catalyst for Radical Social Mobilization: The Case of the Housing Movements of São Paulo 145
Lucy Earle

8 On-Street Upgrading? Assessing the Consequences of Allocation and Regulation Policy in Santiago de Chile's *Ferias Libres* 165
Lissette Aliaga-Linares

9 Of Guns, Ideas, and Taxes: Understanding the Political Logic of Violence-Reducing Policy Innovation in Three Colombian Cities 186
Francisco Gutiérrez Sanín, María Teresa Gutiérrez, Tania Guzmán Pardo, Juan Carlos Arenas Gómez, and María Teresa Pinto

10 Public–Private Co-operation for Gas Provision in Poor Neighbourhoods of Buenos Aires: Assessing the Impact on Housing Improvements and Health 205
Cynthia Goytia, Ricardo A. Pasquini, and Pablo Sanguinetti

11 A New Way of Monitoring the Quality of Urban Life in Latin America 227
Eduardo Lora and Andrew Powell

Part IV Conclusion

12 Towards a New Research Agenda for 21st Century Latin American Urban Development 259
Dennis Rodgers, Ravi Kanbur, and Jo Beall

Index 265

Illustrations

Tables

3.1	Fixed effects regression estimates: construction permits on lagged cocaine production potential: Cochabamba, La Paz, Santa Cruz	74
8.1	Logistic regression for explaining ferias allocation	179
8.2	OLS regression coefficients for the estimated effects of segregation, local unemployment rates on the number of licensed vendors (*feriantes*) and unlicensed vendors (*coleros*)	181
10.1	Evaluation of the differences between the treatment and control groups for selected variables	215
10.2	Evaluation of the differences between the treatment and control groups for selected variables: post-treatment survey data	218
10.3	Summary of econometric results: intention-to-treat estimator	219
10.4	Summary of the results on the instrumented treatment estimator	220
11.1	Significant house and neighbourhood characteristics revealed in house prices, selected cities	234
11.2	Hedonic estimation of implicit prices for housing and neighbourhood characteristics, metropolitan area of San José de Costa Rica	236
11.3	Ranking of districts by housing and neighbourhood characteristics, using hedonic prices to construct a QoL index, Metropolitan San José, Costa Rica	238
11.4	Using hedonic prices to construct a QoL index, by neighbourhood, City of Buenos Aires	240
11.5	Overall life satisfaction regressions for the six case cities: summary of results and significant factors	244
11.6	Values of neighbourhood characteristics in selected Buenos Aires neighbourhoods	246

Figures

3.1 Potential cocaine production in South America by country, 1997–2007 62
3.2 Model of the effects of drug exports on urban land markets 69
3.3 De-trended series of cocaine production potential and construction activity: Cochabamba, La Paz, and Santa Cruz, 1998–2008 73
8.1 Number of licences and *Coleros* per *feria* according to the year of set-up, 1939–2004 176

Maps

4.1 Income distribution in Santiago 82
4.2 Location of low-income housing, 1990–2006 83
4.3 Time–space map of Bernardo's journey 87
4.4 Time–space map of Marta's journey 91
8.1 Location of ferias and supermarkets in Santiago de Chile according to the percentage of low SES households in the neighbourhoods 174

Photos

4.1 Bernardo walks to the bus terminal in the morning 88
4.2 Inside the bus in the morning 89
4.3 Bernardo on the bus in the afternoon 90
4.4 Marta and Patricia walk to school 91
4.5 Marta on the bus 92
4.6 A different Santiago: La Dehesa 93
4.7 The bus arriving back at night 93

Acknowledgements

The editors would like to thank Anne Ruohonen and Lorraine Telfer-Taivainen of UNU-WIDER for their excellent support in the preparation of this volume. They are also grateful to Gareth A. Jones, Melanie Lombard, and three anonymous reviewers for their constructive comments, as well as to the participants at the UNU-WIDER workshop 'Beyond the Tipping Point: Latin American Development in an Urban World' held in Buenos Aires, 22–24 May 2009, where many of the contributions to this volume were first presented and discussed. We are especially grateful to Beatriz Cuenya, Director of the Centro de Estudios Urbanos y Regionales (CEUR-CONICET), for hosting the workshop.

This volume is a product of the broader UNU-WIDER research project 'Development in an Urban World'. We thank both the former and current directors of UNU-WIDER, Tony Shorrocks and Finn Tarp, for supporting this research.

Dennis Rodgers, Geneva
Jo Beall, London
Ravi Kanbur, Ithaca

Foreword

The 20th century was a century of unprecedented rapid urbanization, whether considered in terms of rural–urban migration or natural urban growth. By the dawn of the 21st century, for the first time in human history, more than half of the world's population was living in urban areas, and demographic forecasts for the decades ahead estimate that by 2030, almost five billion people – out of a total world population of eight billion – will be living in towns and cities. In 2009, UNU-WIDER launched a large-scale interdisciplinary research project to try to gain a better understanding of what this urbanization will most likely mean for human development. Although the project explored the nature of the new urban reality in general, an area of particular interest was how the consequences of urbanization are different for different parts of the developing world.

This collection presents a range of studies focused on Latin America. According to UN-Habitat, Latin America is the developing world's most urbanized region, with over 75 per cent of its population residing in towns and cities at the beginning of the 21st century – a figure that it is estimated will rise to almost 85 per cent by the middle of this century. As such, Latin America, in many ways, arguably constitutes something of an 'urban laboratory'. Although many of the consequences of contemporary global urbanization are regionally specific, common trends and issues that cut across regions clearly also exist. Thus, much can be learnt from the Latin American experience. This volume presents an original collection of studies, drawn from a range of disciplines, which highlight some of the key issues regarding the changing nature of contemporary urban life in the region, and the consequences of its transformation for development more generally.

I would like to conclude by expressing my gratitude to Dennis Rodgers, Jo Beall, and Ravi Kanbur for their first-rate academic and professional skills in successfully bringing this thought-provoking volume to fruition, as well as to the contributors to this collection for providing such a stimulating set of studies.

UNU-WIDER gratefully acknowledges financial contributions to the research programme by the governments of Denmark (Royal Ministry of

Foreign Affairs), Finland (Ministry for Foreign Affairs), Sweden (Swedish International Development Cooperation Agency – Sida), and the United Kingdom (Department for International Development – DFID).

Finn Tarp
UNU-WIDER Director, Helsinki

Contributors

Lissette Aliaga-Linares is a Peruvian sociologist who graduated from the Universidad Nacional de San Marcos, Lima (2001). A PhD candidate from the Department of Sociology at the University of Texas (UT) at Austin, she specializes in demography, urbanization and migration. Aliaga-Linares has served as a consultant to various international development agencies and has participated in various Latin American comparative research projects. Her main research focus is the informal economy, a topic that she studies by combining qualitative methods with spatial and non-spatial statistical techniques.

Juan Carlos Arenas Gómez is Professor and Researcher at the Instituto de Estudios Políticos, Universidad de Antioquia. He is a sociologist and a political scientist, and is currently Co-ordinator of the MA programme in Political Science. His research interests focus on political parties and electoral processes in urban scenarios, and he has published many articles on these issues in Medellín, Colombia.

Jo Beall is Director, Education and Society, and a member of the executive board of the British Council. She was formerly Deputy Vice Chancellor at the University of Cape Town, prior to which she was Professor of Development Studies at the London School of Economics. Her work in the field of international development spans over twenty years. She has undertaken research on urban development and local governance in low- and middle-income countries and has worked extensively in Africa, Asia, and Latin America. Her most recent research has been on the role of cities in conflict and fragile situations.

Diane E. Davis is Professor of Urbanism and Development in the Program on Urban Planning and Design at Harvard University, in its Graduate School of Design. Before joining Harvard she was Professor of Political Sociology and head of the International Development Group (IDG) in the Department of Urban Studies and Planning at MIT, where she also served as Associate Dean of the School of Architecture and Planning. Davis is the author of *Discipline and Development: Middle Classes and Prosperity in East Asia and Latin America* (2004; Best Book of the Year, ASA Political Sociology Section 2005) as well as the co-editor of *Irregular Armed Forces and Their Role in Politics and State Formation*

(2003) and *Cities and Sovereignty: Identity Conflicts in Urban Spaces* (2011). Her research examines relations between cities and national economic development, the politics of urban policy, urban violence, and conflict cities. Currently, she is undertaking an eight-country study of insecurity in cities of the global south. Davis is a co-founding member of the transnational working group on Urban Resilience in Conditions of Chronic Violence (URCV) and an active participant in a network of scholars who study informality in large metropolises of the Americas (RECIM).

Lucy Earle is a social development advisor for the UK Government's Department for International Development (DFID). Her work on São Paulo was undertaken for her doctorate at the Development Studies Institute of the London School of Economics and Political Science. It was then refined and expanded upon while she was a post-doctoral fellow at the African Centre for Cities, Department of Environmental and Geographical Science at the University of Cape Town. Alongside work on the engagement of the São Paulo housing movement with the Brazilian state, she has also undertaken research on the interaction between residents of informal settlements and local government in Maputo, Mozambique.

Cynthia Goytia is Professor of Applied Urban and Regional Economics and Director of the MA programme in Urban Economics at the Universidad Torcuato Di Tella (UTDT) in Buenos Aires, Argentina. Her research is focused on the interface between urban economics and urban/regional planning, institutional economics and development, for addressing many of the critical issues facing contemporary urban areas. Her recent research has focused on empirically revising and enriching the application of urban economics principles in order to understand how urban places function in developing countries. This includes the economics and political economy of land use regulation and its effects, its association with informality in the land and housing market, the welfare and capitalization impacts of infrastructure and local development programmes, the determinants of informal institutions (such as trust) in informal neighbourhoods and its causal effects in urban and economic development. She is the author of many policy articles and reports on these issues.

María Teresa Gutiérrez is an anthropologist with an MA in History. She is a member of the research group 'Institutions and Conflict from a Comparative Perspective' at IEPRI (Instituto de Estudios Politicos y Relaciones Internacionales), Universidad Nacional de Colombia, with which she has researched issues such as public policies, political parties, land conflicts, and Colombian political history. She is currently doing a PhD in History at UNAM, Mexico.

Francisco Gutiérrez Sanín is a researcher at the Instituto de Estudios Políticos y Relaciones Internacionales, Universidad Nacional de Colombia. He has directed projects sponsored by the London School of Economics, the Social Science Research Council, Oslo University, and Oxford University, among others. He has published in top journals on civil war, democracy and conflict, and social/political indicators.

Tania Guzmán Pardo is co-ordinator of the research team that wrote the National Human Development Report 2011 for Colombia, entitled *Rural Colombia: Reasons for Hope*, which was sponsored by the United Nations Development Programme. She was a researcher for the Regional Human Development Report for Central America, *Open Spaces for Public Safety and Human Development*, and was part of the research team that prepared the Human Development Report for Bogota (Colombia). She is Professor of Political Science at the Universidad Javeriana in Bogota (Colombia), and in recent years her work has focused on topics linked to development, governance, and gender. She is a lawyer, specializing in public law and economics, and has an MA in Political Science from the Universidad Nacional de Colombia.

Paola Jirón is an academic at the Institute of Housing (INVI), Faculty of Architecture and Urbanism (FAU), University of Chile. She holds a BComm from Concordia University, Canada, an MA from University College London, and a PhD in Urban and Regional Planning from the London School of Economics and Political Science. Her work is mainly focused on Latin American cities. She currently co-ordinates the Fondo Nacional de Desarrollo Científico y Tecnológico (FONDECYT)-funded research project N°1090198 on urban daily mobility and social exclusion. Her main areas of research relate to urban daily mobility, everyday life, gender in human settlements, urban exclusion, urban quality of life, and research methodologies for urban issues.

Ravi Kanbur is T.H. Lee Professor of World Affairs, International Professor of Applied Economics and Management, and Professor of Economics at Cornell University. He holds a Bachelor's in Economics from Cambridge, and a PhD in Economics from Oxford. He has taught at the universities of Oxford, Cambridge, Essex, Warwick, Princeton, and Columbia. He has served on the senior staff of the World Bank, including service as Principal Advisor to the Chief Economist of the World Bank.

He has also served as Director of the World Bank's World Development Report. Kanbur's main areas of interest are public economics and development economics. His work spans conceptual, empirical, and policy analysis. He is particularly interested in bridging the worlds of rigorous analysis and practical policy-making. He has been published in leading economics journals such as *American Economic Review, Journal of Political Economy*, and *Economic Journal*.

Eduardo Lora is the Chief Economist a.i., and General Manager of the Research Department at the Inter-American Development Bank (IDB) in Washington DC. He received his MA from the London School of Economics in 1982 and was a visiting researcher at Oxford University in 1989. Prior to joining the IDB in 1996, he served five years as Executive Director of Fedesarrollo, one of the most important research centres in Latin America. He has written various textbooks and edited a dozen books on economic and social policy issues. He has been the academic coordinator of several issues of the IDB's flagship annual publication. He has a regular column in the Colombian magazine *Dinero* and has published numerous academic articles. His academic and professional awards include the title of Distinguished Alumnus of the London School of Economics.

Ignacio A. Navarro is Assistant Professor of Public Policy and Applied Research Methods at California State University, Monterey Bay. His research interests include local governance and land economic issues in Latin America, with an emphasis on property rights and redevelopment investment decisions.

Ricardo A. Pasquini is an economist and independent researcher, currently affiliated to the School of Government at Universidad Torcuato Di Tella and to the Center for Financial Stability (Buenos Aires). His research interests are particularly related to the use of empirical and applied economics for the design of public policies. He has authored articles in academic journals, chapters in books, and numerous working papers, on the subjects of urban economics, development economics, and finance. His experience includes having worked as a consultant for multilateral organizations such as the World Bank, the Inter-American Development Bank, the Andean Corporation (CAF), and other national and local government agencies, and with the support of specialized research institutes such as the Lincoln Institute of Land Policy.

María Teresa Pinto is a researcher at the Instituto de Estudios Políticos y Relaciones Internacionales (IEPRI) at the Universidad Nacional de

Colombia, and teaches at the Universidad del Valle. She is a political scientist by training, with MA degrees from IEPRI and the Université Marne la Vallée, France. Her research focuses on social movements and conflict.

Andrew Powell is Principal Advisor of the Research Department of the Inter-American Development Bank. He holds an MPhil and a DPhil in Economics from the University of Oxford. He has been a professor at the Universidad Torcuato di Tella, Buenos Aires, and previously held academic posts at the universities of London, Warwick, and Oxford, all in the UK. During the period 1996–2000 he was Chief Economist of the Central Bank of Argentina. He has held visiting positions at Harvard University, the IMF, and the World Bank. He has published widely on diverse issues including commodity markets, international finance, banking, the role of international financial institutions, and the cost of natural disasters. His current interests focus on policy issues in emerging economies, capital flows, and banking regulation as well as quality of life issues.

Helene Risør is an anthropologist and holds a PhD from Copenhagen University. She is Assistant Professor on the Anthropology Program at the Institute of Sociology, Universidad Católica de Chile, and post-doctoral fellow at Copenhagen University. Her research focuses on political and urban anthropology, in particular issues of civil (in)security, violence and post-conflict, citizenship, generational politics, and migration. Her regional specialization is Latin America, and she has done extensive fieldwork in Chile and Bolivia.

Dennis Rodgers is Professor of Urban Social and Political Research in the School of Social and Political Sciences at the University of Glasgow. He was previously a senior research fellow in the Brooks World Poverty Institute (BWPI) at the University of Manchester, UK, where he led their programme on Urban Poverty and Conflict. He is also a research fellow at the Centre on Conflict, Development and Peacebuilding (CCDP) at the Graduate Institute of International and Development Studies (Geneva, Switzerland), and previously taught at the London School of Economics (2000–07). A social anthropologist by training, his research focuses on the interdisciplinary study of urban development, conflict and violence (in particular youth gangs), and the politics of urban planning in Nicaragua, Argentina, and India. He has published widely on these topics, and was previously Associate Editor of the *European Journal of Development Research,* and is currently an editor of *Urban Studies.*

Pablo Sanguinetti is Research Director of Socioeconomic Investigations at CAF (Corporación Andina de Fomento [Andean Development Corporation]). He is Professor of Economics at Universidad Torcuato Di Tella in Buenos Aires. He holds an MA (1989) and PhD (1992) in Economics from the University of California, Los Angeles. His research interests include international trade and integration, economic development, and fiscal federalism. He has published articles in *Economics and Politics*, *Journal of International Economics*, and *Journal of Development Economics*, as well as several other journals and books. He has occupied visiting scholar positions at University of New Mexico (1994), University of Texas (A&M) (1999), and University of Bonn (2004). He has been a member of the editorial board of Latin American Research Review (LARR). He has worked as consultant for the World Bank, Inter-American Development Bank, the Economic Commission for Latin America and the Caribbean (ECLAC), and CAF. He served as Member of the Board of the International Trade Commission of Argentina from 1996 to 2000 (Comisión Nacional de Comercio Exterior).

Part I
Introduction

1
Re-thinking the Latin American City

Dennis Rodgers, Jo Beall, and Ravi Kanbur

Cities, like dreams, are made of desires and fears.
Italo Calvino, *Invisible Cities* (1972)

1 Introduction

According to UN-Habitat (2007: 337), Latin America is the most urbanized region in the world. Over three-quarters of its population resided in cities at the turn of the 21st century, a proportion that is estimated to rise to almost 85 per cent by 2030. By comparison, just over 36 and 37 per cent of the populations of Africa and Asia were urban dwellers in 2000. In many ways, this state of affairs is not surprising. Urbanization and urban culture have long been features of the Latin American panorama, with the Mayas, Incas, and Aztecs – to name but the best-known pre-Columbian societies – all associated with the construction of large urban centres, even if none of these societies were urban per se (see Hardoy 1973).[1] Furthermore, Iberian colonialism – which held sway over the region for over three hundred years – was administered by means of a widespread network of cities from which power and control were projected, both materially and symbolically (see Hoberman and Socolow 1986). At the same time, however, the region's contemporary urban condition is very much a consequence of 20th-century developments: 'in 1900, most Latin Americans lived in the countryside and only three cities had more than half a million inhabitants' (Gilbert 1994: 25). Industrialization and the introduction of capitalist modes of production in rural areas from the 1930s onwards triggered a process of concentrated urbanization that within 70 years had led to a majority of the societies in the region crossing the urban threshold (Valladares and Prates Coelho

1995), as well as the emergence of over forty cities with more than one million inhabitants (Angotti 1995: 14).

This rapid urbanization – which has 'no parallel in the history of the world' (Kemper 2002: 91) – fostered a particular 'quality and distinctiveness about the Latin American city', according to Gilbert (1994: 21). Until the beginning of the 20th century, the region's urban imaginary largely reflected the ideas expounded in Sarmiento's celebrated work *Civilizacíon y Barbarie: Vida de Don Facundo Quiroga*, first published in 1845. This famously contended that the central tension of Latin American society was 'the dialectic between civilization and barbarism' (González Echevarría 2003: 2), and posited that the latter was inherently associated with the unbridled violence of life in the countryside, while the former was linked to the law and order of urban contexts (see Sarmiento 2003). Latin American urban centres were consequently widely seen as 'cities of hope' (see Pineo and Baer 1998), and were considered the focal points for a burgeoning modernity that led many in the latter half of the 19th century to see the region as 'the land of the future' (Dunkerley 2000: 142). The unprecedented urban growth that characterized Latin America from the 1930s onwards gradually transformed this utopian urban imaginary, however, and promoted a much more negative conception of cities, which manifested itself in a variety of guises over the years, from the popular theory of 'over-urbanization' in the 1940s and 1950s (see Germani 1973), to the currently predominant vision of the Latin American city as a 'city of walls' (Caldeira 2000).

As Baiocchi (2001) has remarked, the problem with such utopian and dystopian representations of urban contexts is that both tend to obscure the fact that cities are multifaceted spaces, simultaneously integrating both positive and negative tendencies. Certainly, Mumford (1996 [1937]: 185) famously observed that 'the city in its complete sense…is a…collective unity', and argued that it could only be understood through a consideration of the ways in which opposing aspects of urban life articulated together, rather than by simply emphasizing one or the other. To a large extent, this particular trend is a function of the fact that 'most of our knowledge about Latin American urbanization has been pieced together from case studies of a variety of analytical units examined in a wide range of urban (and non-urban) contexts', and that 'rarely have comparative data been gathered', with 'relatively little attention given to the longitudinal dimensions of urban processes' (Kemper 2002: 96). In other words, the dearth of a generally synoptic literature is due to the fact that the overwhelming majority of the research that has been conducted on Latin American cities has tended to be quite specialized and has not really attempted to get to grips with the dynamics of urbanization per se, at best considering these epiphenomenally (Leeds 1994: 235).[2]

Understanding the broader patterns of Latin American urban development research is critical, however, especially if we are to conceive of cities as part of the solution rather than part of the problem – something that is particularly important in a world that has inexorably moved beyond its urban 'tipping point' (see Beall et al. 2010). To this extent, this volume offers a range of perspectives on contemporary urban dynamics in the region, drawing on empirical examples from Argentina (Buenos Aires), Bolivia (Cochabamba, El Alto, La Paz, Santa Cruz), Brazil (São Paulo), Chile (Santiago de Chile), Colombia (Bogotá, Cali, Medellín), and Mexico (Mexico City). Contrary to the overwhelming majority of past characterizations of urban contexts in the region, it explicitly argues for a more systemic engagement with Latin American cities, contending that the time has come to reconsider their unity in order to nuance the 'fractured cities' perspective that has widely come to epitomize the contemporary urban moment in the region (see Koonings and Kruijt 2007), and which has arguably led to something of a Latin American urban 'impasse'.

This introduction provides a current review of the literature on Latin American urban development in order to frame the contributions to this volume. It begins by offering a broad-brush overview of regional urban development trends, before exploring changing concerns and predominant issues in order to illustrate how the underlying imaginary of the city has critically shifted over the past half-century. Focusing particularly on the way that slums and shanty towns have been conceived in the Latin American urban imagination, it highlights how thinking about cities in the region has been subject to a pendulum movement that has seen them become increasingly considered as fundamentally fragmented spaces rather than unitary systems within which the majority of the region's population now reside. It then outlines how this particular vision has had critically negative ramifications for urban development agendas, and calls for a renewed vision of Latin American urban life, before providing an overview of the contributions to this volume.

2 Patterns of Latin American urban development

Although cities were an important feature of pre-Columbian societies in Latin America, the shape of contemporary regional urbanization owes more to the 'common history and the strong cultural roots that were laid during almost three hundred years of Iberian rule' (Gilbert 1994: 21). Spanish – and to a much lesser extent, Portuguese – colonizers either destroyed or superimposed their own settlements over existing indigenous urban centres, and rapidly built a network of new ones through which they imposed their political control and administered their conquered territories. As Goldstein (2004: 6–8) summarizes, 'colonial cities were planned and constructed to reflect ... the hierarchical racial and political-economic organization of [colonial] society itself. These cities were to be highly ordered, regular, and governable, their streets uniform, and the functions assigned to particular areas of the city (e.g., housing, commerce, government) predetermined and restricted to those areas. Thus emerged the famous grid pattern of the Latin American city, which persists to this day: the ideal of rationality, of order reflected in the physical layout of the city ... in symmetrical fashion with a series of straight streets emanating from a central plaza or square endowed with a church, a town hall, a prison, and the *picota*'.

The post-colonial period saw an intensification of efforts to rationalize and order Latin American urban landscapes. Cities were consolidated and, to a certain extent, reorganized as the region moved from being a quasi-self-sufficient settler economy to gradual integration into the world market as a producer of primary goods. Consequently, urban development during this period was principally connected to the changing commercial functions of cities. Towards the latter half of the 19th century, large-scale international migration also began to play a prominent role in shaping patterns of urbanization in the region, as the region saw significant human inflows from all over the world. Most immigrants, however, came from impoverished areas of Europe – in particular Italy and Spain – and were seeking to start afresh in a Latin America that was very much viewed as a virgin land of opportunity. The population of Buenos Aires, for example, grew from just under a quarter of a million in 1869 to over two million in 1914, and this was mainly a result of migration, as is well evidenced by the fact that three out of four inhabitants of the city in 1910 had been born abroad (Gilbert 1994: 39).

This international migratory flow tapered off following the First World War, but internal rural–urban migratory flows soon took over as a new – and even more consequent – source of urban growth (Kemper 1971). The broader impulse for this development was the implementation of import substitution industrialization (ISI) policies in most of Latin America from the 1930s onwards. Industrial clustering generated significant labour opportunities in cities which, together with the transformation of traditional modes of production in the countryside, fuelled massive population movement from the countryside to urban settlements, to the extent that the region became demographically urban within less than two generations (Lattes et al. 2003). Due to industrial clustering,[3] urban growth initially tended to be concentrated in one or two cities per country, and led to a 'primacy' effect, whereby the populations of these principal urban centres far exceeded those of secondary urban centres.[4] Writing in 1980, Lloyd (1980: 4) noted how 'at the end of the eighteenth century, Arequipa, Peru's second city, was two-thirds the size of Lima (and in fact had a larger "Spanish colonist" population). Today Lima is 15 times the size of its nearest rival. The capital contains almost a quarter of the country's population, compared with only 5 per cent at the earlier period'.

Urban primacy is a feature of most developing countries, but Latin America stands out when compared to other regions of the world, with several of its countries displaying some of the highest primacy indices in the world (see Cerrutti and Bertoncello 2003: 14). Perhaps not surprisingly, Latin America currently has two of the five largest 'mega-cities' worldwide, despite accomodating less than 15 per cent of the planet's urban population (Kruijt and Koonings 2009: 10). At the same time, however, urban growth began to be less concentrated in large cities from the end of the 1970s onwards, as Latin America witnessed a 'broadening of the urban hierarchy' (Roberts 1989: 673) due to the proliferation of middle-sized cities with more than fifty thousand but less than one million inhabitants (Cerrutti and Bertoncello 2003). This new trend was partly linked to the end of ISI policies and the widespread introduction of a new free market model throughout the region which emphasized deregulation and decentralization, including the end of industrial policy and other forms of state-sponsored macro-economic management. As Portes and Roberts (2005: 76) describe: 'Traditional urban primacy...declined almost everywhere, giving rise to the rapid growth of secondary centers and to more complex urban systems whose future evolution remains uncertain. The relative decline of traditional primate cities has been due, among other factors, to their loss of attraction as a magnet for internal or international migrants, lower levels of fertility, and the economic attraction of new growth poles created by local or regional export booms promoted by the new model. Internal migration flows...responded rapidly to these developments, leading to the growth of secondary cities in Brazil, Chile, and, in particular, along the Mexico-USA border'.

The rise of middle-sized cities also coincided with a decline in rural–urban migration flows. While rural–urban transferences were estimated to make up almost half of all urban growth in the 1950s, this proportion was thought to have declined to just over a third by the 1990s (Lattes et al. 2003). The process was not experienced homogeneously throughout Latin America, however, with some countries such as Bolivia and Paraguay still displaying high levels of movement from the countryside to the city. Indeed, the phenomenon clearly remains significant, although it is now arguably mainly due to 'push' rather than 'pull' factors, insofar as access to social services and labour opportunities in rural areas continue to be much worse than in urban areas. At the same time, the predominant form of spatial movement within contemporary Latin America is undoubtedly urban-urban migration.[5] 'In Mexico, for example, between 1987 and 1992, 50 per cent of interstate movements (excluding intra-metropolitan movements) had urban areas as origin and destination ...; and between 1995 and 2000, 70 per cent of all municipal movements took place between urban areas and only 14 per cent were rural-city movements' (Cerrutti and Bertoncello 2003: 11). Moreover, urban-urban migration displays very different characteristics to rural–urban movement, in that urban-urban migrants tend to be more educated than their rural–urban counterparts (and even, in some cases, more educated than non-migrants).

This latter trend is by no means surprising in view of the evolution of urban labour markets in post-ISI Latin American cities, which, more often than not, have seen rates of unemployment and informal employment increase significantly due to the demise of old industries and the contraction of public employment, particularly from the 1980s onwards. This has had clear repercussions on the evolution of urban poverty and inequality trends in the region's cities. As Portes and Roberts (2005: 77) remark, 'the trend common to all countries was the persistence of or rise in levels of inequality prompted by the appropriation of larger income shares by the dominant classes, and the stagnation or at least lower growth in the slice of the economic pie going to the working classes. In most countries, the informal proletariat is the largest class of the population, exceeding by several multiples the combined size of the dominant classes. The informal proletariat bore the brunt of economic adjustment both through its numerical growth, due to the contraction of the formal sector, and the stagnation or decline in real average wages, which, in most cases, failed to lift working-class families out of poverty'.

Perhaps not surprisingly, in view of the widely noted relationship between crime and inequality (Fajnzylber et al. 2002) Latin American cities generally experienced a sustained rise in violence and insecurity during the 1990s and beyond (Moser and McIlwaine 2006). This increasing insecurity of urban life has had a critical impact on cities, in particular generating a 'new urban segregation', most evident in the proliferation of 'fortified enclaves', that is to say 'privatized, enclosed, and monitored spaces of residence, consumption, leisure, and work' (Caldeira 1999: 114), designed to isolate their occupants from criminality and therefore minimize their insecurity. These typically take the form of self-sufficient gated communities and closed condominiums, characterized by high walls, sophisticated surveillance technology, and round-the-clock private security that, in addition to making residences secure, also protect on-site amenities such as shops, sports clubs, restaurants, and bars.[6] Fortified enclaves can vary considerably, however. In Buenos Aires, for example, the 'countries' – from the English-language term 'country club' – are purpose-built on the northern periphery of the city, and spread over very large areas, often including polo grounds and football pitches within their boundaries (Svampa 2001). By contrast, in Santiago de Chile fortified enclaves tend to be concentrated in the north-east of the city, and involve the piecemeal 'closing off' of areas through the privatization of streets and squares in order to constitute 'closed communities' (Fischer et al. 2003; Sabatini and Arenas 2000).

In some Latin American cities, such as Managua, the capital city of Nicaragua, the phenomenon has gone even further than enclaves, with urban segregation developing through an active process of 'disembedding' rather than fragmentation (Rodgers 2004). Partly because of the small size of the Managua urban elite, what has emerged instead of gated communities and closed condominiums is a 'fortified network', which has been established through the selective and purposeful construction of high-speed roads connecting the spaces of the elites within the city: their homes, offices, clubs, bars, restaurants, shopping malls, and the international airport. The poor are excluded from these locations by private security, but are also excluded from the connecting roads, which are cruised at breakneck speeds by expensive 4x4 cars and have roundabouts instead of traffic lights, meaning that those in cars avoid having to stop – and risk being carjacked – but those on foot risk their lives whenever they cross a road. The general picture, in other words, is one whereby a whole 'layer' of Managua's urban fabric has been 'ripped out' for the exclusive use of the city elites, thereby profoundly altering the cityscape and the relations between social groups within the metropolis by exacerbating socio-spatial polarization, dismantling previous forms of community cohesion, and effectively disrupting the unity of the city.[7]

3 Key issues in Latin American urban development

As Valladares and Prates Coelho (1995) have noted, there has been a clear evolution in the overall thematic focus of research on Latin American urban contexts. The first major wave of studies in the 1950s and 1960s was very much focused on the general demographic dynamics of cities, in particular, rural–urban migratory flows. Studies focused principally on migrants' relations with the city, and the emergent ways of life in the 'marginal settlements' they rapidly became associated with (see Roberts 1978; Lloyd 1979). During the 1970s this led to a more specific focus on the economic aspects of urban life, including an emphasis on the study of informal land and housing markets (see Gilbert and Varley 1991), as well as employment and labour market dynamics, partly consequent to the worldwide economic crisis brought on by the oil shock of 1973 (see Rodgers 1989). By the 1980s, however, politics – and in particular those associated with the mobilization of the poorer strata of urban society – became the predominant theme of the majority of studies (see Kowarick 1994),[8] before finally giving way, from the 1990s onwards, to a hegemonic concern with the social dynamics of city life, most evident in the proliferation of investigations into the dynamics of urban violence and insecurity (see Rotker 2002).[9]

It is obviously beyond the scope of this introduction to attempt to systematically map all the different iterations of this particular intellectual evolution, and we will limit the scope of discussion to the way that it unfolded in relation to one specific, but arguably very important, aspect of Latin American urban development over the past 70 years or so, namely the phenomenon that is variably called slums, shantytowns, squatter settlements or, in the Latin American vernacular, *asentamientos, favelas, barriadas, poblaciones*, and *villas miserias*.[10] Not only has this topic recently been very much in vogue globally (see UN-Habitat 2003; Davis 2006) but as Fischer et al. (forthcoming) point out, it also arguably offers an 'x-ray' of Latin America's urban development in a way that few other issues can, as shantytowns and slums have been either the focus or the site for a significant proportion of scholarly studies of urban contexts in the region. As such, the key themes and issues that have emerged from shantytown research over the years offer us a critical window onto the general trajectory of predominant thinking about Latin American urban development, and in particular the way that this has generally moved from considering cities as utopian to a more dystopian perspective (see also Eckstein 1990).

Indeed, the initial concern with slums can, in many ways, be seen as the beginning of this critical shift in the Latin American urban imaginary. As Kemper (2002: 95) points out, early studies of slums and shantytowns in the 1940s and 1950s tended to see such aggregations as 'festering sores' or 'cancers' within otherwise booming Latin American cities. Although they were understood to be a 'natural' consequence of the influx of migrants from the countryside seeking opportunities in cities along the lines generally theorized by Lewis (1954), they were also effectively seen as a traditional throwback that could potentially impede the perceived forward march of modernization. This concern became all the more acute when studies increasingly reported that far fewer jobs were being created in urban centres than were necessary to accommodate the migrant-fuelled growth of their economically active populations.[11] This imbalance came to be referred to as a problem of 'over-urbanization' (Germani 1973), and was widely considered a key threat to potentially achieving a balanced development process in Latin America during the 1950s (Gugler 1982). After being severely critiqued – in particular by Sovani (1964) – the notion of 'over-urbanization' was subsequently refined, and the issue became less that there were too many people and not enough jobs in cities, but rather that there were too many people involved in the wrong kinds of economic activity, as migrants from low-productivity rural agricultural employment took up low-productivity urban employment or ended up underemployed. This came to be known as the 'tertiarization' phenomenon (Gilbert 1994: 60).

By the end of the 1960s, however, the problematic nature of slums was seen to be less that their populations were ill-adapted to urban labour markets, and more that, as a result of their inferior – but ultimately necessary – jobs, shantytown dwellers could not participate 'properly' in the working of the city; in other words, they were 'marginal' to mainstream urban development (see Kowarick 1980). The concept of marginality was quickly extended from an economic notion to a sociological and psychological one that explained the difficulties displayed by the hordes of rural migrants in adjusting to city life as being related to their 'incapability' to adopt an urban way of life. This idea gained particular traction in the wake of the work of Lewis (1959, 1961, 1966), and more specifically his notion of the 'culture of poverty', which suggested that the material circumstances of impoverishment characteristic of the slums and shantytowns of Latin American cities inevitably generated a series of cultural adaptations that led to the constraints of poverty being internalized by those caught up in its vicissitudes, in order to make them ontologically more acceptable. The inhabitants of marginal squatter settlements thus displayed 'helplessness', and rarely engaged in long-term strategizing, preferring to pursue 'instant gratification' instead, something that effectively kept them in a 'vicious cycle' of impoverishment (Lewis 1966: 53).

This 'culture of poverty' cemented a particular perception of Latin American cities, which came to be widely seen as constituted, on the one hand, of bustling, modernizing, progressive areas – generally in the centre – and problematic, unproductive, and backwards areas – generally on the periphery – on the other (Kruijt and Koonings 2009). The notion of the 'culture of poverty' provoked enormous debate (see Valentine 1968; Hannerz 1969; Leacock 1971), however, and was derided as 'a "blame the victim" strategy' (Lancaster 1988: 75). The idea that poor people passively accepted their fate and could not become active participants in urban life was particularly criticized, including by Perlman (1976) who, on the basis of extensive ethnographic research in Rio de Janeiro *favelas*, argued that the prevailing wisdom about those living in contexts of marginality was completely wrong:

> Socially, they are well organized and cohesive and make wide use of the urban milieu and its institutions. Culturally, they are highly optimistic and aspire to better education for their children and to improving the condition of their houses. The small piles of bricks purchased one by one and stored in backyards for the day they can be used is eloquent testimony to how *favelados* strive to fulfill their goals. Economically, they work hard, they consume their share of the products of others (often paying more since they have to buy where they can get credit), and they build – not only their own houses but also much of the overall community and urban infrastructure. They also place a high value on hard work, and take great pride in a job well done. Politically, they are... aware of and keenly involved in those aspects of politics that most directly affect their lives, both within and outside the favela.... In short, *they have the aspirations of the bourgeoisie, the perseverance of pioneers, and the values of patriots.* (ibid.: 242–43, emphasis in original)

Many studies reported similar findings in other major Latin American cities, including Mexico City (Lomnitz 1977) and Lima (Lobo 1982), for instance, and contributed to the emergence of a new debate concerning slum life, in particular related to the nature of poor people's involvement in urban economic development (see Butterworth and Chance 1981; Mangin 1970). This issue crystallized around the notion of the 'informal economy' (see Thomas 1995), and in particular the question of whether such forms of economic enterprise simply constituted a form of survival, prone to exploitation or enabling minimal capital accumulation (see Moser 1978), or else something that had the potential to be 'a dramatic "bootstrap" operation, lifting the underdeveloped economies through their own indigenous enterprise' (Hart 1973: 89). A clear consensus concerning the fundamental nature of the informal economy has yet to emerge (see Guha-Khasnobis et al. 2006; Rakowski 1994), although it should be noted that the notion that informal economic activities can potentially be developmentally positive has been more influential in Latin America than anywhere else in the world as a result of the work of de Soto (1989), which has been strongly championed by the World Bank (see, for example, Maloney 2001).

The economic potential of slum dwellers continues to be a major bone of policy contention, but the situation is very different with regards to what might be termed the 'politics of poverty'. Perlman's research was particularly critical in the context of the general intellectual trajectory of thinking about Latin American cities because it blew apart the widespread notion that shantytown dwellers were politically apathetic and unengaged, bringing politics centre-stage in the study of urban poverty, something that had not been the case previously, except, to a certain extent, in relation to eviction processes (e.g. Peattie 1970). Perlman (1976: 243) particularly noted how *favelados* were 'responsive to the ... parameters in which they operate[d]', often bargaining astutely with politicians, exchanging their votes for services, and very much actively participating in what were usually patron-client forms of politics (see also Auyero 2000). A number of scholars subsequently began to explore grassroots political mobilization in the slums and shantytowns of the region (e.g. Eckstein 1977; Velez-Ibañez 1983; Smith 1989). This became a veritable flood in the wake of the wave of democratization that swept Latin America during the 1980s, as the region's slums and shantytowns increasingly came to be seen as privileged spaces for the emergence of radical forms of political action (see Stokes 1991; Jones 1994; Hernández et al. 2010).[12]

The new political turn in Latin American slum studies drew largely on Castells' (1983) ground-breaking theories, which turned the classic Marxist notion of class on its head and offered consumption and life, rather than work, experiences as the basis for collective consciousness and therefore action. Most studies focused their attention on what came to be known as 'social movements' (see Cardoso 1987; Eckstein 1989; Escobar and Alvarez 1992). These were conceived less as directed forms of protest than as broader instances of political being that had more indistinct consequences than traditional class-based movements. As Whittier (2002: 289) summarizes: 'social movements are neither fixed nor narrowly bounded in space, time, or membership. Instead, they are made up of shifting clusters of organizations, networks, communities, and activist individuals, connected by participation in challenges and collective identities through which participants define the boundaries and significance of their groups'. The social movement literature was extremely prolific, and inspired a whole generation of urban scholars to focus their attention on a range of different identity-based social movements emanating from slums, including religious (e.g. Burdick 1992), racial (e.g. Gomes da Cunha 1998), gendered (e.g. Jelin 1990), and sexual (e.g. Wright 2000), amongst others. Such movements were widely portrayed as potentially key political players in the new post-authoritarian democratic Latin America, insofar as it was argued that they would inherently transcend the region's traditionally patronage-based and corporatist politics.[13]

However, an issue that rapidly emerged as critical with regard to the politics of slum-based social movements was the way that they interfaced with the state, whether in its local urban manifestation or its national incarnation, since it indisputably remained the single most important social actor in Latin American society (Lehmann 1991). Although social movements were widely theorized as being a potential means for involving the poor in decision-making processes, as well as holding states to account (see Avritzer 2002), in fact numerous studies reported that if such movements failed to interface meaningfully with the state, they tended to have little in the way of long-term constructive impacts on the lives of their participants and wider society (e.g. Auyero 2000; Goldstein 2004; Gutmann 2002; Melucci 1996). This concern led debates around slum and shantytown dweller politics to engage with the issue of citizenship, and more specifically the relationship that social movements could have with what was generally considered to be the basic building block of post-authoritarian Latin American urban political society (see Holston and Appadurai 1999). In particular, within a broader Latin American context where it was becoming increasingly common to talk of the existence of a 'crisis of governance' (see, for example, de Rivero 1998; Galeano 1998; Gledhill 1996; O'Donnell 1999) – more often than not linked to 'neoliberalism' (Perreault and

Martin 2005) – it was widely speculated that slum-based social movements might have the potential to take on some of the institutional functions of retreating states (see Earle 2009).[14]

The main focus of this line of thinking concerned slum-based forms of 'insurgent citizenship' (Holston 1999, 2008) or, in other words, bottom-up initiatives that 'offer proposals and conceive concrete alternatives – and ... realize them despite the state apparatus and ... against the state' (Lopes de Souza 2006: 329).[15] There have been studies of such practices all over Latin America during the past decade and a half, but a veritable (cottage) industry developed in relation to the 2001 crisis in Argentina which, as López Levy (2004: 10) remarked, was widely seen as 'a heady time steeped in a sense of shared destiny when people bypassed politics as usual', and engaged in a range of innovative forms of collective action, including *piqueteros* (organized groups of unemployed workers), *asambleas barriales* (spontaneous neighbourhood assemblies), *clubes de trueque* (barter clubs), and *empresas recuperadas* ('recovered', i.e. worker-occupied, enterprises). At the same time, however, although such forms of collective action are often undoubtedly a significant feature of slums and shantytowns throughout contemporary urban Latin America, more often than not their study has also been pervaded by a significant element of romanticism, to the extent that they are generally perceived as 'a social miracle' (Wolff 2007: 6). This has obscured the critical fact that contrary to the social movements of the 1980s, their contemporary successors tend to operate in the absence of, rather than in opposition to, the state.

Kruijt and Koonings (1999: 11) have described such circumstances as 'local governance voids', and contend that far from generating new forms of political participation and inclusion, more often than not they lead to a 'democratization' of violence, whereby brutality 'ceases to be the resource of only the traditionally powerful or of the grim uniformed guardians of the nation ... [but] increasingly appears as an option for a multitude of actors in pursuit of all kinds of goals' (see also Koonings and Kruijt 2004; Méndez et al. 1999). Certainly, it has been widely reported that post-Cold War Latin America has seen a sharp rise in levels of violence (see Londoño et al. 2000; Pearce 1998), and the overwhelming majority of this brutality is clearly concentrated in urban slums and shantytowns (Moser and McIlwaine 2004). Indeed, it has arguably become *the* defining feature of life in such settlements at the beginning of the 21st century. As Perlman (2010) dramatically documents in her landmark re-study of her original Rio de Janeiro *favela* fieldwork sites from the late 1960s, contemporary violence turned the 'myth of marginality' into a 'reality of insecurity and violence', thereby fundamentally undermining the possibilities for social mobilization and the political empowerment that she had famously previously observed. Similarly, Robert Gay (2009) describes how the '*favelas* of hope' he studied in Rio, which had been characterized by vibrant grassroots organizations in the past, have become '*favelas* of despair', dominated by extralegal armed actors spreading terror and mistrust. An equivalent picture emerges from other contemporary studies of Rio de Janeiro's slums (e.g. Arias 2006; Goldstein 2003; McCann 2006; Penglase 2005), as well as studies of slums and shantytowns in other Latin American cities (e.g. Goldstein 2004; Hume 2009; Moser 2009).

The most prominent actors within this new panorama of urban violence are the youth gangs that are a ubiquitous feature of almost every major city in Latin America (Rodgers 1999; Jones and Rodgers 2009), particularly in contemporary Central America (Arana 2005; Liebel 2004; Rodgers 2006a; Rodgers and Muggah 2009). Often portrayed as a form of modern-day barbarism, they are a particularly visible element of slum and shantytown life in the region's cities, with many studies explicitly linking the phenomenon's emergence to the social, spatial, economic, and political exclusion that characterize such urban areas (Rodgers 2009). At the same time, however, it is also increasingly noted that youth gangs are being superseded or subsumed into more organized forms of crime, such as drug dealing, which are much more violent (see e.g. Leeds 1996; Rodgers 2007; Zaluar 2004). This intensification of brutality is primarily attributed to the particularly repressive policies often enacted by state authorities to counter urban violence in general – and gangs in particular (see Jütersonke et al. 2009) – that clearly aim, more than anything else, to contain it in the slums and shantytowns of Latin American cities in order to allow urban elites to live in comfortable and 'splendid segregation' (Rodgers 2006b; Davis 2009, 2010). This has helped cement a contemporary vision of slums and shantytowns as 'precarious peripheries' (Rolnik 2001), ever more cut off from the rest of the metropolis, something that is starkly symptomatic of the fact that Latin American cities are 'splitting...into divergent economic and cultural universes' (Bayat and Biekart 2009: 817).

4 Beyond pendulum swings

The above overview of the key trends and issues that have emerged concerning the role played by slums in relation to urban development in Latin America reveals a distinct pendulum movement between utopian and dystopian conceptions of shantytowns, sometimes seeing them as drivers of progress, while at other times more as obstacles. Economically, for example, slums went from initially being seen as reserve armies of labour to being regarded as zones of exclusion and abandonment. Politically, they moved from being considered marginal and apathetic to being sources of alternative collective action. Socially, shantytowns were seen to have evolved from being integrative demographic melting pots into nests of crime and violence that threaten to spill over to the rest of the city.[16] At the same time, however, a common point to all of these different conceptualizations of slum dynamics is an underlying dualism, insofar as they are predicated on a basic understanding of the Latin American city as a fundamentally dichotomous entity – slums versus the rest. To a certain extent, this is by no means a new observation. For example, Walton (1978) famously qualified the Latin American city as a 'divided city', focusing on the way that urban services in Guadalajara, Mexico, were distributed in a way that favoured the elite and 'forgot' slum dwellers. This has, however, clearly become increasingly marked over time, with slums now seen as almost pathological social formations that are implicitly not considered to be properly part of the city per se.

In turn, this has fostered a vision of urban development as promoting very piecemeal, and often reactive, policy initiatives that fail to take into account the unity of the cities and only consider one aspect of the urban equation, so to speak. At best, this has led to narrowly targeted urban development programmes that focus either on one issue or else on a limited geographical area. At worse, it has encouraged the proliferation of small-scale, bottom-up local initiatives that take no account of the broader urban context. At the same time, the above overview also highlights how slum life is part and parcel of Latin American modernity, and that shantytowns are not an accidental offshoot of political and economic development, or an external phenomena; rather they are critical elements of the urban development of cities, albeit clearly within a broader dynamic of ever-growing inequality and exclusion (Davis 2006). Even the currently dominant Latin American 'city of walls' vision can be said to be based on an imaginary that inherently brings together those both inside and outside the walls into a conceptually symbiotic relationship, albeit a rather tense one. This tension notwithstanding, such a vision starkly highlights the fundamental fact that cities are collective sociological units, and this needs to be made much more explicit in contemporary thinking about Latin American urban development.

Without wanting to come across as calling for a renewed optimism about the city – the empirical evidence with regard to the purposeful nature and extent of urban exclusion in contemporary Latin America unambiguously militates against such naivety (see Roberts and Wilson 2009) – it can nevertheless be contended that it is critical that the underlying epistemology of the contemporary Latin American urban imaginary swings back towards a more holistic notion of the city. Certainly, the current vision of 'fractured cities' obscures the fact that cities are social, economic, political, and cultural systems that bring different (and often contradictory) processes together, and unless we focus our attention more on the interrelatedness of these different processes within cities, our analyses – and concomitant policy initiatives – will unavoidably remain inadequate. As Toynbee (1970: vii) presciently pointed out in a now-forgotten but highly original study of global urban history, the 'urban explosion' calls for 'the unified study of human settlements', because piecemeal analysis will inevitably miss the 'big picture' of things to come (which he speculated to be the rise of a world city, or 'ecumenopolis'). When seen from this perspective, it is clear that we must adopt a renewed perspective on cities in order to truly understand the underlying nature and challenges of Latin American urban development in the 21st century, especially if we are to see them as part of the solution, rather than part of the problem, of contemporary development in an world that is inexorably becoming increasingly urban.

5 This volume

The contributions that make up this volume all illustrate this issue by considering a range of social, economic, and political processes affecting contemporary Latin American cities in an explicitly systemic manner. They approach the different facets of urban development in contemporary Latin America from a range of disciplinary perspectives, but always looking for broader city-wide connections rather than trying to circumscribe issues in order to consider them in isolation. The contributions are broadly divided into two parts. Part II brings together chapters that attempt to re-conceptualize processes conventionally associated with urban fragmentation in a more systemic manner, focusing on the ways in which they are situated within a broader urban political economy, and how they therefore contribute to constituting the city as a collective entity. Part III focuses on different practices and modes of connection, exploring how a range of different approaches and policies seeking to draw on the notion of the city as a unitary social, political, and economic form contribute to reconnecting 'divided cities', both in theory and practice.

The opening chapter of the collection, by Diane Davis, starts by examining the transformation of the urban social infrastructure in Mexico City as a result of rising insecurity. Contrary to the vast majority of the literature on urban violence in Latin America, Davis offers a framework that assesses the social, physical, economic, and political consequences of urban violence for urban dwellers from both negative and positive perspectives, highlighting that there are always trade-offs. She then takes a step back and offers an assessment of the aggregate picture for city living, focusing in particular on the implication for policy. Davis considers whether further advances can be made in reinforcing positive changes (and reversing negative ones), even without clear progress on crime and insecurity, and concludes by discussing several promising avenues for further innovation and action that have been implemented in Mexico City, specifically including some that might indirectly feed back on the violence–insecurity nexus in unexpected yet positive ways.

Ignacio Navarro's contribution on 'Cocaine Cities' explores the relationship between urbanization and the drugs trade in Bolivia. Although drug trafficking has long been a focus of interest in urban Latin America, its non-violent connection to city life has been generally overlooked, particularly in respect of the economic impact that the drugs trade can have, such as on urban land markets. Navarro explores two avenues through which the drugs trade impacts on urban development: through an employment multiplier effect similar to that of other legal exports, and also through money laundering using urban real estate. He finds that urban growth patterns are closely related to fluctuations in cocaine production, thereby highlighting how an activity that is often portrayed as fundamentally disconnected from general city dynamics is actually very much embedded within these – although it should be noted that he also suggests that the urban employment generated by the drugs trade only has a modest effect, and most of the phenomenon's impact on the city is due to money laundering through real estate purchase.

Paola Jiron's contribution explores the way that mobility impacts upon the lives of Latin American city dwellers, drawing on innovative ethnographic research. She argues that current urban interventions tend to neglect the importance of mobility as a fundamental structuring vector of urban living, and that paying attention to the mobility practices of urban inhabitants can challenge traditional analyses of city life. In particular, she focuses on the issue of urban inequality, which in Latin America is often made synonymous with urban segregation and, more specifically, residential segregation. Paying attention to the increase in urban daily mobility questions the way this concept ought to be understood, analysed, and diagnosed. The view of urban inequality moves from fixed enclaves in the city to 'mobile gradients' through the city, thereby shifting the conceptualization of the problem and highlighting the need to broaden urban analysis to take into account mobility and circulation rather than immobility and interdiction.

The next contribution, by Helene Risør, presents an ethnographically informed exploration of the figure of the *vecino*, or local neighbourhood inhabitant, in urban Bolivia. She argues that the *vecino* is a central agent in the constitution of the modern Bolivian political landscape, a perspective that differs significantly from more widespread assumptions that emphasize indigenous participation as the major vector for contemporary Bolivian politics, particularly in the wake of the election of Evo Morales as president of Bolivia in 2006. Drawing on research in El Alto, a city on the outskirts of Bolivia's capital La Paz, Risør describes how class-based and indigenous traditions of political organization have been re-articulated into a residence-based notion of the urban citizen, and shows how the processes of urban territorialization through which poor urban dwellers have sought to attain their social, economic, and civil rights have crystallized around the figure of the *vecino*. To this extent, Risør argues that rather than focusing on a putative enduring indigenous (and insurrectional) culture, it is important to take into account local urban practices in order to understand citizenship in contemporary Bolivia.

The final contribution to Part II, by Dennis Rodgers, attempts to explain an apparent paradox, namely the fact that many Latin American cities are seats of vibrant and much applauded participatory democratic innovations, despite also being amongst the most segregated in the world, something that is widely considered to fundamentally undermine democracy, and, more specifically, the communicative processes upon which participatory democratic initiatives are founded. By explicitly situating such participatory democratic initiatives within their broader urban political economy, however, he shows how they can in fact actively promote urban segregation – in a way reminiscent of South African apartheid's notorious policy of 'separate but equal development' – and that there is therefore no contradiction between the popularity of such initiatives in Latin American cities and their high levels of socioeconomic segregation. This in turn highlights how putatively democratic and emancipatory urban political practices need to be implemented, first and foremost, within the context of a unifying and integrating framework of urban governance if they are to be truly encompassing, although Rodgers concludes by exploring how emancipatory democratic practices can also emerge as a result of 'extraordinary events' that are, in many ways, only possible due to the very existence of cities as sites of intense social interaction and exchange.

The first chapter of Part III of the collection, by Lucy Earle, focuses on the interrelation between 'irregular urbanization' and radical social mobilization by the urban poor in the city of São Paulo, Brazil. Based on ethnographic fieldwork with the Alliance of Housing Movements, or Uniao de Moradores Municipaes (UMM), this contribution describes how São Paulo grew as a socially segregated city during the 20th century, partly due to the calculated neglect of municipal authorities. Highlighting the city's socio-spatial inequality, degradation of the central districts, and widespread irregularity, it illustrates how these factors have negatively affected the urban poor whilst also providing a catalyst for social mobilization, stimulating slum dwellers to assert their claims to land and to regularize tenure. The chapter describes how social movements such as the UMM resort to existing legal provisions, both at the municipal and the national level, which they radically reinterpret in order to justify theoretically illegal acts of civil disobedience which put pressure on city authorities to respond to their claims. As such, Earle highlights the interrelation between legal, political, and social processes within urban contexts, and in particular how city-wide legal provisions can have unexpected consequences and serve to promote the interests of otherwise marginalized and excluded groups.

The next chapter, by Lissette Aliaga-Linares, looks at the socio-spatial implications of street market regulation in Santiago de Chile. Contrary to most other Latin American cities, this metropolis' street vendors, or *feriantes*, gained legal recognition early in the 20th century, and the local municipal authorities provide vendors with individual patents as well as assigned spaces and times during which they may operate according to a clear set of rules. Although theoretically promoting a more rational organization of the urban economy, Aliaga-Linares contends that this regulation is currently promoting processes of market segmentation within the city. In particular, based on an analysis of their spatial distribution in the city, she shows how *feriantes* seem to be increasingly relocated to poorer, and therefore less profitable, areas of the city. She identifies two factors that have led to this situation, namely the encroachment upon *feriantes'* space by supermarkets, as well as the resurgence of unlicensed vendors, or *coleros*, which has led to an increasing stigmatization of street vendors generally, which is then reflected in the municipal authorities' location rationale. At the same time, Aliaga-Linares highlights how the number of *coleros* has decreased radically within socio-economically less segregated neighbourhoods, and suggests that a location rationale taking this into account would prevent further market segmentation, benefiting both consumers and street vendors.

The contribution by Francisco Gutiérrez Sanín, María Teresa Gutiérrez, Tania Guzmán Pardo, Juan Carlos Arenas Gómez, and María Teresa Pinto explores the political dynamics underpinning efforts to reduce violence in three Colombian cities: Bogotá, Medellín, and Cali. The first two have been the theatres of 'metropolitan miracles', whereby a series of new policy initiatives have been widely associated with a radical decline in homicide rates. In Cali, however, similar innovations have not had a significant impact on levels of violence. The generally accepted explanation for the 'miracles' is that the new policies triggered an urban cultural revolution, but as Gutiérrez and his co-authors point out, this fails to get to grips with why Cali did not undergo a 'miracle' – unless it is culturally different to Bogotá and Medellín, which is not (significantly) the case. Instead, they propose an alternative explanation for the success of the new policies in Bogotá and Medellín and their failure in Cali, based on a generic understanding of the specific political processes that allow for the rise of policy innovators. In particular, the chapter illustrates how politics operate very similarly in Bogotá and Medellín, but completely distinctly in Cali. As such, this contribution highlights the need to understand urban politics in a holistic manner as a means of comprehending the social outcomes of urban governance.

Cynthia Goytia, Ricardo Pasquini, and Pablo Sanguinetti's chapter explores the impact of a public–private initiative providing piped gas to poor neighbourhoods in Buenos Aires. The *Redes Solidarias* programme connected 4,000 households to natural pipelined gas in the Great Buenos Aires Area in 2005. Using the programme as something of a 'natural experiment', Goytia, Pasquini, and Sanguinetti estimate its causal effects with regard to more than just the provision of gas, but also housing improvements, health, and happiness, basing their study on survey data collected in 2006 and 2007. They find that the *Redes Solidarias* programme generated significant improvements in housing, including in relation to dwellings' walls and the installation of hot water in bathrooms but, most interestingly, also produced a significant reduction in cases of flu, fever, and other respiratory diseases, thereby highlighting the interrelatedness of different aspects of city living and the need to consider urban processes holistically.

The final chapter of Part III (and of the collection), by Eduardo Lora and Andrew Powell, similarly reinforces the message that a holistic and systemic approach to city life is necessary if we are to truly understand the possibilities for processes of sustainable urban development. More specifically, they describe how a growing number of cities around the world are trying to establish systems to monitor the quality of urban life that combine both objective and subjective information and attempt to cover a wider range of issues than the eternal standards of housing, service provision, and employment. They offer a simple method which takes advantage of both types of information and provides criteria to identify and rank the issues which are potentially most important for urban dwellers. Their major innovation is to combine the so-called 'hedonic price' and 'life satisfaction' approaches used to value public goods, thereby effectively treating the city as common property rather than simply as an epiphenomenal context within which urban dwellers live their lives. They summarize the results of pilot case studies carried out in six Latin American cities before discussing various possible policy applications.

Finally, drawing on the insights of these different contributions, a brief conclusion offers some thoughts regarding the possible construction of a new research agenda for 21st century Latin American urban development. This fourth 'Re-' to the initial triptych of 'Re-thinking', 'Re-conceptualizing', and 'Re-connecting' the Latin American city offered in this introduction will draw out connections between the different contributions to this volume, highlighting common themes and insights in order to lay out a number of potential avenues for future investigations about cities in Latin America.

Notes

This introduction was published in a modified form as an article in the *European Journal of Development Research*, (2011) 23(4): 550–68. Thanks to Gareth A. Jones and Melanie Lombard for their very useful comments on an earlier draft.

1. Tenochtitlan, the Aztec capital, was – with an estimated population of 300,000 – very likely the largest city in the world around the year 1400 (Low 1995: 756).
2. At the same time, there have been surprisingly few comprehensive overviews of the scholarly research on Latin America's urban development, and none very recently. Following Hauser's (1961) and Morse's (1965, 1974) pioneering surveys, the most extensive reviews have undoubtedly been those produced by Hardoy and Gilbert, both individually (Hardoy 1975; Gilbert 1994) and in collaboration (Gilbert, Hardoy, and Ramirez 1982; see also Morse and Hardoy

1992), as well as Cornelius and Kemper (1978). Otherwise, there have been a handful of isolated – and generally short – stand-alone papers (e.g. Walton 1979; Valladares and Prates Coelho 1995; Kemper 2002). A partial exception is the joint Princeton–University of Texas at Austin research programme on 'Latin American Urbanization at the end of the Twentieth Century' that has (so far) produced a collection of six individual city case studies (Portes, Roberts, and Grimson 2005), as well as two articles that focus on the specific consequences of neo-liberalism and political mobilization respectively for Latin American urban contexts (Portes and Roberts 2005; Roberts and Portes 2006).

3. Government policies also led to the creation of new urban centres in previously marginal regions, either explicitly to stimulate regional economic development or else to serve as administrative capitals. Examples include Brasilia in Brazil (see Holston 1989), as well as Ciudad Lázaro Cárdenas in Mexico or Ciudad Guayana in Venezuela.
4. Colombia is a partial exception, and had a more balanced urban network, at least during the 1960s (see Valladares and Prates Coelho 1995).
5. International migration, particularly to the USA and, to a lesser extent, Western Europe, has been an ever-growing phenomenon since the 1980s (see Castles and Miller 2009). Remittances sent back by migrants often have a significant impact on urban land and housing markets, and returnee migrants significantly change local urban culture. Also, although tangential to the remit of this introduction, it is interesting to note that the overwhelming majority of this migration is ultimately urban-urban migration, since most immigrants come from cities in Latin America, and end up in cities abroad. Similarly, another important, but often overlooked urban migration is the historical movement of Jewish, Japanese, and Arabic ('Lebanese') populations to Latin American cities in (respectively) Argentina, Brazil, and Venezuela and Colombia, and which have significantly shaped the urban cultural and economic dynamics of a number of cities in these countries (see Klich and Lesser 1998; Tsuda 2001). Finally, there also exist long-standing migratory links between cities within the Latin American region, including, for example, Bolivians moving from Cochabamba to Buenos Aires in Argentina, which have had a significant impact on local labour markets in the latter (see Bastia 2007).
6. An often overlooked but very much related and extremely significant urban development that has proliferated concurrently with gated communities and closed condominiums in Latin American cities, are the numerous semi-private malls and other 'mega-projects' catering exclusively for the rich (see Jones and Moreno-Carranco 2007).
7. Such urban developments are often linked to broader processes of globalization, although as Crot (2006) has pointed out, it is important to realize that the territorial impact of globalizing forces will inevitably be mediated by the city system. In particular, she shows how the territorial transformations that have taken place in Buenos Aires over the past two decades cannot be simplistically related to, or blamed on, global pressures, but rather are the result of their specific articulation with local urban configurations, and in particular the local Buenos Aires planning process. The same is arguably true of the 'disembedding' of Managua, although the planning process here has clearly been much more exclusive than its Buenos Aires equivalent (see Rodgers 2008).

8. An important strand of research on the urban politics of the poor focused on the racial and the cultural (Wade 1997: 63; Jones 2006).
9. It is interesting to note that a burgeoning literature has recently emerged which merges a concern with urban indigenous politics and violence (see Goldstein 2004; Lazar 2008; Risør 2010).
10. For convenience's sake, we will use these terms interchangeably in this chapter, although we realize that they do not necessarily all refer to equivalent phenomena under all circumstances, and moreover that they are often highly charged labels (see Gilbert 2007).
11. As Portes and Benton (1984: 593) note, 'between 1950 and 1980, the total Latin American economically active population grew at an annual rate of 2.5 per cent, but the urban labour force increased at a rate of 4.1 per cent per year'.
12. There had been some earlier interest in slum dweller politics, of course, including in particular attention from left-leaning academics during the 1960s and 1970s. This, however, was not sustained, partly because, as Portes (1972: 282) noted, while 'few theories have been more widely held than that of slum radicalism[,] few have met with more consistent rejection from empirical research. Studies in almost every Latin American capital have found leftist extremism to be weak, or even nonexistent, in peripheral slums'.
13. A particularly fruitful avenue of investigation in this regard has been the work of Santos (1995) and Fernandes and Varley (1998) on the way that slum dwellers increasingly resort to the law in order to access resources and challenge their informal status, as well as the burgeoning literature around the 'right to the city' in Latin America (e.g. Fernandes 2007).
14. An opposite but related debate which emerged from the late 1980s onwards concerned the possibility of developing alternative forms of democratic governance that linked grassroots social movements more meaningfully with the state, including in particular more participatory forms of politics that could include spatially and economically excluded shantytown dwellers (Fung and Wright 2003; Chavez and Goldfrank 2004). The ubiquitous example of such democratic innovation was participatory budgeting and, more specifically, its implementation in Porto Alegre, Brazil, which was widely held up as an empirical example that 'another world is possible' (Abers 2000; Baiocchi 2005). However, interest in such processes has begun to wane as numerous instances of practice either failed to work or else failed to institutionalize over the long term, including the paradigmatic Porto Alegre case (see Koonings 2009; Rodgers 2010).
15. This perspective can be related to earlier debates about self-help housing during the late 1960s and early 1970s; see, for example, Mangin (1967), and especially Turner (1968, 1969).
16. See Roberts (2010) for an exemplification of all these trends in relation to low-income neighbourhoods in Guatemala City.

References

Abers, R. (2000). *Inventing Local Democracy: Grassroots Politics in Brazil*. Boulder: Westview.

Angotti, T. (1995). 'The Latin American metropolis and the growth of inequality'. *NACLA Report on the Americas*, 28(4): 13–18.

Arana, A. (2005). 'How the street gangs took Central America'. *Foreign Affairs*, 84(3): 98–110.

Arias, E.D. (2006). *Drugs and Democracy in Rio de Janeiro: Trafficking, Social Networks, and Public Security*. Chapel Hill: University of North Carolina Press.

Auyero, J. (2000). *Poor People's Politics: Peronist Survival Networks and the Legacy of Evita*. Durham: Duke University Press.

Avritzer, L. (2002). *Democracy and the Public Space in Latin America*. Princeton: Princeton University Press.

Baiocchi, G. (2001). 'Brazilian cities in the nineties and beyond: new urban dystopias and utopias'. *Socialism and Democracy*, 15(2): 41–61.

Baiocchi, G. (2005). *Militants and Citizens: The Politics of Participatory Democracy in Porto Alegre*. Stanford: Stanford University Press.

Bastia, T. (2007). 'From mining to garment workshops: Bolivian migrants in Buenos Aires'. *Journal of Ethnic and Migration Studies*, 33(4): 655–69.

Bayat, A., and K. Biekart (2009). 'Cities of extremes'. *Development and Change*, 40(5): 815–25.

Beall, J., B. Guha-Khasnobis, and R. Kanbur (eds) (2010). *Urbanization and Development: Multidisciplinary Perspectives*. Oxford: Oxford University Press.

Burdick, J. (1992). 'Rethinking the study of social movements: the case of Christian base communities in urban Brazil'. In A. Escobar and S.E. Alvarez (eds), *The Making of Social Movements in Latin America: Identity, Strategy, and Democracy*. Boulder: Westview.

Butterworth, D., and J.K. Chance (1981). *Latin American Urbanization*. New York: Cambridge University Press.

Caldeira, T.P.R. (1999). 'Fortified enclaves: the new urban segregation'. In J. Holston (ed.), *Cities and Citizenship*. Durham: Duke University Press.

Caldeira, T.P.R. (2000). *City of Walls: Crime, Segregation and Citizenship in Sao Paulo*. Berkeley: University of California Press.

Cardoso, R. (1987). 'Movimentos sociais na América Latina'. *Revista Brasileira das Ciências Sociais*, 3(1): 27–37.

Castells, M. (1983). *The City and the Grassroots: A Cross-Cultural Theory of Urban Social Movements*. Berkeley: University of California Press.

Castles, S., and M.J. Miller (2009). *The Age of Migration: International Population Movements in the Modern World*. New York: The Guilford Press.

Cerrutti, M., and R. Bertoncello (2003). 'Urbanization and internal migration patterns in Latin America'. Paper presented at the Conference on African Migration in Comparative Perspective, 4–7 June, Johannesburg, South Africa.

Chavez, D., and B. Goldfrank (eds) (2004). *The Left in the City: Participatory Local Governments in Latin America*. London: Latin American Bureau.

Cornelius, W.A., and R.V. Kemper (eds) (1978). *Metropolitan Latin America: The Challenge and the Response*. Beverley Hills: Sage Publications.

Crot, L. (2006). '"Scenographic" and "cosmetic" planning: globalization and territorial restructuring in Buenos Aires'. *Journal of Urban Affairs*, 28(3): 227–51.

Davis, D.E. (2009). 'Non-state armed actors, new imagined communities, and shifting patterns of sovereignty and insecurity in the modern world'. *Contemporary Security Policy*, 30(2): 221–45.

Davis, D.E. (2010). 'The political and economic origins of violence and insecurity in Latin America: past trajectories and future prospects'. In E.D. Arias and D.M. Goldstein (eds), *Violent Democracies in Latin America*. Durham: Duke University Press: 35–62.

Davis, M. (2006). *Planet of Slums*. London: Verso.

de Rivero, O. (1998). *El Mito del Desarrollo: Los Paises Inviables en el Siglo XXI*. Lima: Mosca Azul.

de Soto, H. (1989). *The Other Path: The Invisible Revolution in the Third World*. New York: Harper and Row.

Dunkerley, J. (2000). *Americana: The Americas in the World, around 1850*. London: Verso.

Earle, L.O. (2009). 'Occupying the illegal city: urban social movements and social citizenship in Sao Paulo'. Unpublished PhD dissertation, Development Studies Institute, London School of Economics and Political Science.

Eckstein, S. (1977). *The Poverty of Revolution: The State and the Urban Poor in Mexico*. Princeton: Princeton University Press.

Eckstein, S. (ed.) (1989). *Power and Popular Protest: Latin American Social Movements*. Berkeley: University of California Press.

Eckstein, S. (1990). 'Urbanization revisited: inner-city slum of hope and squatter settlement of despair'. *World Development*, 18(2): 165–81.

Escobar, A. and S.E. Alvarez (eds) (1992). *The Making of Social Movements in Latin America: Identity, Strategy, and Democracy*. Boulder: Westview Press.

Fajnzylber, P., D. Lederman, and N. Loayza (2002). 'Inequality and violent crime'. *Journal of Law and Economics*, 45(1): 1–40.

Fernandes, E. (2007). 'Constructing the "right to the city" in Brazil'. *Social and Legal Studies*, 16(2): 201–19.

Fernandes, E. and A. Varley (eds) (1998). *Illegal Cities: Law and Urban Change in Developing Countries*. London: Zed Books.

Fischer, B., B. McCann, and J. Auyero (eds) (forthcoming). *Cities from Scratch: From Villas Miseria to Colonias Populares in Latin America*. Durham: Duke University Press.

Fischer, K., J. Jäger, and C. Parnreiter (2003). 'Transformación económica, políticas y producción de la segregación social en Chile y México'. *Scripta Nova*, VII(146): 127, http://www.ub.es/geocrit/sn/sn-146(127).htm.

Fung, A., and E.O. Wright (eds) (2003). *Deepening Democracy: Institutional Innovations in Empowered Participatory Governance*. London: Verso.

Galeano, E. (1998). *Patas Arriba: La Escuela del Mundo al Revés*. Madrid: Siglo Veintiuno.

Gay, R. (2009). 'From popular movements to drug gangs to militias: an anatomy of violence in Rio de Janeiro'. In K. Koonings and D. Kruijt (eds), *Mega-Cities: The Politics of Urban Exclusion and Violence in the Global South*. London: Zed.

Germani, G. (1973). 'Urbanization, social change, and the great transformation'. In G. Germani (ed.), *Modernization, Urbanization, and the Urban Crisis*. New York: Little, Brown and Co.

Gilbert, A. (1994). *The Latin American City*. London: Latin American Bureau.

Gilbert, A. (2007). 'The return of the slum: does language matter?' *International Journal of Urban and Regional Research*, 31(4): 697–713.

Gilbert, A. and A. Varley (1991). *Landlord and Tenant: Housing the Poor in Urban Mexico*. London: Routledge.

Gilbert, A., J.E. Hardoy, and R. Ramirez (eds) (1982). *Urbanization in Contemporary Latin America*. Chichester: John Wiley and Sons.
Gledhill, J. (1996). 'Putting the state back in without leaving the dialectics out: social movements, Elites, and Neoliberalism'. Paper presented to a session on 'Gramsci, Hegemony and the Critique of Anthropology', American Anthropological Association Meeting, San Francisco, November, http://jg.socialsciences.manchester.ac.uk/gramsci.pdf [accessed 8 May 2010].
Goldstein, D.M. (2003). *Laughter Out of Place: Race, Class, Violence and Sexuality in a Rio Shantytown*. Berkeley: University of California Press.
Goldstein, D.M. (2004). *The Spectacular City: Violence and Performance in Urban Bolivia*. Durham: Duke University Press.
Gomes da Cunha, O.M. (1998). 'Black movements and the politics of identity in Brazil'. In S.E. Alvarez, E. Dagnino, and A. Escobar (eds), *Cultures of Politics, Politics of Cultures: Revisioning Latin American Social Movements*. Boulder: Westview Press.
González Echevarría, R. (2003). 'Facundo: an introduction'. In D.F. Sarmiento (ed.), *Facundo: Civilization and Barbarism*. Berkeley: University of California Press.
Gugler, J. (1982). 'Overurbanization reconsidered'. *Economic Development and Cultural Change*, 31(1): 173–89.
Guha-Khasnobis, B., R. Kanbur, and E. Ostrom (eds) (2006). *Linking the Formal and Informal Economy: Concepts and Policies*. Oxford: Oxford University Press.
Gutmann, M.C. (2002). *The Romance of Democracy: Compliant Defiance in Contemporary Mexico*. Berkeley: University of California Press.
Hannerz, U. (1969). *Soulside: Inquiries into Ghetto Culture and Community*. New York: Columbia University Press.
Hardoy, J.E. (1973). *Pre-Columbian Cities*. London: Allen and Unwin.
Hardoy, J.E. (ed.) (1975). *Urbanization in Latin America: Approaches and Issues*. New York: Anchor books.
Hart, J.K. (1973). 'Informal income opportunities and urban employment in Ghana'. *Journal of Modern African Studies*, 11(1): 61–89.
Hauser, P.M. (ed.) (1961). *Urbanization in Latin America*. Paris: UNESCO.
Hernández, F., P. Kellett, and L.K. Allen (eds) (2010). *Rethinking the Informal City: Critical Perspectives from Latin America*. New York: Berghahn Books.
Hoberman, L.S., and S.M. Socolow (eds) (1986). *Cities and Society in Colonial Latin America*. Albuquerque: University of New Mexico Press.
Holston, J. (1989). *The Modernist City: An Anthropological Critique of Brasília*. Chicago: University of Chicago Press.
Holston, J. (2008). *Insurgent Citizenship: Disjunctions of Democracy and Modernity in Brazil*. Princeton: Princeton University Press.
Holston, J., and A. Appadurai (1999). 'Cities and citizenship'. In J. Holston (ed.), *Cities and Citizenship*. Durham: Duke University Press.
Hume, M. (2009). *The Politics of Violence: Gender, Conflict, and Community in El Salvador*. Chichester: Wiley-Blackwell.
Jelin, E. (ed.) (1990). *Women and Social Change in Latin America*. London: Zed.
Jones, G.A. (1994). 'The Latin American city as contested space: a manifesto'. *Bulletin of Latin American Research*, 13(1): 1–12.
Jones, G.A. (2006). 'Culture and politics in the "Latin American" city'. *Latin American Research Review*, 41(1): 241–60.

Jones, G.A., and M. Moreno-Carranco (2007). 'Megaprojects: beneath the pavement, excess'. *City*, 11(2): 144–64.

Jones, G.A., and D. Rodgers (eds) (2009). *Youth Violence in Latin America: Gangs and Juvenile Justice in Perspective*. New York: Palgrave Macmillan.

Jütersonke, O., R. Muggah, and D. Rodgers (2009). 'Gangs, urban violence, and security interventions in Central America'. *Security Dialogue*, 40(4–5): 373–97.

Kemper, R.V. (1971). 'Rural-urban migration in Latin America: a framework for the comparative analysis of geographical and temporal patterns'. *International Migration Review*, 5(1): 36–47.

Kemper, R.V. (2002). 'Urbanization in Latin America'. In M. Ember and C. R. Ember (eds), *Encyclopedia of Urban Cultures: Cities and Cultures around the World*. Danbury: Grolier Publishing.

Klich, I., and J. Lesser (eds) (1998). *Arab and Jewish Immigrants in Latin America: Images and Realities*. London: Frank Cass.

Koonings, K. (2009). 'Surviving regime change? Participatory democracy and the politics of citizenship in Porto Alegre, Brazil'. In P. Silva and H. Cleuren (eds), *Widening Democracy: Citizens and Participatory Schemes in Brazil and Chile*. Leiden: Brill.

Koonings, K., and D. Kruijt (eds) (2004). *Armed Actors: Organised Violence and State Failure in Latin America*. London: Zed Books.

Koonings, K., and D. Kruijt (eds) (2007). *Fractured Cities: Social Exclusion, Urban Violence and Contested Spaces in Latin America*. London: Zed.

Kowarick, L. (1980). *A Espoliação Urbana*. Rio de Janeiro: Paz e Terra.

Kowarick, L. (ed.) (1994). *Social Struggles and the City: The Case of São Paulo*. New York: Monthly Review Press.

Kruijt, D., and K. Koonings (1999). 'Introduction: violence and fear in Latin America'. In K. Koonings and D. Kruijt (eds), *Societies of Fear: The Legacy of Civil War, Violence and Terror in Latin America*. London: Zed.

Kruijt, D., and K. Koonings (2009). 'The rise of megacities and the urbanization of informality, exclusion and violence'. In K. Koonings and D. Kruijt (2009) *Mega-Cities: The Politics of Urban Exclusion and Violence in the Global South*. London: Zed.

Lancaster, R.N. (1988). *Thanks to God and the Revolution: Popular Religion and Class Consciousness in the New Nicaragua*. New York: Columbia University Press.

Lattes, A.E., J. Rodríguez, and M. Villa (2003). 'Population dynamics and urbanization in Latin America: concepts and data limitations'. In T. Champion and G. Hugo (eds), *New Forms of Urbanization: Beyond the Urban-Rural Dichotomy*. Aldershot: Ashgate.

Lazar, S. (2008). *El Alto, Rebel City: Self and Citizenship in Andean Bolivia*. Durham: Duke University Press.

Leacock, E. (1971). *The Culture of Poverty: A Critique*. New York: Simon and Schuster.

Leeds, A. (1994). *Cities, Classes, and the Social Order*. Ithaca: Cornell University Press.

Leeds, E. (1996). 'Cocaine and parallel polities in the Brazilian Urban periphery: constraints on local-level democratization'. *Latin American Research Review*, 31(3): 47–83.

Lehmann, D. (1991). *Democracy and Development in Latin America: Economies, Politics and Religion in the Postwar Period*. Cambridge: Polity Press.

Lewis, O. (1959). *Five Families: Mexican Case Studies in the Culture of Poverty.* New York: Basic Books.
Lewis, O. (1961). *The Children of Sánchez: Autobiography of a Mexican Family.* New York: Random House.
Lewis, O. (1966). *La Vida: A Puerto Rican Family in the Culture of Poverty – San Juan and New York.* New York: Random House.
Lewis, W.A. (1954). 'Economic development with unlimited supplies of labor'. *Manchester School of Economic and Social Studies,* 22(2): 139–91.
Liebel, M. (2004). 'Pandillas juveniles en Centroamérica o la difícil búsqueda de justicia en una sociedad violenta'. *Desacatos,* 14: 85–104.
Lloyd, P. (1979). *Slums of Hope? Shanty Towns of the Third World.* London: Penguin.
Lloyd, P. (1980). *The 'Young Towns' of Lima: Aspects of Urbanization in Peru.* Cambridge: Cambridge University Press.
Lobo, S. (1982). *A House of My Own: Social Organization in the Squatter Settlements of Lima, Peru.* Tucson: University of Arizona Press.
Lomnitz, L.A. (1977). *Networks and Marginality: Life in a Mexican Shantytown.* New York: Academic Press.
Londoño, J.-L., A. Gaviria, and R. Guerrero (eds) (2000). *Asalto al Desarrollo: Violencia en América Latina.* Washington, DC: IADB.
Lopes de Souza, M. (2006). 'Together with the state, despite the state, against the state: Social movements as "critical urban planning agents"'. *City,* 10(3): 327–42.
López Levy, M. (2004). *We Are Millions: Neo-liberalism and New Forms of Political Action in Argentina.* London: Latin American Bureau.
Low, S.M. (1995). 'Indigenous architecture and the Spanish American plaza in Mesoamerica and the Caribbean'. *American Anthropologist,* 97(4): 748–62.
Maloney, W. (2001). 'Informality revisited'. *World Bank Policy Research Working Paper,* 2965, Washington, DC: World Bank.
Mangin, W. (1967). 'Latin American squatter settlements: a problem and a solution'. *Latin American Research Review,* 2(3): 65–98.
Mangin, W. (ed.) (1970). *Peasants in Cities: Readings in the Anthropology of Urbanization.* Boston: Houghton Mifflin.
McCann, B. (2006). 'The political evolution of Rio de Janeiro's Favelas: recent works'. *Latin American Research Review,* 41(3): 149–63.
Melucci, A. (1996). *Challenging Codes: Collective Action in the Information Age.* Cambridge: Cambridge University Press.
Méndez, J.E., G. O'Donnell, and P.S. Pinheiro (eds) (1999) *The (Un)Rule of Law and the Underprivileged in Latin America.* Notre Dame: University of Notre Dame Press.
Morse, R.M. (1965). 'Recent research on Latin American urbanization: a selective survey with commentary'. *Latin American Research Review,* 1(1): 35–74.
Morse, R.M. (1974). 'Trends and patterns of Latin American urbanization, 1750–1920'. *Comparative Studies in Society and History,* 16(4): 416–47.
Morse, R.M., and J.E. Hardoy (eds) (1992). *Rethinking the Latin American city.* Washington, DC and Baltimore: Woodrow Wilson Center Press and Johns Hopkins University Press.

Moser, C.O.N. (1978). 'Informal sector or petty commodity production: dualism or dependence in urban development?', *World Development*, 6(9–10): 1041–64.

Moser, C.O.N. (2009). *Ordinary Families, Extraordinary Lives: Assets and Poverty Reduction in Guayaquil, 1978–2004*. Washington, DC: Brookings Institution Press.

Moser, C.O.N., and C. McIlwaine (2004). *Encounters with Violence in Latin America: Urban Poor Perceptions from Colombia and Guatemala*. London: Routledge.

Moser, C.O.N., and C. McIlwaine (2006). 'Latin American Urban Violence as a Development Concern: Towards a Framework for Violence Reduction'. *World Development*, 34(1): 89–112.

Mumford, L. (1996 [1937]). 'What is a city?'. In R.T. LeGates and F. Stout (eds), *The City Reader*. London: Routledge.

O'Donnell, G. (1999). *Counterpoints: Selected Essays on Authoritarianism and Democratization*. Notre Dame: University of Notre Dame Press.

Pearce, J. (1998). 'From civil war to "civil society": Has the end of the Cold War brought peace to Central America?', *International Affairs*, 74(3): 587–615.

Peattie, L.R. (1970). *The View from the Barrio*. Ann Arbor: University of Michigan Press.

Penglase, R.B. (2005). 'The shutdown of Rio de Janeiro: the poetics of drug trafficker violence'. *Anthropology Today*, 21(5): 3–6.

Perlman, J.E. (1976). *The Myth of Marginality: Urban Poverty and Politics in Rio de Janeiro*. Berkeley: University of California Press.

Perlman, J.E. (2010). *Favela: Four Decades of Living on the Edge in Rio de Janeiro*. Oxford: Oxford University Press.

Perreault, T., and P. Martin (2005). 'Geographies of neoliberalism in Latin America'. *Environment and Planning A*, 37(2): 191–201.

Pineo, R.F., and J.A. Baer (eds) (1998). *Cities of Hope: People, Protests, and Progress in urbanizing Latin America, 1870–1930*. Boulder: Westview Press.

Portes, A. (1972). 'Rationality in the slum: an essay on interpretive sociology'. *Comparative Studies in Society and History*, 14(3): 268–86.

Portes, A., and L. Benton (1984). 'Industrial development and labor absorption: a reinterpretation'. *Population and Development Review*, 10(4): 589–611.

Portes, A., and B.R. Roberts (2005). 'The free-market city: Latin American urbanization in the years of the neoliberal experiment'. *Studies in Comparative International Development*, 40(1): 43–82.

Portes, A., B.R. Roberts, and A. Grimson (2005). *Ciudades Latinoamericanas: Un Analysis Comparativo en el Umbral del Nuevo Siglo*. Buenos Aires: Prometeo Libros.

Rakowski, C.A. (ed.) (1994). *Contrapunto: The Informal Sector Debate in Latin America*. Albany: State University of New York Press.

Risør, H. (2010). 'Twenty hanging dolls and a lynching: defacing dangerousness and enacting citizenship in El Alto, Bolivia'. *Public Culture*, 22(3): 465–85.

Roberts, B.R. (1978). *City of Peasants: The Political Economy of Urbanization in the Third World*. Beverly Hills: Sage.

Roberts, B.R. (1989). 'Urbanization, migration, and development'. *Sociological Forum*, 4(4): 665–91.

Roberts, B.R. (2010). 'Moving on and moving back: rethinking inequality and migration in the Latin American city'. *Journal of Latin American Studies*, 42(3): 587–614.

Roberts, B.R., and A. Portes (2006). 'Coping with the free market city: collective action in six Latin American cities at the end of the twentieth century'. *Latin American Research Review*, 41(2): 57–83.

Roberts, B.R., and R.H. Wilson (eds) (2009). *Urban Segregation and Governance in the Americas*. New York: Palgrave.

Rodgers, D. (1999). 'Youth gangs and violence in Latin America and the Caribbean: a literature survey'. *Latin America and Caribbean Region Sustainable Development Urban Peace Program Working Paper* 4, Washington, DC: World Bank.

Rodgers, D. (2004). 'Disembedding the city: crime, insecurity, and spatial organization in Managua, Nicaragua'. *Environment and Urbanization*, 16(2): 113–24.

Rodgers, D. (2006a). 'Living in the shadow of death: Gangs, violence, and social order in urban Nicaragua, 1996–2002'. *Journal of Latin American Studies*, 38(2): 267–92.

Rodgers, D. (2006b). 'The state as a gang: conceptualising the governmentality of violence in contemporary Nicaragua'. *Critique of Anthropology*, 26(3): 315–30.

Rodgers, D. (2007). 'Managua'. In K. Koonings and D. Kruijt (eds), *Fractured Cities: Social Exclusion, Urban Violence and Contested Spaces in Latin America*. London: Zed.

Rodgers, D. (2008). 'An Illness called Managua'. *London School of Economics Crisis States Research Centre Working Paper* 37.2, London: CSRC, http://www2.lse.ac.uk/internationalDevelopment/research/crisisStates/download/wp/wpSeries2/wp372.pdf [accessed 27 March 2011].

Rodgers, D. (2009). 'Slum wars of the 21st century: gangs, Mano Dura, and the new urban geography of conflict in Central America'. *Development and Change*, 40(5): 949–76.

Rodgers, D. (2010). 'Contingent democratization: the rise and fall of participatory budgeting in Buenos Aires'. *Journal of Latin American Studies*, 42(1): 1–27.

Rodgers, D., and R. Muggah (2009), 'Gangs as non-state armed groups: the Central American case'. *Contemporary Security Policy*, 30(2): 301–17.

Rodgers, G. (ed.) (1989). *Urban Poverty and the Labour Market: Access to Jobs and Incomes in Asian and Latin American Cities*. Geneva: ILO.

Rolnik, R. (2001). 'Territorial exclusion and violence: the case of the state of São Paulo, Brazil'. *Geoforum*, 32(4): 471–82.

Rotker, S. (ed.) (2002). *Citizens of Fear: Urban Violence in Latin America*. New Brunswick: Rutgers University Press.

Sabatini, F., and F. Arenas (2000). 'Entre el Estado y el mercado: Resonancias geográficas y sustentabilidad social en Santiago de Chile'. *EURE*, 26(79): 95–113.

Santos, B. de S. (1995). *Toward a New Common Sense: Law, Science and Politics in the Paradigmatic Transition*. London: Routledge.

Sarmiento, D.F. (2003). *Facundo: Civilization and Barbarism*. Berkeley: University of California Press.

Smith, G. (1989). *Livelihood and Resistance: Peasants and the Politics of Land in Peru*. Berkeley: University of California Press.

Sovani, N.V. (1964). 'The analysis of "over-urbanization"'. *Economic Development and Cultural Change*, 12(2): 113–22.

Stokes, S.C. (1991). 'Politics and Latin America's urban poor: reflections from a Lima Shantytown'. *Latin American Research Review*, 26(2): 75–101.
Svampa, M. (2001). *Los que Ganaron: La Vida en los Countries y Barrios Privados*. Buenos Aires: Editorial Biblos.
Thomas, J.J. (1995). *Surviving in the City: The Urban Informal Sector in Latin America*. London: Pluto Press.
Toynbee, A. (1970). *Cities on the Move*. London: Oxford University Press.
Tsuda, T. (2001). 'When identities become modern: Japanese immigrants in Brazil and the global contextualization of identity'. *Ethnic and Racial Studies*, 24(3): 412–32.
Turner, J.C. (1968). 'Housing priorities, settlement patterns, and urban development in modernizing countries'. *Journal of the American Institute of Planners*, 34(6): 354–63.
Turner, J.C. (1969). 'Uncontrolled urban settlement: problems and policies'. In G. Breese (ed.), *The City in Newly Developing Countries: Readings on Urbanism and Urbanization*. Englewood Cliffs: Prentice Hall.
UN-Habitat (2003). *The Challenge of the Slums: Global Report on Human Settlements 2003*. London: Earthscan.
UN-Habitat (2007). *Enhancing Urban Safety and Security: Global Report on Human Settlements 2007*. London: Earthscan.
Valentine, C.A. (1968). *Culture and poverty: Critique and Counter-Proposals*. Chicago: University of Chicago Press.
Valladares, L., and M. Prates Coelho (1995). 'Urban research in Latin America: towards a research agenda'. *UNESCO Management of Social Transformations (MOST) Discussion Paper* 4, http://www.unesco.org/most/valleng.html [accessed 25 April 2010].
Velez-Ibañez, C.G. (1983). *Rituals of Marginality: Politics, Process, and Culture Change in Central Urban Mexico*. Berkeley: University of California Press.
Wade, P. (1997). *Race and Ethnicity in Latin America*. London: Pluto.
Walton, J. (1978). 'Guadalajara: creating the divided city'. In W.A. Cornelius and R.V. Kemper (eds), *Metropolitan Latin America: The Challenge and the Response*. Beverley Hills: Sage Publications.
Walton, J. (1979). 'From cities to systems: recent research on Latin American urbanization'. *Latin American Research Review*, 14(1): 159–69.
Whittier, N. (2002). 'Meaning and structure in social movements'. In D.S. Meyer, N. Whittier, and B. Robnett (eds), *Social Movements: Identity, Culture and the State*. Oxford: Oxford University Press.
Wolff, J. (2007). '(De-)Mobilising the marginalised: a comparison of the Argentine Piqueteros and Ecuador's indigenous movement'. *Journal of Latin American Studies*, 39(1): 1–29.
Wright, T. (2000). 'Gay organizations, NGOs, and the globalization of sexual identity: a Bolivian case'. *Journal of Latin American Anthropology*, 5(2): 89–111.
Zaluar, A. (2004). *Integração perversa: Pobreza e Tráfico de Drogras*. Rio de Janeiro: Editora FGV.

Part II

Reconceptualizing Urban Fragmentation

2
Urban Violence, Quality of Life, and the Future of Latin American Cities: The Dismal Record So Far and the Search for New Analytical Frameworks to Sustain the Bias towards Hope

Diane E. Davis

1 Introduction

The depressing fact of growing violence across major cities in Latin America is hardly news to scholars and practitioners in the region.[1] In recent years, the number of reports and publications devoted to violence or insecurity and their impact on urban quality of life has grown exponentially. Most of this work is hugely pessimistic, if not outright despairing, about the near intolerable urban conditions for large swathes of the urban population in Latin American cities. Even those whose scholarship is directed towards remedying these conditions are considerably humbled by the task at hand, given the interrelationships between violence, insecurity, un- and underemployment, and deteriorating quality of urban life, none of which can be easily reversed with conventional policy tools. This is not to say that efforts at reform have been entirely absent, or that scholars and policymakers in Latin America have not devoted considerable energy to formulating and/or implementing reform policies to reverse the problems of crime and insecurity. Recent work has highlighted the importance of concerted efforts to reform policing and the judicial system, as well as the importance of relying on financial or legal support from multilateral agencies and international human rights non-governmental organizations (NGOs) fighting impunity and insecurity. Calls for reforms or policy changes to accelerate the arrest capacities or crime-fighting activities of federal agents and the local police have been equally popular. Finally, the crafting and advocacy of community-level programmes that build local capacities to hold police and governments responsible, that educate citizens about their rights and responsibilities, and that offer new forms of citizen monitoring of criminal behaviour have also garnered widespread policy attention and support in recent years (Moser 2004; Arias and Rodrigues 2006).

But even with all these efforts, on-the-ground success has remained elusive, especially as measured by degrees of public confidence in the police and the latter's capacities to reduce violence and guarantee public security, let alone reverse crime rates. Crime, insecurity, and police impunity in the major cities of Latin America – most notably Rio de Janeiro, São Paulo, Buenos Aires, and Mexico City – remain at unprecedented levels, standing as one of the most serious problems facing the continent's urban citizenry. Part of the problem is due to structural constraints, including the fact that a corrupt police force and a weak judicial system are interrelated problems that together undermine the rule of law, further fuelling the likelihood of violence and insecurity. When one factors into this equation the globalization of illegal trade activities (in guns and drugs, for example) that foster or sustain new forms of criminality, and a neoliberal environment in which income inequality is on the rise and poverty continues unabated, the deck seems almost completely stacked against tangible progress. It should also be remembered that police or juridical reform and effective crime fighting generally entail concerted, labour-intensive actions that involve bureaucratic restructuring, individual retraining, new forms of recruiting, and daily (not to mention costly) vigilance to assess the robustness and permanence of these programmes and institutional modifications (Ungar 2002).

Even in those few situations where high-profile reform efforts have been universally recognized as having been relatively successful in eliminating the sources of violence and insecurity, they have generally had a short shelf life. In El Salvador, for example, which is considered a model case of police reform because it was actively coordinated and overseen by the UN and a bevy of international NGOs all working towards the same aims, initial gains pretty much disappeared within three years of completion (Call 2003: 828–9), with insecurity and impunity rapidly returning to pre-reform levels. In light of such initiatives, it is tempting to conclude that the content and sweep of those policy changes intended to reverse the violence-insecurity nexus are more important in symbolic than in substantive terms, mainly because their chief effect has been to give citizens a sense that efforts are being made, while serious progress remains elusive. In light of this sorry state of affairs, what is to be done other than throwing in the towel? In this chapter I offer an alternative framework for assessing and potentially remedying the violence-insecurity nexus in Latin American cities, one that entails a focus on the ways that cities are changing as a result of this nexus. I hope that these trends might serve as the starting point for generating novel policy ideas and/or renewed hope for bettering the future of Latin American cities. Specifically, rather than focusing directly on the structural causes of rising crime and violence, or on the institutional conditions of the state, economy, or administration of justice systems that mitigate against measurable gains in fighting crime and reducing insecurity, I turn my attention to effects, and use a closer focus to evaluate which urban policies have (or have not) worked in reducing the problems of crime and violence, how, and why.

This strategy serves as the analytical equivalent of a magician's sleight of hand to some degree: it redirects scholarly attention away from crime and violence per se, and towards the ways that citizens, business firms, and the city itself have actually responded to these threats. By jumping analytical tracks, so to speak, I try to lay the foundation for hope. Rather than miring the analysis in a study of the corrupt and self-sustaining vicious cycle of violence and impunity from which exit appears almost impossible, and in which government policymakers are routinely thwarted, our attention is turned to other aspects of urban life and livelihood that are changing in the context of growing crime and violence, perhaps even for the better. To do so is not to deny the existence of these terrible problems, but to recognize that cities and their citizens can (and have) shown resilience and pragmatism, both of which can help create positive urban change in ways that may cultivate greater scope for optimism and new opportunities for productive policy action – if not directly in the area of insecurity, then perhaps in other significant dimensions of urban life that can help compensate for or diminish the magnitude of these problems.

To accomplish these conceptual aims, I have developed a three-fold framework to assess recent urban changes in violent and crime-ridden Latin American cities. First, I assess the *character* of recent urban transformations: whether there have been positive or negative developments, both with respect to the security situation and the overall quality of urban life. Second, I consider the *permanence and sustainability* of recent changes. The mere exercise of trying to distinguish between ephemeral and lasting changes in crime-ridden Latin American cities is valuable because it underscores the importance of cultivating a deeper appreciation of the institutions, actors, wider socioeconomic conditions, and processes involved in transforming the urban landscape, as well as the likelihood that they will continue, as opposed to being reversed or thwarted. Third, and perhaps most important, I analyse recent urban transformations along several distinct dimensions of urban life, rather than trying to assess the city as a whole. Specifically, I develop a four-fold focus on the *physical, economic, social,* and *political* aspects of life in Latin American cities, and how greater insecurity and violence affect them. By analysing and disaggregating urban changes through this sectoral lens, we can see which aspects of urban life have been most egregiously transformed by the violence-insecurity nexus.

The chapter draws on data, ethnographic materials, primary and secondary documents, and personal interviews collected through my own long-term studies of crime, violence, and urban development in Mexico City. The chapter starts by examining transformations in the city's urban social infrastructure, offering an overview of the social consequences of the violence-insecurity nexus for residents. It then looks at the three other domains of urban life (physical, economic, political) in turn; each examination begins with the negative aspects and then moves onto the positive developments. After examining all four sectors, the next section takes a step back and offers overall assessments of the aggregate picture presented in the narrative, both with respect to the positive and negative character of urban transformations in the city as a whole, as well as with respect to their permanent or ephemeral nature. This exercise leads to a final section on policy recommendations, which builds on the understanding of where the recent violence/insecurity-led urban transformations have been most positive. In particular, it considers whether further advances can be made in reinforcing positive changes (and reversing negative ones), even without clear progress on crime and insecurity, and concludes by discussing several promising avenues for further innovation and action, especially those that might indirectly feed back on the violence-insecurity nexus in unexpected yet positive ways.

2 The urban social consequences of the violence-insecurity nexus

Among those who study the urban social consequences of the rising rates of violence and insecurity in Latin America, there seems to be an overwhelming consensus that the picture is extremely negative. Several of the most harmful and socially destructive changes in Latin American cities, and which have sparked the most discussion and concern, are the acceleration of a climate of fear, both in terms of physical and psychological wellbeing (Rotker 2002), the increasing turn to violence as a means for routine problem solving – whether at the level of the family, the neighbourhood, or across the city as a whole (Moser 2004) – and an attendant reduction in the quality of public life, neighbourliness, and community cooperation (Concha-Eastman 2002). According to one scholar of the subject, 'violence generates changes in social behaviour [and the] production and erosion of social capital', which in turn makes it more difficult to sustain cooperation and collaboration within families, communities, and at other levels of society (ibid.: 49; see also Ratinoff 1996). Although these changes are often considered to be individual responses, one must not forget that other mediating institutions and practices play a role in exacerbating fear, and thus in cultivating an urban social climate in which violence may become relatively 'normalized'. Two sets of actors and institutions are key here: the media and the police. Recent studies have shown that media attention to violence and crime, although grounded in real statistical evidence, can accelerate perceptions of fear, thereby driving the vicious cycle of insecurity and social withdrawal (Martín-Barbero 2002). This dynamic owes much to the logic of media production and consumption (i.e. the types of stories selected for presentation; their framing as news, which drives sensationalism; the inability of consumers to differentiate the ordinary from the sensational; and so forth). Moreover, the routine reporting of crime-related occurrences in newspapers and on television can give the sense that such actions are the norm, which may help foment a habitual recourse to violence in all domains of social life.

The police also play a mediating role in producing a climate of fear and in privileging the use of force as the single most legitimate means for remedying the problems of criminality, thereby 'normalizing' violence as a response to violence (de la Barreda Solórzano 2007). To a great degree, police involvement in criminal activities, either in collusion or through corruption, is as much the effect as the cause of further violence and insecurity, and this is true for both public and private police. On the public side, the problems of crime have accelerated so rapidly that police and citizens alike have begun advocating for greater arrest powers, tougher crime-fighting laws, and reduced restrictions on police discretion. In Mexico, upon the advice of Rudolph Giuliani, a form of 'zero tolerance' was recently adopted, leading to the criminalization of a wide variety of behaviours long associated with urban street life, including the activities of 'squeegee men' who cleaned car windshields at stop signs, and the street-selling of petty traders and vendors in certain key locations of the city (Davis 2007). Although such restrictive measures might create a greater sense of security among potential victims, especially those of the middle and upper classes, they also increase a sense of insecurity among certain more politically disenfranchised (and mainly low-income) citizens who now are identified as likely criminal suspects when they seek to earn a living, and those whose life may be more socially precarious (Koonings and Kruijt 2007).

Still, with a long history of corruption and impunity among the police, even those citizens who are not likely to be socially confused with criminals may find themselves at the end of an extortion chain in which police (sometimes in collusion with criminals) hit them up for bribes, further fuelling the overall sense of insecurity (Bergman 2007). In such conditions, many turn to private police; however, the proliferation of private police has not reversed the problems of crime or reduced feelings of insecurity. In my own interviews with citizens in Mexico, many complained that while they felt compelled to employ private police because of the general problems of insecurity and accelerating crime, they knew that private police were often involved in criminal activities as well. Some even argued that private police were a magnet for crime, because they 'advertised' to the public both the resources and prosperity of their employers, thus making themselves more likely targets for crime. This is a bit of a paradox, especially when one considers that citizens and businesses began to absorb the servicing and protection duties that had long been the legitimate charge of 'public' police precisely because the 'official' forces were unable to stop the rise in crime. To be sure, citizens cannot be faulted for turning to the private sector to solve problems that the government and local police are incapable of tackling. Yet the decision to bypass public police in favour of private security forces has its clear downside in social terms. For example, it often translates into less accountability and less social engagement between citizens and governing officials, insofar as there is the question of to whom private police are accountable – and what this means for social equity, justice, and the rule of law more generally.

But there are also some clear positives in the social arena of Latin American cities, especially if we look for collective – and not merely individual – responses to violence and insecurity. For one, growing concern about the deteriorating conditions has fostered new forms of citizen participation and new incentives for social mobilization. With support from global and/or local NGOs, citizens are developing new ways to work together at the level of the community, ranging from 'mapping' local delinquency and crime patterns to new forms of interaction with police. Although the idea of community policing is not new, it is arriving in Latin American cities with a great fanfare, and many of these programmes offer new ways for citizens to gain intimate knowledge of how local police departments work. What is most positive about these trends is not merely the collective claim-making or the resurgence of an active citizenry. What remains key to the issue of crime and insecurity is that new social alliances are being forged behind this issue, because it permeates all of urban society, often to the point of bringing the middle classes together with the rich and poor in a single coalition around similar complaints. This type of alliance can potentially form the basis for a new social project in an era of social and political transition, by uniting citizens around issues that are less divisive and polarizing than those associated with the ideologies and models of politics that dominated in earlier eras. At a minimum, though, it can force elected officials and political leaders to move beyond old ways of doing politics – whether it be clientelism, state-centrism, or a myopic preoccupation with economic development – and compel them to find programmes, languages, ideas, and alliances that will address some of the strongly articulated concerns about insecurity advanced by the urban citizenry.

3 Urban spatial consequences of the violence-insecurity nexus

On the physical and spatial front, violence and insecurity have transformed Latin American cities in a variety of visible ways. From the point of view of classical urbanism, most of these changes are considered to be negative, if not out-and-out horrifying. The list of questionable physical transformations seen as a response to unprecedented levels of crime ranges from the rise of gated communities and other guarded urban and suburban enclaves, where citizens fortress themselves in order to keep out the forces of crime, to the increased use of cars and other private modes of transport (owing to the high rates of robbery and rape on public transport), to the reduced availability and use of public space (Valenzuela 2007). Stated simply, citizens have become so fearful of crime that they are changing where and how they live, travel, and interact with their fellow citizens. In Mexico City, there is considerable fear and anxiety associated with being in public spaces (Jiménez

Ornelas 2005: 124; de la Barreda Solórzano 2007). These sentiments are reflected in recent surveys, which show that 39 per cent of Mexico City's residents (and 20 per cent nationally) are fearful of public spaces; a startling 77 per cent will not go out at night, and 48 per cent consistently avoid public transport (Jiménez Ornelas 2005: 124–6).

The combined impact of these fears and avoidance strategies has reduced the scope for face-to-face interaction, whether in streets, parks, or buses. It has also reinforced the privatization and atomization of urban social life in ways that depart from the past, when a vibrant urban physical environment and culture was characteristic of life and livelihood in most Latin American cities. In prior epochs, central plazas, parks, and downtown streets served as the lifeblood of public communication and interaction, contributing (in a modest way) to what Jürgen Habermas has called the 'public sphere'. In Mexico City, some of the most public and open spaces were in downtown areas, where Habermas's notion of public life and public opinion (the latter evidenced through parades, protests, and marches on Constitution Plaza, also known by its Indian name, Zócalo) often have achieved their most powerful incarnation. But, over the years the most public of places and experiences, the historic centre, has been transformed by rising crime. Downtown areas now host some of the city's most dangerous streets, where informality and illegality collide to create a 'no man's land' where citizens fear to tread. As a result, the 'public' character of downtown and other key areas of the city have become ever more circumscribed as fewer and fewer people stroll its streets (Valenzuela 2007).

One can also view the negative effects of fear and violence on the spatial form and character of the city through the lens of environmental sustainability. With citizens turning to private cars and gated suburban developments as escape hatches, metropolitan sprawl continues; there is increased demand for new suburban infrastructure, thus more consumption of green spaces and an upward trend in overall pollution levels. In Mexico City, the expansion of the city to the far reaches of the valley of Mexico has also had a negative impact on the water supply, and has hiked the demand for other basic services like sewerage and electricity. The turn towards private automobile use is not trivial, especially by women and the middle classes, who are among the most fearful of using public transportation. Whatever the origins, the upshot is a fragmented, sprawled, and environmentally challenged urban agglomeration that, while potentially safer for individual residents, leaves much to be desired in terms of urban sustainability.

Nonetheless, all is not lost on the spatio-physical front. Perhaps one of the most interesting positive consequences of the dystopian urbanism that hovers over many crime-ridden cities of Latin America is the new-found support for urban renewal, jump-started by massive public and private sector commitment to reviving the built environment of the city, especially old areas of downtown long dominated by informal and illegal activities. The recent programme to 'rescue' or redevelop downtown Mexico City, with support from purveyors of iconic architecture and one of the world's richest men, Carlos Slim, is a case in point (Davis 2006a). Mexico City's problems with growing crime, delinquency, and violence began to accelerate dramatically in the mid-1990s. Between 1990 and 1996, reported rates of robbery, property damage, fraud, and extortion more than doubled from 1,059.0 to 2,434.3 incidents per 100,000 inhabitants (*Fundación Mexicana* 1997: 16). In this same time period, the percentage of robberies involving violence increased from 38.5 per cent to 55.5 per cent (ibid.: 17). By the late-1990s and early 2000, citizens who used to buy goods in the historic centre and stroll through the downtown plazas and boulevards surrounding the government offices, museums, and national cathedral were increasingly fearful of venturing downtown.[2] This held true not only for middle-class residents; as time passed, even the city's poor found that they too were afraid to venture into these areas because of the high levels of violence and the total absence of a rule of law. And with few customers venturing downtown, even the informal vendors, who had long relished the dilapidated areas because they could sell their goods in peace and without threat of eviction, supported efforts for change.

In response, a coalition of private and public actors joined together to invest huge sums of money in the development of downtown. Today, a scant six years after the formal announcement of the 'rescue', Mexico City's historical centre has experienced a major cultural revival, with new investments in hotels, restaurants, museums, public buildings, parks, and housing. The mixed land use, the historical revival of colonial buildings and monuments, and the vibrant cultural life that now spills into cafes, streets, and entertainment venues have generated kudos from professional urbanists and residents alike. Others have gone so far as to suggest that these urban transformations, by reinvigorating land use and reviving public spaces, have helped reduce downtown crime rates and the unwillingness to venture into the streets. Granted, some of the latter improvements are the result of the deployment of a special police force that has been mounted in order to protect the new downtown developments and give the public a sense of security, as well as innovations in high-tech surveillance, including video cameras posted in key streets and public buildings with direct hook-up to a police monitoring centre. But the gains in reducing crime and increasing security cannot be attributed merely to new policing and surveillance programmes that target criminals per se, but also to the larger project of revitalizing public space and land use, and the beneficial effects that accrue from these combined efforts.

4 Urban economic consequences of the violence-insecurity nexus

One recent line of research in the study of crime-ridden cities is the impact of violence and insecurity on the local economy, especially private sector investment. Although systematic data are hard to find, the general view is that crime and insecurity do have a dampening effect on certain sectors of the economy. The most obvious is the potential impact on investor confidence. Both domestic and foreign firms become anxious about the potentially negative impacts on their activities associated with high crime and violence, ranging from material losses through robbery and assault, to higher costs for security personnel to protect physical and human capital, to the threat of catastrophic loss associated with the kidnapping of executives. In Mexico, the latter problem has reached epidemic proportions, with many criminal gangs devoted entirely to kidnapping. In such an environment, foreign investors are likely to think twice about moving their firm's activities or headquarters to Mexico, or at least to the most crime-ridden cities. This has meant that potential investment revenues, and conceivably new areas of economic growth, may have been lost because of the larger environment of insecurity.

But private sector firms are not the only ones facing potential loss of revenue. Crime and violence have grown in an environment of informality and illegality, in which black markets tend to flourish. This not only poses a potential obstacle to investors in the formal economy, who will avoid investing in commercial, manufacturing, or trade activities that are provided at much lower costs in the informal sector; it also means that the public sector will miss out on tax revenue from those formal firms. To the extent that more funds in the public coffers help pay for crime-fighting measures, the loss of revenue associated with the rise of illegality and informality may push a vicious cycle in which formal investors withdraw and crime increases. To be clear, not all informal sector activities are illegal or criminal, and thus the relationship between crime and informality is neither automatic nor direct. But many of those who work in the informal sector prefer the dilapidated and inaccessible back alleys and streets where their clandestine activities can remain hidden from view, and where police often fear to tread. As a result, informal sector workers frequently oppose urban renewal plans promoted by real estate developers, thereby finding themselves in conflict with public and private sector actors when it comes to desired changes in the character of the built environment (Davis 2006b).

However, even though violence and insecurity may serve as disincentives for investment in manufacturing, commerce, or other traditional sectors of the Latin American urban economy, they also are producing new avenues of servicing, employment, and product development. Specifically, the negative security environment in Latin America has helped jump-start the development of the private security industry, which relies on new technologies and human capital to service a burgeoning clientele. The exponential proliferation of private security firms in Mexico City, which started in 1994, took many observers by surprise; since then it has translated into enormous growth, not just for global firms involved in high-end security services for wealthy or corporate clientele, but also for local firms that work for neighbourhood organizations, small business associations, and other more modest consumers. Security guard positions and other low-skilled security services offer a growing source of employment, especially for unskilled and minimally educated workers whose prospects of employment have declined as economic globalization has changed the character and traditional industrial options for low-wage employment in Mexico. The potential downside, of course, is that the growth of the security industry feeds itself to a great degree, with the proliferation of firms offering security services driving the perception that crime and violence are out of control.

5 Urban political consequences of the violence-insecurity nexus

The final sector to assess is the political, a domain to which surprisingly little attention has been paid. How have the violence- and insecurity-led transformations in Latin American cities affected local – and possibly even national – politics? If we defined politics from the point of view of civil society, we would highlight the emergence of new forms of collective organization that empower citizens to engage with the state about solving security issues, a trend already noted above. But has the crime and security situation affected politics 'from above', as well as from below? Has it impacted upon the activities and orientations of political parties and elected officials? In Mexico it clearly has, but not always in positive ways. One of the most visible consequences of the growing problem of insecurity is the acceleration of internecine political conflict between the Partido de la Revolución Democrática (PRD), the Partido Acción Nacional (PAN), and the Partido Revolucionario Institucional (PRI) over which is the most effective party in rooting out crime and impunity. Likewise, the fact that crime and insecurity conditions tend to transcend formal territorial jurisdictions has brought new intrastate political conflicts and tensions, which either map with partisan tensions (when different parties control different jurisdictions) or exacerbate policymaking tensions within the same party. Both situations create organizational stalemate and/or conflict, which in turn limits the capacity for successful reform and the implementation of effective crime-fighting programmes (Davis 2006a).

Evidence of all this is clear from a closer look at partisan infighting and political conflict over crime fighting in Mexico City over the last decade. In 1997, three years into the city's unparalleled upsurge of crime and violence, the newly elected PRD government of Cuauhtémoc Cárdenas sought to assert greater control over Mexico City police, seeing them as the key to impunity and crime fighting. But political conditions and institutional goals on the national level did not follow suit, because a different party (PRI) maintained its monopoly on the national executive. The PRI then used its reservoir of institutional capacities to undermine police reform efforts in the capital, leading to partisan conflict.[3] And even when the PRI lost on the federal level, and yet a third party (PAN) came into power nationally, political conflict continued, coming to a head in a particularly high-profile case of vigilantism in late 2004, in which federal police were lynched by a group of citizens (*El Universal* 2004). During the official outcry over the event it became clear that one of the reasons the federal policemen had lost their lives at the hands of the crowd was that the local riot police, who answered to Mexico City (and not federal) authorities, had not actively intervened to save the attacked officers.

In response to the lynching, Mexico's two most important elected politicians, President Vicente Fox and Mexico City Mayor Manuel López Obrador, turned this troubling event into a pre-presidential electoral dogfight. Rather than uniting forces in the common search for a policy solution to the problems of police conflict and citizen vigilantism, these bitter rivals – from competing political parties, controlling the two most significant levels of governance in the nation, and locked in a treacherous struggle for the hearts and minds of Mexico City's residents and the national electorate more generally – sought to use the situation to humiliate each other so as to score points with the electorate, as they had done with many other high-profile incidents of violence, police corruption, and impunity (CNI en Linea, 7 December 2004; 8 December 2004). For his part, President Fox used the lynching as a pretext for forcing the resignation of Mexico City's very popular police chief, Marcelo Ebrard, a key ally of Fox's main political rival, Mayor López Obrador. In response, López Obrador retaliated by charging Fox with playing dirty politics, even as he set out on his own independent search for a new round of police reforms and alternative security policies to show that he, as mayor, was better able to gain control of the situation than the president (CNI en Linea, 7 December 2004).

This political picture is far from positive, but there have been signs of hope in Mexico City since Marcelo Ebrard was subsequently elected mayor of the city. In particular, he built on his prior efforts at police reform, seeking to break the stranglehold of corruption and introduce new means of making police more accountable. He created new programmes and political alliances that wreaked havoc on the old hierarchies of political power in long-standing governance and police institutions, while also linking previously antagonistic state and civil society actors in a common project of reducing crime. Specifically, a few months after coming to office, Mayor Ebrard established and empowered a brand new political authority in Mexico City named the *Autoridad del Centro Histórico* (Historic Centre Authority), and charged it to deal with problems of policing, crime, and urban quality of life in the highly circumscribed but critical and economically vibrant area of downtown near the historic centre of the city. The targeted area had long been associated with crime and police corruption, but was also the setting for real estate efforts to 'rescue' downtown and its built heritage so as to increase property values, upgrade the commercial clientele, draw tourist and other affluent populations downtown, and minimize crime by offering new sources of income and employment to local residents.

The newly empowered *Autoridad del Centro Histórico* was given the task of managing and coordinating all activities that occurred within this circumscribed area, such as policing, street cleaning, granting construction permits, monitoring air quality, regulating transport, and accommodating cultural tourism (Ruiz Healy 2007). As such, it came to supplant all other institutional hierarchies and established levels of governance. New forms of regulation and reform in terms of accountability consequently accrued not only to police activity, but also to other public services offered in this area which had previously been coordinated sectorally, at the level of the whole of the city, or even federally, but not at this sub-territorial level. Finally, the *Autoridad* also undertook the coordination and regulation of public activities in conjunction with private sector developers and NGO activists who were driving new investment and cultural or social projects in the area.

This experiment has been moderately successful in eliminating old institutional practices in urban public service delivery and in bettering the conditions of public security in this highly troubled area. Citizens have come back to the historic centre to shop, eat, and live in ever greater numbers, and the general sense is that crime rates in the area have stopped accelerating. But, more importantly, this experiment offered a new model for enhancing police accountability, vis-à-vis citizens and authorities, as well as local businesses, leading to a less corrupt police force and greater confidence in the local police. Much of this is due to the fact that a special police force, designated only to the historic centre, has special institutional oversight of this circumscribed territory. At the same time, it is important to note that many of the personnel recruited for this specially designated police personnel had personal ties to the mayor. This not only ensured them high salaries and special privileges, which helped mitigate against the temptation of corruption, but it also meant they were politically tied to a political team that wanted the experiment to succeed. Although clearly important, this personalized element of the project clearly raises some questions about reproduction and the possibility of clientelism.

6 Assessing the overall picture: gains and losses in the short and long terms

Through the above narrative analysis of sectoral transformations in crime-ridden Mexico City over the past decade, we can observe both gains and losses in terms of urban quality of life, as understood in social, physical, economic, and political terms. It is difficult to say whether the overall urban balance is positive or negative. There have been some clearly beneficial changes in land use, urban redevelopment, employment, social mobilization, and economic growth, but these changes have not eliminated social anxiety: they are still accompanied by political dissatisfaction and disenfranchisement, and they have unfolded in an environment where the growth of the 'security-industrial complex' has brought more individuals into a world of criminality while further reinforcing a public sense of fear and insecurity rather than eliminating it. In terms of whether these changes will have short- versus long-term impacts on the Latin American city, the jury is not yet out, partly because immediate changes in one sector can produce long-term changes in another, some of which may exacerbate rather than eliminate insecurity and crime. This is clear with a focus on the rise of private security forces, a phenomenon related to both citizen dissatisfaction with public police and the growth of the security industry as a source of employment and technological innovation.

With a growing market for the production and consumption of security-related goods, the future of these activities is practically assured. In fact, private security services appear to be making a long-term mark on Latin American cities because they are bringing new corporate investors, new technologies, and new patterns of employment into an environment where other options are limited. This also means that the private security industry is unlikely to disappear on its own, even if crime and insecurity conditions were to improve automatically. And to the extent that the proliferation of these activities can reinforce citizen fears by their very presence, and thus help cultivate an environment of insecurity, their persistence – although good for the economy and unemployment – may have unanticipated but long-term negative consequences on the urban experience and quality of life. In order to balance the gains and losses, both short and long term, policymakers need to pay more attention to the security industry and its present and future role in Latin American cities. At present, the trend suggests problems ahead, and a call for policymakers to think more carefully about regulating, monitoring, and taxing private security services in ways that may help to mitigate the negative externalities associated with this sector.

A second, complex area that warrants further temporal assessment is the domain of spatial and physical changes in the city. On the upside, efforts at urban renovation and the revitalization of previously crime-ridden areas have been successful in the short term, at least in bringing citizens and public life back to areas that had been abandoned. The short-term impact on city form – including sprawl, which accelerated as a result of population movement away from these abandoned areas and other problematic public spaces (and modes of transport) – is less clear, although one could imagine that the revitalization of old downtown areas in crime-heavy Latin American cities might offer new residential alternatives and diminish the trend towards suburbanization.

However, in the longer term, these revitalization programmes may produce their own set of problems and priorities. One reason is that such programmes count on strategies for 'securing' these newly revitalized public spaces, either through more attentive policing or other surveillance methods. Yet these mediating actors and technologies may actually be eliminating public space as much as reclaiming it. Because few public or private investors have the resources to totally transform more than a few buildings or streets at a time, partial efforts are necessary, which in turn means that any heavy policing or surveillance strategies designed to protect these few redeveloped pockets of space will also be scattered and targeted. This means that persons or activities in properties or areas outside the redeveloped parcels will most likely be subject to excess policing, surveillance, and, most probably, social exclusion if not extreme insecurity (both relative and actual), owing to the spillover effects in contiguous areas as a result of keeping criminals outside of a few protected zones.

The long-term result of this dynamic may be a more diminished – or at least narrowed or segmented – public sphere, in the sense that in the city's overall high-crime environment, those public spaces that are utilized are also less likely to host class and income diversity. One might even go so far as to say that with targeted urban redevelopment, a city is more likely to host two 'publics' in its domain: one comprising those citizens who use the streets and other public locales (even though problems of crime and insecurity put them at risk when they go public, thereby limiting their freedom of movement), and another comprising citizens who move through a semi-privatized urban world accompanied by surveillance cameras, security personnel, and private armoured cars, all of which allow them a degree of free movement in public spaces, but keep them physically or technologically separated from the 'other public'. All this will unfold, moreover, in a city that still suffers from violence and insecurity, thereby suggesting that more policy attention be paid to the larger social and spatial consequences of successful urban redevelopment projects. Can the positive gains associated with urban renewal programmes be scaled to the city as a whole? Will security conditions be improved if redevelopment remains only partial? What are the limits, in short, of targeted urban redevelopment when most of a city remains poor, dilapidated, and socially excluded from these areas?

With regard to social exclusion/inclusion, a third arena in which greater consideration of long- and short-term gains and losses would be valuable is precisely that of the new social conditions of Latin American cities. As noted above, one positive development in response to growing violence and insecurity is the emergence of new forms of collective claim-making and a general citizen consciousness that creates new forms of unity and common social projects. But these developments also have their limits, especially in the long run, owing to the fact that citizens who use the route of social mobilization rather than the formal political process show themselves to be disenfranchised – if not cynical – about the possibilities for fundamental reform. To be sure, with many grassroots groups taking the problems of police corruption and public insecurity to heart, and seeking alternative solutions and community practices at the neighbourhood level, there is evidence that citizens are both building on and reinforcing the democratic practices and advances that resulted from many years of struggle against authoritarianism. In recent years the Mexico City government has supported citizen security meetings at the level of the delegation, with the goal of bringing residents and police together in democratic dialogue about how best to guarantee public security. Yet the results have been highly circumscribed, and perhaps more ornamental and symbolic than substantive as citizens do not speak frankly about police corruption and criminal impunity in their neighbourhood when those very same police are sitting across the table, armed with their note pads and badges (and potentially identifying citizens by face and address), and known to be involved in crime as much as fighting it.

Given the limits to individual – and even neighbourhood – action, among those social organizations making most headway in tackling crime and police corruption are those operating on a city-wide basis, something which guarantees a larger scale and greater scope for action and organization. In Mexico, the most high-profile organizations operating on this scale tend to work in collaboration with private sector businesses. One such organization – actually funded by the private sector – is the Instituto Ciudadano de Estudios Sobre la Insecuridad (ICESI), which has developed a massive public relations campaign about police corruption; its efforts have included publishing the names of police officials known to be involved in illegal activities. Organizations like ICESI have considerable clout because of their connections with the wealthier elite in society, as well as a great deal of legitimacy because they are independent from the institutions of government that are all too often implicated in police corruption or the failure to stem its tide. But these types of organization also have a narrowly defined view of the problem of insecurity, why it occurs, how best to solve it, and to whom they should be accountable. In particular, those linked to business often care about crime and police corruption primarily because they create an environment in which economic gains are put in jeopardy, either by creating location disincentives for private investors, or by driving away potential consumers. Within this framing, concerns about justice and human rights are sidelined, while the techniques these organizations favour are often more consistent with an authoritarian, eliminate-the-problem-no-matter-what-it-takes ethos.

This has included pushing for harsher legislative penalties against criminals and greater powers of arrest for police; political parties in Mexico have clearly begun to jump on this bandwagon, as evidenced by the fact that the administration of President Felipe Calderón empowered the military to work in the arena of crime fighting, giving them unparalleled powers to use military weapons and techniques to confront crime and insecurity, no matter the consequences. These trends suggest the need for greater policy attention to human rights violations and to social inequities or exclusions being reinforced through the positive development of business and politicians' involvement in crime fighting. They also suggest a critical rethinking of the increasingly militarized context in which the war on crime is being fought. Although there may be short-term gains in buttressing arrest rates and making headway against organized crime and other major players by using military personnel and tactics, the long-term trade-offs in empowering the armed forces, in criminalizing low social status individuals and activities, in minimizing human rights abuses, and in reinforcing a political regime built on the dedicated use of violence (even when directed against criminals), suggest that the future will be marked by more social conflict and political tension.

7 Building a new institutional framework for enabling progress on the violence-insecurity nexus

Precisely because the long-term prospects on the social, economic, spatial, and even political fronts continue to remain mixed, it is easy to get excited about clear progress, and especially about those few innovations that do seem to have produced some positive gains while also laying the groundwork for long-term gains. Along these lines, let us return to the institutional reforms introduced by Mexico City Mayor Ebrard and analyse their dynamics with an eye to the larger policy progress and lessons they embody. As noted above, the gains in fighting crime and creating an environment of greater security in Mexico City's troubled downtown areas was not only due to the urban redevelopment efforts introduced by public and private sector actors, or to the mayor's personal capacity to reduce corruption among the city police. Both were significant, but the programme's short-term successes were also owed to the organizational innovations in local governance introduced by the mayor, which introduced new forms of politics capable of transcending old patron-client practices by offering new vertical connections as much as horizontal ones. This organizational innovation centred around the establishment of an entirely new type of authority, the *Autoridad del Centro Histórico*, which bounded a territorial entity for policy action that allowed for new forms of coordination and self-reinforcing commitments to reducing crime from a variety of stakeholders.[4]

What is important about this experiment, analytically speaking, is the way that the new lines of authority generated by the establishment of the *Autoridad* – which were also reinforced by the network of loyalties within and between a small but focused group of public and private actors – cross-cut old corrupt institutions and lines of decision-making so as to diminish the individual and institutional influences of the past, including those built on patronage politics. Freed from old power structures, the *Autoridad* was in a position to promote and strengthen anti-crime and security priorities on the basis of new networks, new loyalties, and a new territoriality. Its capacities in this regard are not just related to controlling and monitoring the police, who have been effectively wrenched out of the old, still-corrupt structures of policing, but also relates to other services. For decades, decisions about the police, and other downtown services necessary to better the area, were made at the level of the city as a whole (or also at the level of the nation), creating large 'mafias' of city-wide service providers and patronage networks of loyalty and employment that made institutional reform difficult to implement due to the expansive urban domain and the large flows of resources involved. In general, these service contracts were not tailored to the problems and concerns of neighbourhoods or more localized areas. With such a large scale for urban policy provision and decision-making, and with so many powerful networks and bureaucratic influences involved, accountability was difficult and power became entrenched.

In contrast, under the *Autoridad* decisions are made for a territorial unit smaller than the city, but larger than the neighbourhood, and in such a way as to bypass old patronage power networks (and long-standing political jurisdictions). In this environment, there is scope for the growth of new, horizontal connections of reciprocity. To the extent that this new authority also has the power to coordinate *among* urban servicing sectors – security, transport, and zoning, for example – for this new and more manageable jurisdiction, it has been further able to break the old vertical structures of patronage and decision-making linked to formal politics or bureaucratic authority that kept reform and accountability at bay vis-à-vis citizens. The fact that these new bonds of reciprocity engage both public and private sector actors – including government officials, local residents, NGOs, private developers, the police, and other service and culture providers – in a common project to create security, reduce crime, and physically transform a key but manageable territorial location in the city is also important. This has meant that the old vertical hierarchies of patronage and politics that developed within the formal political sphere have been partly demobilized, at least with respect to servicing decisions about this central part of the city. They have been replaced by new horizontal networks of reciprocity which link the public sector (or political domain) with the private sector (or market domain), which helps prevent city officials from falling under the sway of those old alliances and relations. This new situation allows authorities and a variety of interested parties to engage in new forms of dialogue and reciprocity, increasing the likelihood of implementing reform efforts to promote the shared objectives of transforming this specific part of the city.

To be sure, such an experiment has limits, in terms of the breadth and extent of overall accountability as well as how much real or lasting impact any gains in the historic centre of Mexico City will have on the problems of police corruption, crime, and insecurity in the metropolitan area as a whole. After all, to a certain degree this experiment could be seen as a glorified version of a business-improvement district (BID), a type of programme that has been widely criticized in the United States and elsewhere for its protection of the private sector and the social and class exclusivity that often results. Thus, we must ask, are the *Autoridad* and its horizontal network of partners (including the police) really more accountable to the local residents, or are they merely responding to their business investment partners and their urban redevelopment concerns? Moreover, how big an impact can changes in just one small area of the city have on the larger problem of lack of accountability in the overall system of policing, which remains massive and fragmented? These are tough questions that need further attention.

Having said that, certain general insights of interest to policymakers concerned with crime, insecurity, and urban quality of life can be gleaned from projects such as the downtown Mexico City initiative. First, it is clear that closer attention needs to be paid to urban scale and the spatial interconnectedness of divergent developments, especially within certain key areas of the city, as well as to the most appropriate territorial scale for policy action. To do so would challenge the principal point of entry used by policymakers and practitioners in Latin American cities, which is either the city as a whole (if it is a single political jurisdiction), the metropolitan area (if the city spills beyond its political borders), or the community/neighbourhood. The latter has been the starting point for considerable policy action, particularly in the decentralized world of Latin American urbanism. But maybe greater policy success can come from bypassing long-standing or traditional territorial units and creating new ones that are not only manageable, but also spatially distinct.

Second, policymakers must pay more attention to the sector-specific trade-offs that might result from crime-fighting efforts. Gains in one arena – as with growth in the security industry, new innovations in technology, or success in urban redevelopment – may lead to losses, or to new and unanticipated problems, in another sector. This in turn means that policymakers must start thinking about the integration or coordination of a variety of policies that work in tandem with each other, maximizing the interaction between economic growth, spatial transformation, social inclusion, and physical security in ways that will be self-sustaining and generative of overall progress. Thinking about the physical scale and context of these new interrelationships will be an important part of the task, too. Of course, exactly what that scale or menu of integrated policies may be will have to be tailored to the history and politics of a given place. Experiments that work in one locale may not work in another. But the point is to learn from some of the few success stories that have brought some clear progress, as with the new authority for downtown Mexico City, and then determine what it would take to expand, scale-up, or transfer the fundamental insights to other Latin American urban contexts.

Notes

Support for portions of the research cited in this chapter comes from the Carnegie Corporation of New York and the John D. and Catherine T. MacArthur Foundation. This is an abridged version of a chapter previously published in Allison M. Garland, Mejgan Massoumi, and Blair A. Ruble (eds) (2007). *Global Urban Poverty: Setting the Agenda*. Washington, DC: Woodrow Wilson International Center for Scholars. Many thanks to the Woodrow Wilson International Center for permission to reprint.

1. For a good overview of this problem, as seen from a variety of disciplinary vantage points, see Rotker (2002). For a review essay on the theme, and a

treatment of some of the most innovative ways that scholars are now examining violence in Latin America, see Davis (2006a).

2. For a comprehensive survey of citizen attitudes about crime and its impact on views of the city and urban life, see ICESI (2005).
3. These resources included a system of federal police forces – still tied to the (PRI-dominated) national executive – with a history of intervening in Mexico City affairs; a military bureaucracy still answering to the PRI and also increasingly worried about what would be exposed in terms of federal armed forces' complicity and impunity if Mexico City police were purged; and considerable federal control of local finances – in the form of a budgetary veto on Mexico City expenditures. Also, the constitution set clear limits on the autonomy of the mayor to name his/her own police chief, with any appointee having to be jointly supported by the president and approved by the national congress.
4. Some of the programme's success also owes to the fact that the head of the *Autoridad*, Alejandra Moreno Toscana, is a respected scholar and historian with a substantial résumé of accomplishments in the city, and has legitimacy and authority because she is not a typical 'political operative', insofar as she was one of Mayor Ebrard's university professors and their ties go back several decades. Both worked together in the administration of Mayor Manuel Camacho (1988–94), who governed Mexico City for the PRI, but she does not have a history of party political partisanship. She has strong personal relations with the private sector, including serving as a board member of an organization headed by Carlos Slim, a key developer of downtown and Mexico's richest man, and has long advocated the use of history and culture to renovate the historic centre (*Milenio* 2006).

References

Arias, D., and C.D. Rodrigues (2006). 'The myth of personal security: dispute resolution, security, and identity in Rio de Janeiro's favelas'. *Latin American Politics & Society*, 48(4): 53–81.

Bergman, M. (2007). *Seguridad pública y estado en México: Análisis de algunas iniciativas*. Mexico City: Fontamara.

Call, C.T. (2003). 'Democratisation, war and state building: constructing the rule of law in El Salvador'. *Journal of Latin American Studies*, 35: 827–62.

Concha-Eastman, A. (2002). 'Urban violence in Latin America and the Caribbean: dimensions, explanations, actions'. In S. Rotker (ed.), *Citizens of Fear: Urban Violence in Latin America*. New Brunswick, NJ: Rutgers University Press.

Davis, D.E. (2007). 'El Factor Giuliani: delincuencia, la "cero tolerancia" en el trabajo policiaco y la transformación de la esfera pública en el centro de la ciudad de México'. *Estudios Sociológicos*, xxv(75) (September–December): 639–83.

Davis, D.E. (2006a). 'Undermining the rule of law: democratization and the dark side of police reform in Mexico'. *Latin American Politics and Society*, 48(1): 55–86.

Davis, D.E. (2006b). 'Conflict, cooperation, and convergence: globalization and the politics of downtown development in Mexico City'. *Research in Political Sociology*, 15: 143–78.

de la Barreda Solórzano, L. (2007). 'Miedo'. *Letras Libres*: 26–30. January.

El Universal. (2004). 'En Tlahuac: Linchan 3 Agentes'. 24 November.
Fundación Mexicana para la Salud. (1997). *La violencia en la Ciudad de México: Análisis de la magnitud y su repercusión económica*. Mexico City: Fundación Mexicana para la Salud.
ICESI (2005). *Tercera encuesta nacional sobre inseguridad 2005 (NESI-3)*. Mexico, DF: Instituto Ciudadano de Estudios Sobre la Inseguridad, AC.
Jiménez Ornelas, R.A. (2005). 'Percepción ciudadana sobre la inseguridad en la globalización: México y el Distrito Federal'. In E. Patiño Tovar and J. Castillo Palma (eds), *Inseguridad, riesgo, y vulnerabilidad*. Guadalajara, Mexico: University of Guadalajara.
Koonings, K., and D. Kruijt. (2007). *Fractured Cities: Social Exclusion, Urban Violence & Contested Spaces in Latin America*. London and New York: Zed Press, Ltd.
Martín-Barbero, J. (2002). 'The city: between fear and the media'. In S. Rotker (ed.), *Citizens of Fear: Urban Violence in Latin America*. New Brunswick, NJ: Rutgers University Press.
Milenio. (2006). 'Dirigirá Alejandra Moreno la nueva Autoridad del Centro', 5 December. Available at http://www.milenio.com/index.php/2006/12/05/20784/.
Moser, C.O.N. (2004). 'Urban violence and insecurity: An introductory roadmap'. *Environment & Urbanization*, 16(2): 3–16.
Ratinoff, L. (1996). 'Delincuencia y paz ciudadana'. *Hacia un enfoque integrado del desarrollo: Etica, violencia, y seguridad ciudadana*. Washington, DC: Inter-American Development Bank.
Rotker, S. (ed.) (2002). *Citizens of Fear: Urban Violence in Latin America*. New Brunswick, NJ: Rutgers University Press.
Ruiz Healy, E. (2007). 'Las noticias de hoy'. 24 January. Available at http://www.radioformula.com.mx/noticias/rf2101.asp?ID=55813.
Ungar, M. (2002). *Elusive Reform: Democracy and the Rule of Law in Latin America*. Boulder, CO: Lynne Rienner Publishers.
Valenzuela Aguilera, A. (2007). 'Inseguridad urbana y control social del espacio en la ciudad de México'. *Inseguridad, riesgo y vulnerabilidad. 3er. Congreso Internacional: Balance y Perspectivas del Análisis Territorial*. Puebla, México: Red Nacional de Investigación Urbana.

3
Cocaine Cities: Exploring the Relationship between Urban Dynamics and the Drug Trade in South America

Ignacio A. Navarro

1 Introduction

Economic studies that empirically explore the connection between urbanization and crime tend to use hedonic methodologies in order to focus on the localized effects of criminal activity on relative property prices. Most of these studies find an inverse relation between crime levels and property values. For example, in one of the first studies of this kind, Thaler (1978) found that a 1 standard deviation increase in the incidence of property crime tends to reduce home values by about three per cent. Similarly, Gibbons (2004) found an average decrease in property values of ten per cent in association with a 1 standard deviation increase in property crime. The evidence seems to confirm that property in neighbourhoods with relatively higher crime rates tends to have lower values than comparable property located in relatively 'safer' neighbourhoods in the same urban area.

It is noteworthy that the connection between urbanization and the drug trade has, within mainstream economics literature, tended to be explored from the perspective of the drug trade's social costs, and there has been very little work which considers it as an economic activity with income multiplier effects and special characteristics arising from its illegal nature. Furthermore, the few studies that measure the economic effect of the cocaine drug trade either focus on the economic impact of coca production on rural peasants in producing communities, or at the country level (Painter 1994; De Franco and Godoy 1992), while the magnitude and mechanisms of the backward and forward linkages between urban centres and coca producing rural centres are still widely unexplored.[1]

South American cocaine generates several billions (US$) of yearly expenditure in consumer countries in North America and Europe; undoubtedly, the massive amount of resources moved by the cocaine trade plays an important role in producer economies. This chapter explores the link between the cocaine trade and urbanization patterns in a producer economy in South America. Understanding the role of the drug trade, which has been so prevalent for the past 30 years in South America, on urbanization patterns can not only help us to understand Latin American urbanization more generally, but also to understand the consequences that particular patterns of drug-fuelled urban growth can have. Furthermore, uncovering the economic effects of the drug trade on producer regions is imperative for the formulation of effective policies against drugs, as well as for policies for economic development, poverty alleviation, and low-income housing strategies.

The aim of this chapter is not to assess the benefits and costs of the drug trade on Latin American drug-exporter regions; several authors have written on that topic (see Thoumi 1994, 2003). This chapter's aim is to provide a framework that explains the economic processes through which the drug trade influences land markets in drug-producing regions. Several observers have written about this influence, but there has been no systematic attempt to explain or quantify these processes. This chapter is organized as follows: the Section 2 provides a brief description of South America's role in the cocaine trade. The Section 3 explores the existing literature that describes the connection between the cocaine trade and urbanization patterns in Latin America, and introduces a model that explains this connection. The Sections 4 and 5 describe the case of Bolivia and provide empirical estimates for the processes through which the cocaine trade impacts upon construction activity in the country's largest cities. The Section 6 concludes the discussion.

2 Coca and cocaine in South America

Cocaine hydrochloride (HCL) is a powerful drug made from an alkaloid extracted from the coca plant leaf. Even though cocaine alkaloids were not isolated until the late 19th century, South America's relationship with coca and the coca trade can be traced back to pre-colonial times. Indeed, one of the first things Americo Vespucci reportedly witnessed on his arrival in South America in 1499 was a group of indigenous people chewing coca leaves (Karch 2006). There is also archaeological evidence of human use of coca dating back to at least 3000 BC (Antonil 1978). To this day, coca leaves are chewed by indigenous populations, mostly of Aimara and Quechua descent, to alleviate the effects of altitude sickness and hunger, and are used to produce other derivatives such as coca tea or 'mate'. However, the majority of coca grown in South America is believed to be used for the production of cocaine hydrochloride (UNODC 2004).

According to the United Nation's Office on Drugs and Crime (UNODC), three countries grow virtually all of the coca used for cocaine production: Colombia, Peru, and Bolivia (UNODC 2008). Figure 3.1 shows the potential cocaine production for each of the major producer countries based on estimates of yearly coca plantations. This figure shows that cocaine production in South America ranged from 800 to 1008 metric tons between 1997 and 2007. Although there was some variation in each of the three countries' share of potential cocaine production, Figure 3.1 shows that Colombia was consistently the largest potential cocaine producer in the 1997–2007 period (with about two-thirds of

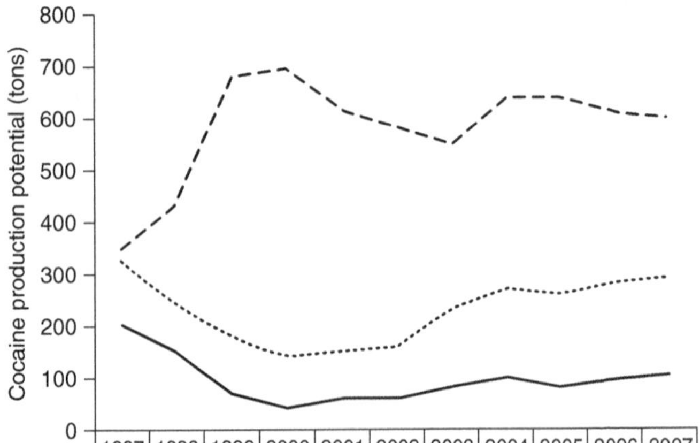

	1997	1998	1999	2000	2001	2002	2003	2004	2005	2006	2007
- - - Colombia	350	435	680	695	617	580	550	640	640	610	600
········ Peru	325	240	175	141	150	160	230	270	260	280	290
—— Bolivia	200	150	70	43	60	60	79	98	80	94	104

Figure 3.1 Potential cocaine production in South America by country (in metric tons), 1997–2007

Source: UNODC (2008).

the region's potential yearly cocaine production), while Bolivia had the smallest share of potential cocaine production (about ten per cent).

Even though there is no agreement regarding the actual size of the cocaine trade and the numbers reported generally tend to be politically manipulated (Thoumi 2005), conservative estimates suggest that cocaine generates anything between US$35–115 billion per year (Reuter and Greenfield 2001). This means that if a country such as Bolivia (which produces about ten per cent of the world's cocaine) received around one per cent of the world's drug trade proceeds, it would amount to between US$0.3–1.15 billion per year. That figure is equivalent to approximately 3–10 per cent of its GDP.[2] In other words, even according to conservative estimates, producer countries receive a considerable influx of dollars from the drug trade.

3 The economic effects of cocaine production on urban dynamics

The literature on the economic effects of drug production and commercialization suggests that they tend to have profound effects on regional economies (Thoumi 1994, 2003). In general, the literature agrees that drug production and commercialization tend to have an impact upon local employment – in areas where drug production and trafficking is concentrated – and also affect investment, consumption, and import patterns, particularly as a result of money laundering mechanisms. In turn, these economic effects can directly impact upon land markets and general urban dynamics. Even though the literature recognizes a relationship between the levels of illegal drug production on the one hand, and commercialization and fluctuation in land markets on the other, these links have not been formally explored or measured. This section reviews some of the most influential literature on the economic effects of the illegal drug trade and develops a framework for exploration of the causal connection between drug exports and fluctuations in land markets.

3.1 Cocaine industry employment and urban land markets

Standard regional economic analysis classifies production activities into basic and non-basic sectors. The former includes the production of goods to be sold primarily outside of the region, while the non-basic sector includes goods produced for sale inside the region. Regional economic theory predicts a multiplier effect from export base activities: as sales in the basic sector of the economy increase as a result of rising demand for products in the region's basic sector, the income generated from the additional exports exceeds the original increase in export income because a portion of each additional unit of income generated by exports is spent on local sector goods. This, in turn, generates income for the local sector of the economy. When applied to cocaine exports, the theory predicts that as the demand for cocaine expands in consumer regions, income in producer regions tends to increase directly through the additional exports and indirectly through the regional multiplier effect. In this sense, the export of illegal goods works in the same way as the export of legal goods – both create income.

A major impact of the increased local income generated by exports is that urban land values also rise as a result. Higher incomes attract labour from other regions, increasing land and housing prices (Wheaton 1974). This relationship is well established in mainstream urban economic theory and has ample empirical support. For example, in a recent large-scale study, McCue and Belsky (2007) found the unemployment rate to be one of the main predictors of short-term house price decline in American metropolitan areas. It is important to note, however, that urban/regional economic theory predicts that the effect of exports on local income and land prices will be directly related to the relative size of the export industry in relation to the local economy and, most importantly, to its relationship with other sectors of the economy. In other words, the stronger the export industry's links with other sectors of the economy, the greater the effect of the export industry on local employment and land prices. The structure of an export industry thus plays an important role with regard to its effect on land prices.

In this regard, Thoumi (2003) argues that most of the direct jobs created by the cocaine trade are concentrated in the first stages of the production chain – coca cultivation and production of cocaine base – as well as in the last stages of the distribution chain – street dealing – while the most lucrative portions of the trade – final production stages and wholesale transportation and sales of cocaine – are generally controlled by a limited number of participants. This suggests that most of the effects of cocaine exports on land markets would logically be concentrated in rural areas where the first stages of the industry and most of the jobs are located, while the effects would be limited in urban centres where marketing and distribution activities are restricted to a small number of individuals.[3]

This would certainly be the case if we were only to consider the effects of cocaine-related export income solely in terms of direct and indirect employment effects. However, those few individuals directly involved in the drug industry in cities clearly constitute a particular group with a very high income, which means that they can invest in real estate and spend in other sectors of the economy in a way that many others cannot. Rodgers (2007), for example, describes how a group of middle-level drug distributors – or *púsheres* – completely transformed a poor Managua neighbourhood through home improvements and real estate investments financed by drug money, leading to high levels of infrastructural inequality in a previously relatively uniform neighbourhood. Dennis (2003) notes a similar investment pattern for cocaine-related proceeds in a Miskitu village on Nicaragua's Caribbean coast, while McDonald (2005) describes how some rural towns in Mexico have experienced dramatic changes as drug money has been used to acquire land mainly as a mechanism to increase status for those in the business.

More generally, many observers have explicitly connected the cocaine trade with real estate market booms in urban centres. Hylton (2007), for example, presents a persuasive case when explaining how the cocaine business has been a major component of Medellin's rapid urban transformation and unprecedented growth. This observation is supported by Marcy (2010), who describes how Medellin's real estate prices doubled in 1986 following a boom in cocaine exports. Clawson and Rensselaer (1998) similarly contend that, in the early 1990s, up to 40 per cent of Cali's construction could be attributed to the cocaine industry (and that the Colombian government's subsequent crackdown on the Cali cartel in 1995 led to a ten per cent decline in construction in the city in that same year). Shams (1992) and Painter (1994) propose equivalent arguments about the Bolivian cities of Cochabamba and Santa Cruz, while Corben (2006) contends that Miami's impressive real estate boom in the 1970s was the result of the city being a major transhipment point for cocaine at that time, with the subsequent real estate bust being caused by Colombian cartels switching their distribution routes during the 1980s and 1990s.

In summary, the weak direct and indirect linkages between the drug industry and other urban industries, both due to the limited number of people involved as well as its illicit nature, would logically predict low effects on land markets in an urban area. However, several authors find a clear connection between cocaine exports and urban land markets, despite the fact that the direct employment created by the cocaine trade and other related industries in urban areas is relatively small. Although the high income of those involved in the drugs trade in cities is one factor explaining this seeming contradiction, there is another, more specific mechanism that could also explain the strong link between exports and urban land prices that is particular to this illicit industry: money laundering.

3.2 Money laundering and urban land markets

As explained in the previous section, the cocaine trade can affect land markets through the employment of those in the cocaine and related industries, but this employment tends to be limited due to the nature of the industry. The illicit character of the industry, however, requires its export proceeds to be introduced into the producer country via money-laundering techniques. These techniques can have a profound effect on land markets on two fronts: indirectly, through the employment they create in the money laundering-supported industry, and directly, by using real estate to layer and integrate laundered money.

3.2.1 Money laundering and urban employment

Money laundering is defined as the process of masking the illegal origin of money. Since drug-related activities tend to generate large amounts of cash, the need to employ mechanisms to evade suspicions about the origin of drug money becomes increasingly important as income from illicit sources increases. Money laundering usually comprises three steps: placing, layering, and integration. In the placing stage, money launderers introduce money into the financial system through various means aimed at avoiding detection of this introduction. The layering stage involves removing the money from the normal flow of institutional and legal monitoring and control in order to make tracking difficult for law enforcing agencies. In the final step, integration, the money re-enters the economy in the form of a legitimate transaction.

The placing stage is one of the most problematic stages because cocaine generates vast amounts of cash that must be moved and disguised before entering the layering stage. Since the early 1980s, banking regulations have become increasingly stringent, and so direct money wires and the acquisition of financial instruments that facilitated placement (such as cashier's cheques, money orders, or traveller's cheques) became more difficult for money launderers to use; as a result, the direct smuggling of money or fraudulent front operations specialized in commercial trade became more common for money laundering (Sultzer 1995). This form of placing laundered money gave rise to substantial imports of all kinds, but especially the import of electro-domestic items and computers in countries such as Colombia and Bolivia. According to Thoumi (2003), these imports mostly occurred in the form of 'technical contraband' (under-invoicing imports and over-invoicing exports), as well as 'physical contraband' (money shipped inside of goods). This resulted in vast amounts of cheap imports being sold in Colombian and Bolivian cities (ibid.; Painter 1994).[4]

This way of laundering money has been particularly effective since selling contraband is socially accepted in many South American countries, and the considerable amount of employment it creates among the urban unskilled labour force makes it hard to control in cities where municipal governments are weak. Further, the amount of jobs created by drug-fuelled contraband can have transformational impacts. For instance, Hylton (2007) concludes that the urban transformation experienced by Medellin in the 1980s and 1990s was, in many ways, caused by a 'rising class' that worked in the smuggled goods commerce industry, which was fuelled by the laundered proceeds of the cocaine trade.[5] Shams (1992) and Painter (1994) make strikingly similar arguments about the effect of cocaine exports in the city of Cochabamba, Bolivia.[6]

3.2.2 Money laundering and real estate

The laundering of drug money can have an effect on land markets through the employment it creates. However, it can also have a direct effect on land markets when real estate construction and transactions are used to launder money. Because real estate transactions usually involve large sums of money, they are generally used in the second and third steps of the money laundering cycle. It is worth noting that before money laundering became subject to elaborate criminal investigation, money launderers often did not have to resort to complex techniques, and real estate transactions were usually only used in the integrating step. Thus, drug dealers would simply buy property using family members or friends to acquire real estate, boats, luxury cars, or other high price items using cash. The city of Miami at the height of the 1980s cocaine boom presents an example of this phenomenon, when one in five real estate transactions were paid in full and in cash (Labaton 1989). Today, however, although real estate transactions are still a major element of money laundering, they are not as straightforward due to increased regulations and more sophisticated international enforcement techniques (FCEN 2008).

Certainly, according to a 2008 Financial Action Task Force (FATF) report, although money laundering techniques involving real estate transactions can vary, the process usually involves the money launderer, a financial institution providing a mortgage, and a third party (either a person or a company). In its simplest version, the money launderer uses a third party to acquire a mortgage loan to buy real estate. The mortgage loan payments are later honoured periodically using direct transfers of drug money from offshore accounts or by money wire transfers either directly to the bank or through the third party. These payments are usually below the amount that would trigger suspicion, and thus they serve as a way to layer and integrate laundered money (FATF 2008).

The more sophisticated the financial crime control, the riskier such a scheme is, and several different potential modifications to such money laundering arrangements exist. One of these is real estate under-valuation. Under such a scheme, a money launderer acquires a mortgage to buy real estate for an amount below the property's market value. The money launderer, however, pays the real market value for the property using the mortgage loan and an 'under-the-table payment' using illicit funds. When the money launderer later sells the property at market value, the illicit money is declared as capital gains and is integrated back into the legal economy. Another option is to use drug money to fund construction projects, and then subsequently recycle it to fund further construction projects. This serves as a layering mechanism that allows money launderers to declare that their capital gains come from construction projects (Thoumi 2003).

The money laundering techniques described above are by no means the only ones used to launder illicit funds using real estate transactions, but serve to illustrate how the real estate market can provide a relatively simple avenue for laundering large amounts of drug money.[7] Furthermore, the examples above illustrate how the local demand for real estate can be artificially inflated when money-laundering activities increase. In turn, this increased demand directly affects short-term real estate prices. Thus, we can expect increases in money laundering activities to produce higher local real estate prices and greater construction activity, and vice versa.

In summary, the effects of cocaine production on urban land markets for regions involved in the trade are well established in the literature. Increased income resulting from the export of illicit substances draws additional population into the cocaine producing region, increasing housing demand and housing prices. This income effect of cocaine production explains at least part of the relationship between drug production and land prices. However, this effect would tend to be small given the structure of this industry. Figure 3.2 below presents an alternative model.

As Figure 3.2 shows, cocaine exports are related to land markets through the employment created by the industry for those involved

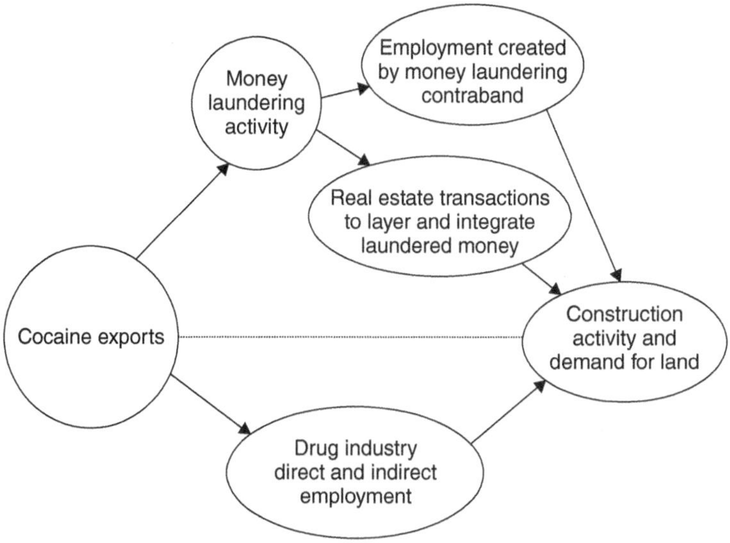

Figure 3.2 Model of the effects of drug exports on urban land markets
Source: Author's own elaboration.

in drug production, trade, and related industries, and through money laundering activities, which can also create employment, as well as the direct use of real estate to layer and integrate drug money. The literature discussed above suggests that cocaine exports create a strong effect on urban land markets in related industries but offers little explanation of the mechanisms governing this relationship. As Healy (1994: 208) puts it: '...there has been no systematic, imaginative research on the dollar laundering activities...', and much less on their effect on land and construction markets. The next two sections present, firstly, a brief overview of drug production trends in Bolivia and, secondly, a measure of the effects and the relative weights of drug-fuelled land and construction in the country's main urban centres between 1997 and 2007.

4 Drug production in Bolivia: a brief overview

According to US government estimates, each kilogram of pure cocaine requires 315–370 kilograms of Bolivian sun-dried coca leaves, which in turn require between 0.11 and 0.15 hectares of coca plantations per year.[8] On this basis, it can be estimated that in 2007, Bolivia grew enough coca to produce between 192 and 262 metric tons of cocaine (UNODC 2008). During the 1930s, about 97 per cent of coca production in Bolivia was concentrated in the Yungas region in the state of La Paz, and two per cent came from the Chapare region in the state of Cochabamba. By the 1960s, however, the ranking of regions in terms of proportion of total production was inverted and Cochabamba became the largest Bolivian coca producer (De Franco and Godoy 1992). Two factors contributed to the emergence of Chapare as the leading coca producing area of Bolivia: (1) its favourable terrain (in particular, having more abundant rivers and a flatter terrain than Yungas); and (2) a policy of colonization of Bolivia's lowlands that encouraged the migration of peasants to the eastern parts of Bolivia following the land revolution in 1952 (ibid.).

Until the 1970s, most of Bolivia's coca production was destined for traditional uses inside its borders (such as chewing, making tea, and medicinal purposes), but a surge in world demand for cocaine opened the door for cocaine exports, which generated higher incomes than any other agricultural product. The fall in cotton and sugar prices in the late 1970s, coupled with one of Bolivia's worst economic crises during the 1980s, further prompted Bolivian farmers to migrate to the Chapare region to farm coca and to produce cocaine (Painter 1994).

The economic and social impact of coca production and the cocaine trade in the rural Chapare region in the 1970s and early 1980s has been the subject of many studies and is amply documented,[9] but the cocaine trade's impact on Bolivia's economy as a whole – and on its urban centres in particular – is less well understood. Using a computable general equilibrium model, De Franco and Godoy (1992) estimate that a ten per cent increase in coca production leads to an increase in real personal income for urban workers of 0.55 per cent. Their results suggest only modest backward and forward linkages between rural producer centres of coca and urban centres, however, most likely because they do not consider the money laundering effects. Painter (1994), on the other hand, uses anecdotal evidence to argue that there are much stronger economic ties between the rural Chapare and its nearest urban centre, the city of Cochabamba.[10] In particular, he suggests that a large portion of cocaine dollars originating from the Chapare region are laundered in Cochabamba's urban economy, and that a large portion of Cochabamba's production and services provide intermediate inputs to the cocaine trade generated in the Chapare. Unfortunately Painter does not provide strong evidence in support of this assertion, despite its intuitive plausibility. The next section offers an empirical evaluation of the effects of cocaine production on urban dynamics in Bolivia's major cities.

5 Modelling the effects of cocaine production in urban Bolivia

As suggested above, the extent to which cocaine production affects urban centres and land markets in particular is a function of the real income generated by the cocaine trade in the urban centre through exports and multiplier effects, but is also a result of the amount of money laundered through the real estate market. Unfortunately, direct measures of money laundering and economic linkages at the regional level are non-existent in Bolivia (and indeed, most of the world). Nonetheless, fluctuations in the real estate market can offer interesting insights into these connections. In order to quantify the relationship between real estate market fluctuations and cocaine production in Bolivia we can rely on two key indicators: (1) yearly urban construction activity, and (2) yearly cocaine production estimates. Time series for these two indicators are available for 1997 for Bolivia's three largest cities – La Paz, Santa Cruz, and Cochabamba – and can be used to model the effects of cocaine production on urban construction. The following sections describe the data, and the econometric approach used, in detail.

5.1 Construction activity measures

In order to test for construction activity and cocaine production we used data on construction permits by city from the Bolivian National Institute of Statistics (INE 2008a). Construction activity trends tend to be very similar across Bolivia's largest cities. Construction was at its highest point for all cities in 1998, but then dropped significantly until 2002. Between 2002 and 2007, however, the cities of Santa Cruz and La Paz experienced a steady increase, while the city of Cochabamba experienced an initial increase followed by a steep decline in 2006.

5.2 Cocaine production data

Measuring the cocaine trade presents several challenges. The illicit nature of cocaine, and in some cases of coca plantations, makes estimation of cocaine production a costly and sometimes politically sensitive endeavour (Thoumi 2005). For this reason, accurate data on cocaine production are limited to a few governments and large organizations, of which the United Nations Office on Drugs and Crime (UNODC 2008) represents one the most reliable (Mejia and Posada 2008). The UNODC uses satellite images to monitor illegal crops in producer countries and complements its estimates with yield and price-monitoring surveys collected by several country offices in conjunction with government agencies in producer countries.

This chapter focuses on two sets of UNODC statistics compiled for coca producing regions, including Bolivia, on a yearly basis since 1997: coca production and cocaine production potential. The coca production statistics reflect the amount of land destined for coca plantations in hectares, while the cocaine production potential introduces other factors such as the legal consumption of coca and regional yield estimates in order to approximate the amount of coca used to produce cocaine.

Bolivia experienced a steady decline in coca leaf production between 1997 and 2000. This decline may be explained by the large political and economic investments in eradication measures, as implemented by President Hugo Banzer Suarez during his term of government. The end of the Banzer era in 2001 saw coca cultivation increase steadily, despite episodes of great political instability, until 2005, when coca production decreased by 8.3 per cent. The US department of state attributes this trend to a government policy that limited coca cultivation to one 'cato' (equivalent to 0.16 hectares) per family, a motion carried by President Mesa (UNODC 2006). Following the accession of Evo Morales – previously leader of the Bolivian coca movement – to the Bolivian presidency, new coca plantations increased rapidly in the Chapare region (by 8.2 per cent in 2006) and this trend continued in 2007.

The UNODC's cocaine potential statistics uses coca production estimates but subtracts the amount of coca destined for traditional uses (i.e. not for cocaine production). Bolivian law currently allows 12,000 hectares of coca plantations to satisfy demand for traditional uses. Plantations in excess of the legal limit are deemed to be destined for cocaine production. It is worth noting that most of the 12,000 hectares of coca production allowed by law are located in the Yungas region. As a result, most of the coca coming out of the Chapare region is directly linked with cocaine production (UNODC 2008). The potential for cocaine production shows a similar trend to that of total coca production; however, since cocaine production is mainly attributed to coca cultivated in the Chapare region, the changes in cocaine production potential are more dramatic than the changes in total coca production. That explains why, despite coca plantations at the national level decreasing by about eight per cent during 2005, the actual potential for cocaine estimate decreased by about 18 per cent.

5.3 Cocaine production and construction in Bolivia's largest cities

Figure 3.3 below presents the 1997–2007 de-trended series of Bolivian cocaine production (1 year lag) and construction permits for the cities of Cochabamba, La Paz, and Santa Cruz.[11] As the figures show, fluctuations in cocaine production during the period under consideration mirror fluctuations in construction activity the following year very closely. The corresponding correlation coefficients for the series are 0.78, 0.92, and 0.91 respectively.

All three panels in Figure 3.3 show a high correlation between the de-trended series, but the panel structure of the data allowed for more precise measures of the effects in the three Bolivian cities under study. Table 3.1 presents a series of regression models to estimate the effects of

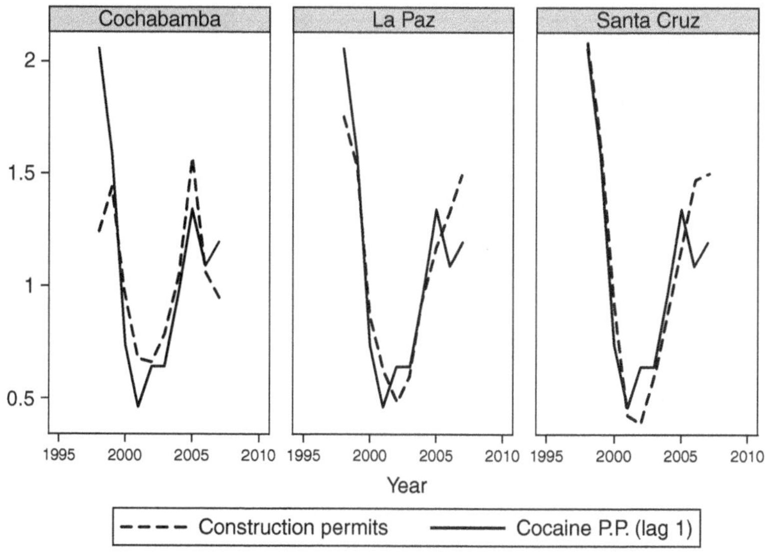

Figure 3.3 De-trended series of cocaine production potential and construction activity: Cochabamba, La Paz, and Santa Cruz, 1998–2008

Source: Author's own calculations using UNODC (2008) and INE (2008a) data.

Table 3.1 Fixed effects regression estimates: construction permits on lagged cocaine production potential: Cochabamba, La Paz, Santa Cruz

	1	2	3	4
	Ln (construction permits)	**Ln (construction permits)**	**Ln (construction permits)**	**De-trended (construction permits) (standardized coefficients)**
Ln (Cocaine production potential (lag1)	0.786	0.687	0.617	0.757
	[0.00]	[0.00]	[0.00]	[0.00]
	(0.05)	(0.07)	(0.04)	(0.06)
Ln (local employment index)		0.030	0.040	0.18
		[0.03]	[0.03]	[0.04]
		(0.01)	(0.04)	(0.04)
Ln (local employment index) (lag1)		0.035	0.046	0.219
		[0.01]	[0.02]	[0.02]
		(0.07)	(0.04)	(0.12)
Trend variable			−0.019	
			[0.39]	
			(0.41)	
Constant	9.34	3.31	40.06	−5.65
	[0.00]	[0.07]	[0.36]	[0.00]
	(0.01)	(0.12)	(0.37)	(0.08)
Observations	30	30	30	30
R-squared (within)	0.7	0.8	0.81	0.83

Note: P values (robust for heteroscedasticity) in brackets; P values (robust for heteroscedasticity and serial correlation) in parentheses.

Sources: Author's own calculations using UNODC (2008) and INE (2008a, 2008b) data.

cocaine production on urban construction in the cities of Cochabamba, La Paz, and Santa Cruz for the 1997–2007 period.

Model 1 shows the regression estimates of the natural logarithm of approved construction permits on potential cocaine production, controlling for city-specific fixed effects. The coefficient on the lagged value of cocaine production potential indicates that, controlling for city-specific effects, a one per cent increase in cocaine production increases construction activity in the following year by about 0.8 per cent ($p<0.01$) on average. Further, cocaine production alone tends to explain about 42 per cent of the variation in construction activity in Bolivia's main cities.

5.4 Separating income multiplier from money laundering effects

It is important to note that the regression coefficients in model 1 are estimates of the *total* effect of cocaine production on urban construction. However, as discussed in previous sections of this chapter, the total effect can be divided into (i) employment effects arising from the income multiplier derived from cocaine exports and (ii) the money laundering effect, which produces artificial shifts in demand for housing.

We separate these effects by introducing measures of city employment collected by the Bolivian National Institute of Statistics (INE 2008b) for each city, in order to isolate those effects of cocaine exports that are not related to employment. As the second model in Table 3.1 shows, the coefficient on the lagged cocaine production potential drops slightly from 0.79 in the first model to 0.69 when employment measures (lagged and current) are introduced in the model. This indicates that only a small portion of the effect of cocaine production on construction in Bolivia's main cities can be explained by formal employment created by the cocaine trade (direct and indirect), and the majority may be explained by money laundering activities that use the real estate sector.[12]

Models 3 and 4 are variations on model 2 which control for the possibility that construction permits and cocaine production might follow the same patterns over time. Model 3 introduces a time trend variable and model 4 uses standardized de-trended measures of construction permits and cocaine production. Thus coefficients in models 3 and 4 represent the association between fluctuations in construction activity and fluctuations in cocaine production. The results are remarkably strong. As model 4 shows, controlling for employment and city specifics, a 1 standard deviation fluctuation in cocaine production in Bolivia tends to produce a fluctuation of 0.74 standard deviations in construction activity. Further, the within R square in model 4 reflects that 82 per cent of the variation in the fluctuations on construction permits in Bolivia's main cities can be explained by city-specific effects, fluctuations in employment, and cocaine production; 50 per cent of that variation can be accounted for by cocaine production alone.

6 Conclusions

This chapter has explored the connection between drug production and land markets in Bolivia. Even though this link has been observed by several studies and in different geographic locations across Latin America since the 1980s, this is the first attempt to explicitly uncover the economic processes that may explain such a link and to measure these quantitatively. The empirical results presented here reveal that Bolivia's construction activity in its main cities is largely influenced by cocaine production. Our estimates show that, between 1997 and 2007, about 50 per cent of the variation in construction fluctuations in Bolivia's main cities is explainable by fluctuations in cocaine production alone. These findings provide evidence of the importance of the drug economy for Bolivia's urban economies.

Interestingly, however, only a modest part of the effect of the cocaine economy on real estate markets can be explained by the number of formal sector direct and indirect jobs it creates in urban areas. On the contrary, our findings suggest that most of the effect of the drug economy on land markets can be explained by direct investments in real estate from those involved in the business, either for money laundering purposes or because real estate represents both a secure investment and a symbol of status, as suggested by McDonald (2005) in his work on Mexican rural villages, or Labaton (1989) in the case of Miami. Another possibility is that our measure of employment is not picking up the effects of employment in the informal sector, which can be directly affected by cocaine exports in the form of increased commerce of smuggled and contraband goods, as suggested by Hylton's (2007) study of Medellin. Irrespective of this, however, it is clear that the drug economy is fundamentally integrated with the legal construction and real estate economy in urban Bolivia.

This basic finding poses an extremely challenging scenario for both economic development and law enforcement policies in countries like Bolivia. On the one hand, drug eradication though law enforcement policies that cut drug exports could potentially cause busts in real estate markets and cause civil unrest. On the other hand, giving a free rein to narco-trafficking activities can lead to inflated land prices, making it harder for the poor to access urban spaces, something that it is often suggested can lead to increased levels of violence. Finding a middle ground between these two unsatisfactory options is clearly a difficult endeavour, especially in a fragile political environment such as that of Bolivia, and this arguably poses one of the most significant urban development challenges for contemporary Latin America.

Notes

The author wishes to thank Dennis Rodgers and participants at the 'Beyond the Tipping Point, Development in an Urban World: Latin America' workshop held in Buenos Aires, May 2009, for their helpful comments and suggestions. All errors and omissions in the chapter are the author's sole responsibility.

1. Moreover, while the crime-property value connection is clear at the neighbourhood level, little has been written about the effect of illicit activities on property values at a macro level, that is to say, for an entire urban area.
2. According to the World Bank's Development Report, Bolivia's GDP for 2006 was US$11.1 billion.
3. Furthermore, the cocaine trade would clearly have limited links with the rest of the urban economy, as a result of the small number of individuals involved in its urban activities. The fact is that the illicit nature of the industry also means that any such links would generally be concealed in nature.
4. The selling of contraband goods is open and usually concentrated in shopping centres that specialize in contraband goods. The largest one in the city of Cochabamba is informally called 'miamisito' (little Miami), making reference to the fact that the same goods available in a shopping mall in Miami could be found in that market – and often at lower prices than in Miami.
5. More specifically, Hylton (2007) argues that cocaine transformed Medellin by providing a 'narco-capital' that translated into greater economic and political power for those directly or indirectly involved in the drug business. This power ultimately had a visible effect on the city's real estate sector through increased jobs and cocaine export earnings.
6. Hylton (2007), Painter (1994), and Healy (1994) go further, and conclude that the urban employment created by money laundering acted as a social stabilizer in times when cocaine producer countries were experiencing economic hardship due to declining industries, such as the textile industry in Colombia and the tin industry in Bolivia during the 1980s. There is no evidence, however, of a counter-cyclical tendency to the drug industry as jobs created by the drug trade or money laundering do not seem to decrease in periods when producer countries are not in downturn. This remains an empirical question that the literature has yet to answer.
7. The examples presented in this section are simplified and for illustrative purposes. For a more comprehensive list of money laundering techniques using real estate transactions, see FATF (2008), and FCEN (2008).
8. Using yield estimates from the Bolivian region of Chapare.
9. See for example Healy (1986).
10. The city of Cochabamba is located at approximately 100 miles from the Chapare region.
11. The de-trended variables were obtained by dividing the series of each city by their smoothed series. The smoothed series were obtained using a standard symmetric moving average smoother of five periods.
12. Using a path diagram analysis (not shown) in the construction permit models, we estimate that only about 13 per cent of the effect of cocaine production on construction permits in Bolivia's main cities could be explained by employment effects.

References

Antonil (1978). *Mama Coca*. London: Hassle Free Press.

Clawson, P.L., and W.L.III Rensselaer (1998). *The Andean Cocaine Industry*. New York: St. Martin's Griffin.

Corben, B. (2006). 'Cocaine Cowboys'. Documentary film by Magnolia Pictures.

De Franco, M., and R. Godoy (1992). 'The economic consequences of cocaine production in Bolivia: historical, local and macroeconomic perspectives'. *Journal of Latin American Studies*, 24(2): 275–406.

Dennis, P.A. (2003). 'Cocaine in Miskitu villages'. *Ethnology*, 42(2): 161–72.

FATF (Financial Action Task Force) (2008). 'Money Laundering & Terrorist Financing Risk Assessment Strategies'. Paris: Financial Action Task Force.

FCEN (Financial Crimes Enforcement Network) (2008). 'Suspected Money Laundering in the Residential Real Estate Industry. An Assessment Based upon Suspicious Activity Report Filing Analysis'. Financial Crimes Enforcement Network.

Gibbons, S. (2004). 'The costs of urban property crime'. *The Economic Journal*, 114: 441–63. Oxford: Royal Economic Society, Blackwell.

Hylton, F. (2007). 'Medellín's makeover'. *New Left Review*, 44: 71–89.

Healy, K. (1986). 'The Boom within the Crisis: Some Recent Effects of Foreign Cocaine Markets on Bolivian Rural Society and Economy'. In D. Pacini and C. Franquemont (eds), *Coca and Cocaine: Effects on People and Policy in Latin America*. Boston: Cultural Survival.

Healy, K. (1994). 'Recent literature on drugs in Bolivia'. In B.M. Bagley and W.O. Walker III (eds), *Drug Trafficking in the Americas*. New Brunswick, NJ: Transaction Publishing/North-South Center.

INE (Instituto Nacional de Estadistica [National Statistics Institute]) (2008a). *Estadísticas de la Actividad de la Construcción 1998–2007.* La Paz: INE.

INE (Instituto Nacional de Estadistica) (2008b). 'Encuesta Trimestral de Empleo, Salario y Remuneraciones'. http://www.ine.gob.bo/empleo/EmpleoSalariosRemuneraciones.aspx, retrieved in December 2008.

Karch, S.B. (2006). *A Brief History of Cocaine*. New York: CRC Press.

Labaton, S. (1989). 'The cost of drug abuse: $60 billion a year'. *New York Times*, 5 December.

Marcy, W.L. (2010). *The Politics of Cocaine: How U.S. Foreign Policy Has Created a Thriving Drug Industry in Central and South America*. Chicago, IL: Lawrence Hill Books.

McCue, D., and E.S. Belsky (2007). 'Why do house prices fall? Perspectives on the historical drivers of large nominal house price declines'. W07–3. Cambridge: Joint Center for Housing Studies, Harvard University.

McDonald, J. (2005). 'The narcoeconomy and small-town, rural Mexico'. *Human Organization*, 64(2): 115–25.

Mejia, D., and C.E. Posada (2008). 'Cocaine production and trafficking: what do we know?'. *World Bank Policy Research Working Paper* 4618. Washington, DC: World Bank.

Painter, J. (1994). *Bolivia and Coca: A Study in Dependency, in Studies on the Impact of the Illegal Drug Trade*. Boulder: Lynne Rienner.

Reuter, P., and V. Greenfield (2001). 'Measuring global drug markets: how good are the numbers and why should we care about them'. *World Economics*, 2(4): 155–73.

Rodgers, D. (2007). 'Managua'. In K. Koonings and D. Kruijt (eds), *Fractured Cities: Social Exclusion, Urban Violence and Contested Spaces in Latin America*. London: Zed.

Shams, R. (1992). 'The drugs economy and anti-drug policy in developing countries'. *Intereconomics*, 27(3): 139–44.

Sultzer. S. (1995). 'Money laundering: the scope of the problem and attempts to combat it'. *Tennessee Law Review*, 63(1).

Thaler, R. (1978). 'A note on the value of crime control: evidence from the property market'. *Journal of Urban Economics*, 5(1): 137–45.

Thoumi, F.E. (1994). 'The size of the illegal drug industry'. In B.M. Bagley and W.O. Walker III (eds), *Drug trafficking in the Americas*. New Brunswick, NJ: Transaction Publishing/North-South Center.

Thoumi, F.E. (2003). *Illegal Drugs, Economy and Society in the Andes*. Washington, DC: Woodrow Wilson Centre.

Thoumi, F.E. (2005). 'The numbers game: let's all guess the size of the illegal drug industry!'. *Journal of Drug Issues*, Winter: 185–200.

UNODC (United Nations Office on Drugs and Crime) (2004). 'Bolivia Coca Cultivation Survey 2003'. Illicit Crop Monitoring Programme Reports. Available at: www.unodc.org/pdf/bolivia/bolivia_coca_survey_2003.pdf.

UNODC (2006). 'Coca Cultivation Surveys for Bolivia, Peru and Colombia'. Illicit Crop Monitoring Programme Reports. Available at: www.unodc.org/unodc/en/crop-monitoring/index.html.

UNODC (2008). 'Coca Cultivation in the Andean Region for 2007: A Survey of Bolivia Colombia and Peru'. Illicit Crop Monitoring Programme Reports. Available at: www.unodc.org/unodc/en/crop-monitoring/index.html.

Wheaton, W.C. (1974). 'A comparative static analysis of urban spatial structure'. *Journal of Economic Theory*, 9(2): 223–37.

4

Mobility Challenges in Santiago de Chile: Improving Diagnosis and the Need to Shift the Understanding of Urban Inequality from Fixed Enclaves to Mobile Gradients

Paola Jirón

1 Introduction

Many urban development interventions currently being implemented in cities in developing countries around the world arguably evidence a major blind spot with regard to their understanding of the ways in which contemporary urban living occurs, and how it is changing under processes related to both globalization and specific national and local issues. In particular, a key factor influencing contemporary forms of urban living relates to the unprecedented manner in which mobility, in its multiple forms, now impacts on urban dwellers' lives, especially when compared to the past. Certainly, as the recent 'mobility turn' in the social sciences – see Cresswell (2006), Hannam et al. (2006), Sheller and Urry (2006a, 2006b), and Urry (2007), for example – has pointed out, the proliferation of different types of mobility – including migration, tourism, residential mobility, and daily mobility, amongst others – unavoidably has an impact on the organization of contemporary everyday life, and therefore constitutes a significant vector for the analysis of urban processes.

Adopting a mobility lens, however, fundamentally challenges certain traditional concepts associated with urban studies. One such concept is that of urban inequality, which in Latin America is often considered synonymous with spatial segregation and, more specifically, with residential segregation (see, for example, Sabatini et al. 2001a, 2001b; Schteingart 2001; Rodríguez and Arriagada 2004). However, an analysis of the various forms of urban daily mobility and their impact clearly challenges the way that this concept ought to be understood, analysed, and diagnosed. Drawing on the example of Santiago de Chile,[1] this chapter shows how, from the perspective of mobility, urban inequality moves from being about spatially-fixed enclaves *in* the city to mobile gradients *through* the city. As such, it highlights the need to broaden the standard urban analyses of inequality in Latin American cities, and also suggests that it is important to question current forms of urban and transport planning in order to open up new avenues for intervening meaningfully in the city.

2 Understanding urban inequality

The way that mobility impacts upon urban inequality has not been incorporated into most analyses of the dynamics of Latin American cities. This is particularly important when it comes to designing and implementing urban interventions, as these are (normally) based on diagnoses and analyses deriving from urban research. Take the case of Chile, for example. Current governmental initiatives aimed at improving social integration in cities use conventional residential segregation analyses to inform policy interventions.[2] These diagnoses are essential and, for the most part, accurate as far as they go, but they are also partial. Current understanding of urban social relations and their implications for urban inequality requires questioning the conceptualization of inequality and broadening traditional analyses of urban segregation.

In particular, most studies of Latin American cities usually consider segregation solely in terms of the residential location of individuals from different income groups (Sabatini et al. 2001a; Caldeira 2001; Borsdorf and Hidalgo 2010; Salcedo and Torres 2004; Roitman 2004; Kaztman 2003).[3] Certainly, this is the case of most studies of Santiago de Chile, which have tended to emphasize how the city is characterized by widespread and very clear patterns of segregated residential location. Some of these studies have argued that this residential segregation has given rise to a poor distribution of services and provision of amenities, which have in turn led to extremely low levels of quality of life, which have contributed substantially to the social exclusion of poor neighbourhoods (Jirón and Fadda 2003).

Sabatini and Salcedo (2005), on the other hand, distinguish between a 'perverse' segregation and a more 'benign' one, depending on the scale of analysis. They argue that at the macro level, segregation in Santiago is extremely perverse because almost all middle-high or high-income neighbourhoods are concentrated in one geographical zone, the northeast (see Maps 4.1 and 4.2). This concentration phenomenon is primarily the consequence of market forces, as well as a legacy of the semi-forceful movement of poor populations from better-off boroughs during the military regime, but it has been aggravated by the implementation of particular types of social housing programmes by the Chilean government, as well as the inadequate coordination of social policies (see Jirón 2007 for further details).

A more micro-vision, however, reveals a lesser degree of segregation within certain areas, according to Sabatini et al. (2001b). They point out that specific residential locations are rarely homogeneous, particularly boroughs with lower land values where middle-high to high-income gated communities have been built. Following

Map 4.1 Income distribution in Santiago

Note: Currency in Chilean Pesos $.

Source: CASEN 2006.

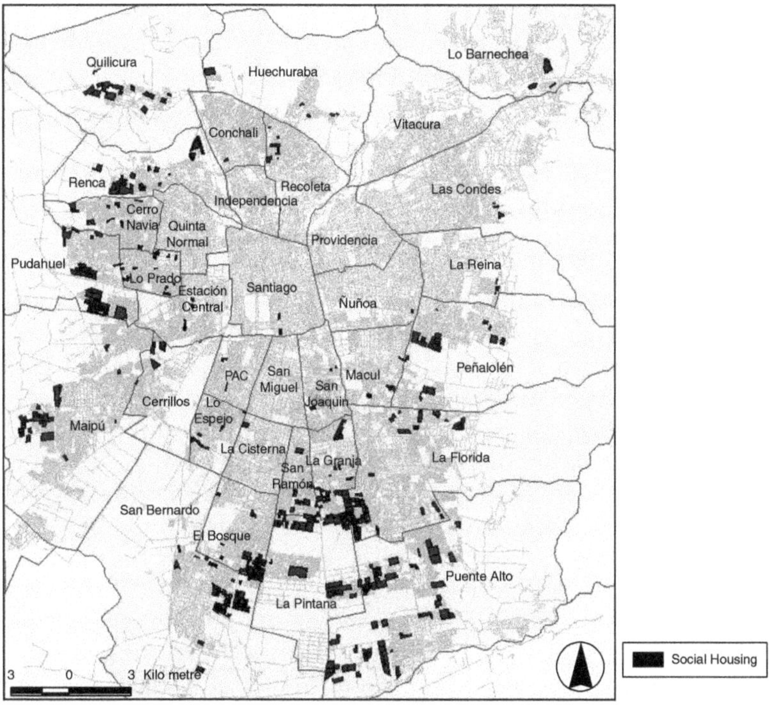

Map 4.2 Location of low-income housing, 1990–2006
Source: INVI-Ude Chile 2008.

international trends (Webster et al. 2002; Caldeira 2001; Low 2005; Roitman 2004), some areas in Santiago have experienced a modification in the traditional distribution of income in the city, where, over the past few years, a portion of middle, middle-high and high-income groups have chosen to live in gated communities located in peripheral boroughs with predominant low-income populations living nearby in social and self-built housing (Hidalgo 2004; Salcedo and Torres 2004). According to Sabatini et al. (2001b), this proximity has led to a more benevolent or benign type of segregation, where, although visibly separated by gates and walls, interaction between the different income groups – mainly in terms of employment – benefits the poor. To this extent, Sabatini et al. (ibid.) claim that certain types of residential segregation are in fact benign, and can bring significant economic, social, and psychological benefits to local communities, and they call for the spatial dispersion of middle or high-income groups throughout the city as a way of combating the exclusion of the poor, even if this goal is reached through investments in the form of gated communities.[4]

Although the logic of this argument is potentially convincing, and perhaps encouraging the location of gated communities in low-income areas and fostering benign segregation may be more convenient than perpetuating perverse segregation, the benefits of such interventions require critical scrutiny. This is because diminishing the physical distance between different socioeconomic groups might not necessarily decrease inequality. Although residential segregation is unquestionably very common in Latin America, it can be analysed in terms other than solely economic – for example, in terms of religion, ethnicity,[5] age or gender. Moreover, other types of segregation beyond the residential exist in Latin America, including segregation with regard to access to public space, education, or employment, for example. Certainly, such an analysis could reveal that encouraging the location of gated communities in lower-income areas could be detrimental in the medium and long term, leading to gentrification and the eventual expulsion of lower income groups (Davidson and Lees 2005),[6] or increased resentment, fewer opportunities for encounters between different social groups, and exacerbated inequalities in the long run. Such consequences would remain hidden if income heterogeneity in residential locations is the only way that urban inequality is observed.

A more careful analysis of social relations within these localities is consequently necessary to truly judge the benevolence of segregation at the micro-level. Residential segregation does not fully explain the ways that people experience inequality in the city, or in their daily lives, and thus getting to grips with urban inequality requires a different type of analysis. More specifically, it is necessary to analyse the new places, activities, and relations that various groups within a given locality have access to, both as a result, as well as despite, their residential proximity. By taking into account everyday practices and their various spheres and spaces of exchange and interaction beyond fixed residential areas, a clearer view of the multiple forms of inequality present in the city can emerge. In this respect, an approach which acknowledges that the experiences of the city are fundamentally mobile – as opposed to fixed in a permanent location – is essential. However, this involves a fundamental revision of concepts, methodologies, and disciplinary approaches, as the next section highlights.

3 Conceptualizing urban mobility

Most urban analysis is based on structured views of the city (Sassen 2001, 2002, 2006; Castells 1996, 2000, 2005; Galetovic 2006; Figueroa 2005), ignoring much of the specificity inherent to the daily experience of urban living. Although such analysis is useful and necessary to understand the broader processes, little is known about the consequences such processes have on daily life, how people respond, react, resent, resignify, or simply ignore such processes, or how alternative processes germinate from below. Analysing daily living experiences and linking these to broader processes can thus provide a new perspective on key urban issues, a perspective that potentially unveils issues that may be rendered invisible by large-scale viewpoints. As such, old concepts and ideas can be questioned and new possibilities emerge.

One potential lens is that of urban mobility. Mobility refers to the social, political, historical, cultural, economic, geographic, physical, communicative, and material dimensions of movement. This involves the actual journeys made and physical distances travelled, but also the expectations, experiences, consequences, and impacts these journeys can have on people's lives. For most people, social life is formed and reformed through intermittent meetings engendered by physical travel (Urry 2003), meaning that although life is networked, it inevitably involves specific encounters at specific times and places. The act of meeting and the different forms and modes of travel are central to much of social life, a life which involves particular combinations of increasing distance and intermittent co-presence (ibid.).

Mobility practices are hybrid, meaning that they involve multiple encounters, bodies, objects, forms, materialities, signs, destinations, and times and, consequently, different experiences. These differentiated experiences often lead to uneven access to the various activities, relations, or places in the city (Delaunay 2007; Rodríguez 2008), and may generate new forms of urban inequality. Accessibility is often referred to as connectivity and transport systems are designed with the aim of maximizing connection (Vigar 2002). However, accessibility involves more than just reaching a certain point in the city; it also involves the ability to participate adequately in the social, cultural, economic, and physical spaces encountered. The way mobility relates to urban inequality cannot only be analysed in terms of connectivity, distance, and time, but must also be conceived in terms of the quality of access, its relation to immobility, and the actual experience of mobility.

Within urban research, much analysis has been conducted on issues such as social exclusion, residential segregation, location of infrastructure, services and housing, place-making, and belonging. Until recently, however, there has been little consideration of the connection between such issues and people's daily mobility (a partial exception is the volume by Savage et al. 2005). In particular, in Latin America, although research on transport has been extensive, from modelling (Martinez and Araya 2000; Fernández et al. 2005; Jara-Diaz and Gschwender 2003) to transport systems (Figueroa 2005; Montezuma 2003; Thomson 2002; Vasconcellos 2001; CAF 2009), mobility studies, as conceived here, are very recent. One area of research has involved exploring the link between housing appropriation and mobility needs (Lazo and Jouffe 2010; Jouffe and Campos 2009), while another strand has involved looking at informal mobility practices (Avellaneda 2007).[7] But generally, there remains a critical need to get to grips with the way that mobility is experienced by different people in the city, and what the consequences of this experience are for their everyday lives. Drawing on the concrete example of a mobility study carried out in Santiago de Chile,[8] the next section illustrates the insights that a mobility approach can generate, with specific reference to the gendered dimensions of urban inequality.

4 Representing differentiated mobility practices

Properly representing mobility practices involves making use of text, photography, and time–space mapping.[9] Time–space maps are used to signal the trajectory taken by each traveller. Specific stations along the way are numbered to correlate with photos of the situation, which is textually narrated. This can be a powerful means of detailing specific mobility practices, particularly when several such descriptions are juxtaposed with the aim of eliciting comparative insight. In order to illustrate this approach, two examples will now be given, which illustrate the fundamentally gendered nature of urban mobility practices. The first narrates the travelling experience of Bernardo, whose journey, though long and bumpy, is more enjoyable than the second case, that of Marta, who, given her gender responsibilities, can only take the bus during rush hour, thus making her experience more uncomfortable than Bernardo's.

Bernardo is 40 years old. He is married to Alicia, who is 39. Bernardo and Alicia have three children: 19-year-old twins, and a seven-year-old boy named Mario. Bernardo works at a print shop close to downtown, and has worked there for the past eight years. Alicia stays home, taking care of the house, Mario, and the new sewing business she is trying to set up (with limited success). Once a month she goes downtown to buy material, but she mostly stays at home and around the neighbourhood.

Every morning Bernardo gets up at 6:00 am, and leaves the house by 6:30 am, while his family is still sleeping. He walks to the bus terminal to catch his bus at the beginning of its route (Station 1 in Map 4.3 depicting Bernardo's journey, and Photo 4.1).

Being one of the first on the bus gives him a choice of seating, and he generally sits by the window in order to make the ride more enjoyable. The bus fills up very quickly, and within a few stops his friend, Mayra, gets on the bus; she stands next to him while he carries her bags on his lap. They talk all the way to work, about their friends, their family, their jobs, other passengers, and life in general (Station 2 in Map 4.3, and Photo 4.2).

Bernardo constantly nods and waves to passengers as they get on and off the bus. The ride lasts over an hour, it is overcrowded, people look tired, and the chances of being pick-pocketed are high, but Bernardo is not bothered. He says that he only gets fed up 'when the vehicle breaks down half way through the journey and we all have to get off and wait for another bus' (Station 3 in Map 4.3). Bernardo generally makes it to work before 8:00 am (Station 4 in Map 4.3), with enough time to buy and eat his breakfast.

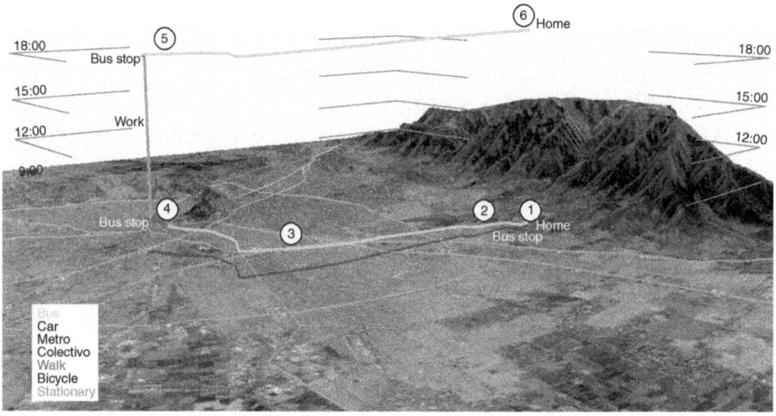

Map 4.3 Time–space map of Bernardo's journey

Photo 4.1 Bernardo walks to the bus terminal in the morning

Bernardo generally stays indoors at work until about 6:00 pm. He knows that the buses are generally very busy at this time, so he walks for about 15 minutes down the main road from his workplace in order to catch his bus before it fills up, and he also gets on it from the back. The ride back home takes an hour and a half and he generally rides standing (Station 5 in Map 4.3, and Photo 4.3). Bernardo finally arrives back home at 7:30 pm (Station 6 in Map 4.3).

This is Bernardo's routine from Monday to Thursday; on Fridays he brings his guitar along, and goes out singing and drinking with his mates after work. He does not get involved in many of the domestic tasks at home, such as cooking, cleaning, grocery shopping, and childminding: 'Alicia is in charge of this'. Instead, Bernardo contributes a monthly amount from his salary, which she then has to manage in order to see the household through the month.[10] Bernardo's limited involvement in household duties is partly what allows him to opt for the best time to find, within the available bus choices, a comfortable and suitable way to get to work early in the morning. He says he would not switch jobs to one closer to home; the ride is not an inconvenience for him. However, those with household responsibilities have to juggle their household

Photo 4.2 Inside the bus in the morning

duties prior to getting on the bus, making their journey more difficult, as the following case of Marta's mobility illustrates well.

Marta is 24 years old, and is married to Ernesto, with one daughter, Patricia, who is 7 years old. She is employed to clean and child-mind

Photo 4.3 Bernardo on the bus in the afternoon

in a house in one of the richest and most exclusive neighbourhoods in Santiago: La Dehesa. Ernesto works as a security guard at a higher-income gated community not far from their neighbourhood. His night shift runs from 8:00 pm until 8:00 am, and repeats on this basis for 5 days, after which he has 3 nights off and then switches to day shifts, from 8:00 am to 8:00 pm. When he is at home during the day, he mostly sleeps. Marta, on the other hand, gets up every morning around 6:30 am. She begins by helping her daughter prepare for school, before setting off at 7:30 am to walk with her through a park, an empty lot, a pedestrian bridge, and a shantytown, in order to make it to school before 8:00 am (Station 1 in Map 4.4, and Photo 4.4).

Once she has dropped Patricia off, Marta walks down the main road to catch the first of the two buses she has to take to get to work (Station 2 in Map 4.4). The buses are already very full, and the few that pass by often do not stop for passengers. Marta generally has to walk past her stop to one further down the street to make sure that a bus stops for her. Pushing and shoving, she gets on it. It is difficult to see inside, let alone outside, as the bus is absolutely packed. 'It's mainly *nanas* [domestic workers] on this bus,' she says, 'going to work to the richer areas of the city, where the better paying jobs are'. Most of the passengers who

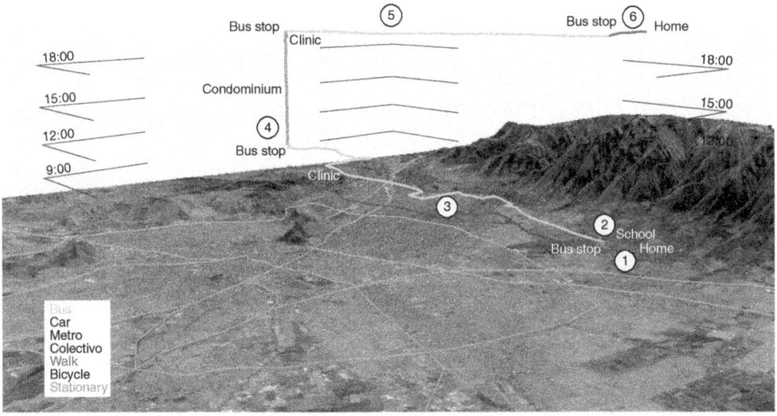

Map 4.4 Time–space map of Marta's journey

Photo 4.4 Marta and Patricia walk to school

are sitting down are sleeping and, except for some initial banter with the driver, the ride is quiet for most of the way. Marta stands for the duration of the ride and gets off before her actual stop to be able walk to catch the next bus. As she explains, 'if I don't do that, the bus is so full, it won't stop for me at the next stop' (Station 3 in Map 4.4, and Photo 4.5).

Marta then travels for another 45 minutes until she finally arrives in a different Santiago to the one she lives in – one that is clean, green and more solitary (Station 4 in Map 4.4, and Photo 4.6).

In total, then, her journey lasts almost two hours, and she makes it to her workplace long after 10:00 am. Her boss often complains about her coming in so late and tells her to get up earlier; 'she doesn't understand that I can't leave earlier, I have to take my girl to school in the morning and it's not a matter of getting up earlier', Marta remarks.

Marta doesn't leave the house all day and finishes around 7:00 pm. She showers at her workplace, and then walks to the bus stop, where she generally waits for the bus for over 20 minutes. However, she often manages to grab a seat when it arrives. She gets off at the end of the route, runs to catch her second bus, and generally manages to obtain a seat on this one as well. She hardly registers the journey itself as she is very tired, although she cannot sleep, even if it is always dark by the time she gets to her home stop. (Station 5 in Map 4.4, and Photo 4.7).

Marta buys tomatoes, bread, and butter in a corner shop on her way home and walks for about 20 minutes, taking the same route she took in

Photo 4.5 Marta on the bus

Photo 4.6 A different Santiago: La Dehesa

Photo 4.7 The bus arriving back at night

the morning. It is very dark and, although she knows her way (Station 6 in Map 4.4), she walks quickly as she is scared. She could take a bus that would leave her closer to home, but it would mean more waiting and paying for another fare, so she prefers to risk the dark road. When she gets home, Patricia is at home alone, watching TV. She has been alone for over an hour, and has had her tea and done the washing up.

It is immediately apparent from these two different mobility patterns that mobility experiences in cities are fundamentally gendered. Although both Bernardo and Marta have fixed work places that require them to be physically present during specific times and with limited possibilities to move during the day, their travelling experiences differ immensely, as do the strategies that they put in place to optimize their travel, despite using the same mode of transport. Bernardo's strategy for a more comfortable seated journey is to be at the bus stop early in the morning, while Marta has to leave later after taking Patricia to school, and therefore has to endure standing in an overcrowded bus. Although Bernardo's son is the same age as Marta's daughter, it is his wife Alicia who prepares the child for school every morning, whereas in Marta's case she is the one in charge of this task.

The daily chore of taking children to and from school has important implications in the daily life of urban dwellers and, in the case of Marta, for the work decisions she makes. During an interview she mentioned how 'I worry about her [Patricia], you see, she's starting second grade and can't read very well yet and I think it's partly because she's alone all the time...but it's hard, you see, I get home tired, the bus takes a long time, the traffic, then walking here...by the time I get home at nine...it's too late, I have to feed her and it's too late to do homework, it's too late...'. At the same time, Marta's concerns oscillate between her daughter and her job. She knows that Patricia should not be staying at home alone as she gets bored, yet the money she makes contributes fundamentally to the household budget.[11]

Marta's strategy to make her ride to work more comfortable is limited mainly to walking further to catch a less full bus. In the afternoon she tries to organize childminding for Patricia with her husband or friends, but her social network is not broad enough and she sometimes ends up paying someone to do this; however, she cannot afford to do so too often, and so she frequently has to leave Patricia home alone.[12] Marta's main concern, therefore, is to find ways for Patricia not to be alone, whereas in Bernardo's case Alicia has this responsibility, which makes his engagement with particular mobility practices easier. This does not mean that Bernardo neglects his children, but his wife is fully in charge of this issue. Alicia, on the other hand, has different issues to face, mainly to do with immobility.

Mobility access in the cases presented above is clearly gendered. Marta faces temporal, organizational, and financial barriers, as she needs to take care of her daughter prior to setting off to work. This forces her to face rush hour in a system that does not operate adequately at such times. This is partly a function of the fact that two salary households invariably face difficulties with regard to childcare, but Marta's organizational barriers are principally based on the fact that she does not have adequate social networks in place to support her in her household responsibilities and thus ease her journey. Marta's lack of connections or networks to help her organize her household life, and her limited time, make her travelling burden a gendered one.

To this extent, Marta's situation can be related to Chant's (2007) discussion about the 'feminization of poverty', which she criticizes as a static view of poverty in terms of income, which overemphasizes female-headed households, and neglects men and the specificities of gender inequality; she suggests looking instead at the 'feminization of responsibility and/or obligation' (Chant 2006, 2007). Although the number of women working outside the home has risen, and men are participating more in household duties, the bulk of unpaid domestic and care work is still carried out by women. In the cases presented this is so, as women (both Marta and Bernardo's wife) are responsible for the household and childcare, and this has an impact upon the time available to carry out their many activities, the decisions they make about employment, and the way these organizational issues, time constraints, and responsibilities have affected their mobility experience in a negative manner. In effect, women in low-income households are not only 'cash poor' but also 'time poor'.

Although it has been broadly recognized that gender differences generate different access to transport, affecting women in particular (Grieco et al. 1989; Levy 1992; Turner and Grieco 2000), the complexity of everyday life means solutions cannot be simplistic in their assumptions. For instance, providing childcare alone will not solve Marta's problem as someone still has to take Patricia to school and be present for moments of crisis, such as illness. On the days that she needs to go to the doctor she has to take a whole day off as she does not know how long it will take for her to be seen at the local surgery. Only by understanding such chains of activities can we develop a better idea of the differentiated difficulties faced by women and men in urban settings.

5 Conclusions

As Sheller and Urry (2003) note, most theorists agree that inclusion and exclusion are spatially and materially fixed, but in doing so they fail to recognize how mobility can undo the divisions between public and private life. To this extent, a more profound understanding of the situations of mobility, and the experiences it creates for those involved, is required. At the same time, a more comprehensive approach to the practices of mobility requires an awareness of the everyday reality of contemporary movement as well as the socio-cultural dimensions that condition these practices, and this chapter has introduced a specific way of capturing the experiences of differentiated mobility in the city.

Analysing urban mobility inevitably highlights the multiple relationships between mobility and inequality. Mobility emerges simultaneously as a *cause*, a *consequence*, and a *manifestation* of urban inequality. These relationships fundamentally question the widespread understanding of urban inequality based on the analysis of spatially-fixed and segregated income groups, as well as challenging the idealist views of social integration, which mainly propose physically mixing social groups in space as the solution to achieving less homogeneous neighbourhoods. Focussing on daily access to activities, people, and places offers a more dynamic way of analysing the disparities in urban areas while in motion.

This experiential information is not currently incorporated into transport, urban, and housing policy and planning, however, in spite of its daily consequences on people's lives. Analysis of the differentiated experiences of mobility can identify the need for better transport systems in terms of affordability, availability, accessibility, comfort, safety, and reliability, for example. Additionally, it can lead to better connected infrastructure and improved housing interventions, and it can also evidence the need to improve access to better working conditions, educational and health services, cultural activities, use of leisure time, and so forth. Making urban daily experiences more visible, and discussing the implications of such interventions on daily mobility practices and experiences, opens up a whole field of research on urban areas that is only now beginning to take place.

The classic vision is that of the fragmentation of daily living through social exclusion which, in Graham and Marvin's (2001) terms, produces a 'splintered city'. Overcoming this has traditionally been thought to necessarily involve reconsidering urban interventions such as peripheral housing locations, or else expanding and connecting ever larger transport networks. One example of such a project is Transantiago, a public urban transportation improvement scheme introduced in Santiago de Chile in 2007. Transantiago was a major public transport plan for the city of Santiago, and it involved the complete restructuring of the inefficient, unsafe, deficient public bus system. Although there was sufficient information prior to the implementation of the new system to understand how patterns of mobility in the capital led to significant inequalities, the plan was conceived solely as a means to improve the efficiency of the system, mainly by reducing congestion and pollution. As a result, it failed to recognize the significance of transport in urban dwellers' daily lives, and in particular its critical impact on urban inequality.[13]

At the same time, the plan did not target inequality, and – partly as a result of this – it has become one of the most poorly evaluated public policies in Chile (Jirón 2012). The lesson in this programme is that as a manifestation, the differentiated use of mobility systems – whether according to income, age, life cycle, disability, or gender – shows that there are broader inequalities in societies which are not merely a function of spatial location or even of income. By looking at these inequalities in terms of mobility and accessibility, they are revealed and new forms of uneven relations within the city are unveiled, potentially enabling more meaningful interventions which go beyond simply trying to change locational or financial factors. As Beaujeau-Garnier (1966: 171) put it, ultimately, 'Man is a mobile creature'.

Notes

1. Research funding was provided by FONDECYT (grant no. 1090198).
2. Examples of this include: MINVU's 'I love My Neighbourhood' programme (*Programa Quiero mi Barrio*), which aims at intervening in 200 existing low-income neighbourhoods; a law modification proposal to include five per cent low-income housing in all real estate proposals; and subsidy for location of low-income housing within urban limits.
3. Residential segregation can potentially have nothing to do with inequality, as in the case of ethnic groups who cluster and prefer to live close to each other, as exemplified by the various Chinatowns or Little Italies in many cities around the world (Musterd 2003).
4. Although numerous authors have warned that the concentration of social housing in some boroughs and the construction of gated communities and closed urbanization in others creates the potential for increased physical deterioration of the city (Ciccolella 1999; Caldeira 2001; Low 2005; Roitman 2004), Hidalgo (2004) concurs with Sabatini et al. (2001b), and suggests that this risk can be eased if new gated community projects built in low-income areas are combined with government initiatives targeted at the poor. This could generate the possibility of modifying the classic pattern

of distribution of social groups in the city, and contribute to reducing the physical distance between rich and poor. However, it should be noted that this may not necessarily lead to lesser degrees of social segregation or greater levels of social integration.

5. For a detailed review of ethnic and racial segregation outside Latin America see Phillips (2007) and Lemanski (2006a, 2006b).
6. In Europe and the USA, one way of generating integration or desegregation has been area-based approaches or residential mixing, often leading to processes of gentrification.
7. Some studies looking at the statistical significance of everyday mobility have also evolved from simply describing movement trends (Escolano et al. 2006), to looking at uneven mobility patterns analysis using various large-scale surveys (Delaunay 2007; Rodríguez 2008). Moreover, some more qualitative studies have touched on the ways that mobility impacts upon social practices (Gutiérrez 2010; Ureta 2009; Jirón 2010a, 2010b).
8. Based on Jirón (2008).
9. For further details about this methodology, see Jirón (2010b).
10. Alicia, for her part, has a hard time realizing that there is a 'life ... happening outside'. Although she knows she could theoretically go out and get a job – her husband would have no say in that –she is afraid of leaving her eight-year-old son alone. She knows other children who have been molested by adults in the community they live in, and does not want to risk this happening to her son. She also wants to be there when Mario gets home from school, and to help him in his development.
11. Marta often talked about quitting her job and finding another one closer by home to avoid travelling for four hours every day in order to be able to spend that time with her daughter. Yet she was also very aware of the fact that even if she did manage to get a job close by, there would still not be anyone to pick Patricia up from school, and the money she would earn was not likely to be as good as what she makes now.
12. The irony, of course, is that Marta takes care of higher-income people's children, yet she does not have the social networks or the money to take care of her own.
13. It's interesting to note that, simultaneous to the ill-prepared implementation of Transantiago, millions of dollars were invested in high-speed urban highways which promoted car use for higher-income groups. When such systems are associated with residential location, a dual inequality is generated based on location in distant poor areas along with limited transport means. Mobility or the lack of mobility possibilities can generate the sense of confinement in a fixed location, which becomes exacerbated when residences are located in segregated areas, and worsened by the restriction of urban mobility systems.

References

Avellaneda, P. (2007). 'Movilidad, Pobreza y exclusión Social: Un Estudio de Caso en la Ciudad de Lima'. Tesis doctoral, Departament de Geografia. Barcelona: Universitat Autònoma de Barcelona.

Beaujeau-Garnier, J. (1966). *Geography of Population*. London: Longman.

Borsdorf, A., and R. Hidalgo (2010). 'From polarization to fragmentation. Recent changes in Latin American urbanization'. In P. Lindert and O. Verkoren (eds), *Decentralized Development in Latin America: Experiences in Local Governance and Local Development*. Amsterdam: Springer.

CAF (Corporación Andina de Fomento [Development Bank of Latin America]) (2009). 'Observatorio de movilidad urbana para América Latina – Información para mejores políticas y mejores ciudades', Corporación Andina de Fomento, Caracas.

Caldeira, T. (2001). *City of Walls: Crime, Segregation, and Citizenship in São Paulo*. Berkeley: University of California Press.

Castells, M. (1996). *The Information Age: Economy, Society and Culture*, vol. I. Oxford: Blackwell.

Castells, M. (2000). 'Materials for an explanatory theory of the network society', *British Journal of Sociology*, 51(1): 5–24.

Castells, M. (2005). *Space of Flows, Spaces of Places: Materials for a Theory of Urbanism in the Information Age: Comparative Planning Cultures*. Oxford: Routledge.

Chant, S. (2006). 'Re-thinking the "feminization of poverty" in relation to aggregate gender indices', *Journal of Human Development*, 7(2): 201–20.

Chant, S. (2007). *Generation and Poverty: Exploring the 'Feminization of Poverty' in Africa, Asia and Latin America*. Cheltenham: Edward Elgar.

Ciccolella, P. (1999). 'Globalizacion y dualizacion en la Region Metropolitana de Buenos Aires. Grandes inversiones y reestructuracion socioterritorial en los anos noventa', *EURE*, 25(76): 22.

Cresswell, T. (2006). *On the Move. Mobility in the Modern Western World*. New York: Routledge.

Davidson, M., and L. Lees (2005). 'New-build "gentrification" and London's riverside renaissance' *Environment and Planning*, 37(7): 1165–90.

Delaunay, D. (2007). 'Relaciones entre pobreza, migración y movilidad: dimensiones territorial y contextual'. *Revista Notas de Población* – CELADE 84: 87–130.

Escolano Utrilla, S., and J. Ortiz (2006). 'Movilidad espacial de la población y cambios recientes del modelo de densidad en ciudades del sistema urbano chileno'. *Geographicalia*, 49: 139–56.

Fernández L, J.E., J. de Cea Ch., and L. de Grange C. (2005). 'Production costs, congestion, scope and scale economies in urban bus transportation corridors'. *Transport Research Part A*, 39: 383–403.

Figueroa, O. (2005). 'Transporte urbano y globalización, políticas y efectos en América Latina'. *Revista EURE*, 31(94): 41–53.

Galetovic, A. (2006). *Santiago. Dónde estamos y hacia dónde vamos*. Santiago: Centro de Estudios Públicos.

Graham, S., and S. Marvin (2001). *Splintering Urbanism: Networked Infrastructures, Technological Mobilities and the Urban Condition*. London: Routledge.

Grieco, M., L. Pickup, and R. Whipp (1989). *Gender, Transport and Employment: The Impact of Travel Constraints*. Aldershot: Gower.

Gutiérrez, A. (2010). 'Movilidad, Transporte y Acceso: Una Renovación Aplicada al Ordenamiento Territorial'. *Scripta Nova*, XIV(331): 86.

Hannam, K., M. Sheller, and J. Urry (2006). 'Editorial: mobilities, immobilities and moorings'. *Mobilities*, 1(1): 1–22.

Hidalgo, R. (2004). 'De los pequeños condominios a la ciudad vallada: las urbanizaciones cerradas y la nueva geografía social en Santiago de Chile (1990–2000)'. *EURE*, 30(91): 29–52.

Jara-Diaz, S., and A. Gschwender (2003). 'Towards a general microeconomic model for the operation of public transport'. *Transport Reviews*, 23(4): 453–69.
Jirón, P. (2007). 'Formalizing the Informal: the evolution of informal settlements in Chile'. In F. Hernández and P. Kellet (eds), *Rethinking the Informal City: Critical Perspectives from Latin America*. Oxford: Berghahn Books.
Jirón, P. (2008). 'Mobility on the Move: Examining Urban Daily Mobility Practices in Santiago de Chile', PhD thesis, London School of Economics.
Jirón, P. (2010a). 'Repetition and difference: rhythms and mobile place-making in Santiago de Chile'. In T. Edensor (ed.), *Geographies of Rhythm: Nature, Place, Mobilities and Bodies*. Ashgate Publishing Limited: 129–143.
Jirón, P. (2010b). 'On becoming "la sombre\the shadow"'. In M. Büscher, J. Urry, and K. Witchger (eds), *Mobile Methods*. London and New York: Taylor and Francis.
Jirón, P. (2012). 'Technology and technicians out of control. The implementation of Transantiago from a daily mobility point of view'. In P. Vannini, L. Budd, O. Jensen, C. Fisker, and P. Jirón (eds), *Mobility and Communication Technologies in the Americas*. New York: Peter Lang Publishing.
Jirón, P., and G. Fadda (2003). 'A Quality of Life Assessment to Improve Urban and Housing Policies in Chile'. World Bank Urban Research Symposium 2003, Washington DC.
Jouffe, Y., and F. Campos (2009). 'Movilidad para la Emancipación o para el Arraigo: Interacción de las Escalas en París y Santiago de Chile'. *Urbano*, 12(19): 7–16.
Kaztman, R. (2003). 'La dimensión espacial en las políticas de superación de la pobreza urbana'. Medio Ambiente y Desarrollo. División de Desarrollo Sostenible y Asentamientos Humanos. Santiago de Chile, CEPAL: 48.
Lazo, A., and Y. Jouffe (2010). 'Las prácticas cotidianas frente a los dispositivos de la movilidad aproximación política a la movilidad cotidiana de las poblaciones pobres periurbanas de Santiago de Chile'. *Revista EURE*, 108(36): 29–47.
Lemanski, C. (2006a). 'Spaces of exclusivity or connection? Linkages between a gated community and its poorer neighbour in a Cape Town master plan development'. *Urban Studies*, 42(2): 397–420.
Lemanski, C. (2006b). 'Desegregation and integration as linked or distinct? evidence from a previously "white" suburb in post-apartheid Cape Town'. *International Journal of Urban and Regional Research*, 30(3): 564–86.
Levy, C. (1992). *Transport: Gender and Development*. London, Routledge.
Low, S. (2005). 'Transformaciones del espacio público en la ciudad latinoamericana: cambio espaciales y prácticas sociales'. Available from: http://www.bifurcaciones.cl/005/Low.htm
Martinez, F., and C. Araya (2000). 'Transport and land use benefits under location externalities'. *Environment and Planning A*, 32.
Montezuma, R. (2003). 'Ciudad y transporte, la movilidad urbana'. In M. Balbo, R. Jordán, and D. Simioni (eds), *La Ciudad Inclusiva*. Santiago de Chile: CEPAL.
Musterd, S. (2003). 'Segregation and integration: a contested relationship'. *Journal of Ethnic and Migration Studies*, 29(4): 623–41.
Phillips, D. (2007). 'Ethnic and racial segregation: a critical perspective'. *Geography Compass*, 1: 1–22.

Rodríguez, J. (2008). 'Movilidad cotidiana, desigualdad social y segregación residencial en cuatro metrópolis de América Latina'. *Revista EURE*, XXXIV(103): 49–71.

Rodríguez, J., and C. Arriagada (2004). 'Segregación Residencial en la Ciudad Latinoamericana'. *EURE*, 30(89): 5–24.

Roitman, S. (2004). 'Urbanizaciones cerradas: estado de la cuestión hoy y propuesta teórica'. *Revista de Geografía Norte Grande*, 32: 5–19.

Sabatini, F., and R. Salcedo (2005). 'Gated Communities and the Poor in Santiago, Chile: Functional and Symbolic Integration in a Context of Aggressive Capitalist Colonization of Lower Class Areas'. International symposium on Territory, Control and Enclosure: The Ecology of Urban Fragmentation, Research Network: Private Urban Governance, Pretoria.

Sabatini, F., G. Cáceres, and J. Cerda (2001a). 'Residential Segregations Pattern Changes in Main Chilean Cities: Scale Shifts and Increasing Malignancy'. International seminar on Segregation in the City, Lincoln Institute of Land Policy, Cambridge MA.

Sabatini, F., G. Cáceres, and J. Cerda (2001b). 'Segregación residencial en las principales ciudades chilenas: Tendencias de las últimas décadas y posibles cursos de acción'. *Revista EURE*, 27(82): 1–23.

Salcedo, R., and A. Torres (2004). 'Gated communities in Santiago: wall or frontier?'. *International Journal of Urban and Regional Research*, 28(1): 27–44.

Sassen, S. (2001). *The Global City* (second edition). Princeton: Princeton University Press.

Sassen, S. (ed.) (2002). *Global Networks, Linked Cities*. London and New York: Routledge.

Sassen, S. (2006). *Cities in a World Economy*. Thousand Oaks: Pine Forge Press.

Savage, M., G. Bagnall, and B. Longhurst (2005). *Globalization and Belonging*. London: Sage.

Schteingart, M. (2001). 'La División Social del Espacio en las Ciudades'. *Perfiles Latinoamericanos*, 19.

Sheller, M., and J. Urry (2003). 'Mobile transformations of "public" and "private" life'. *Theory, Culture and Society*, 20(3): 107–25.

Sheller, M., and J. Urry (2006a). 'The new mobilities paradigm'. *Environment and Planning*, A38: 207–26.

Sheller, M., and J. Urry (2006b). *Mobile Technologies of the City*. London: Routledge.

Thomson, I. (2002). 'Impacto de las tendencias sociales, económicas y tecnológicas sobre el transporte público: investigación preliminar en ciudades de América Latina'. Santiago: División de Recursos Naturales e Infraestructura, CEPAL.

Turner, J., and M. Grieco (2000). 'Research note: gender and time poverty: the neglected social policy implications of gendered time, transport and travel'. *Time and Society*, 9(1): 129–36.

Ureta, S. (2009). 'Manejando por Santiago. Explorando el uso de automóviles por parte de habitantes de bajos ingresos desde una óptica de movilidad sustentable'. *Revista EURE*, XXXV(105): 71–93.

Urry, J. (2003). 'Social networks, travel and talk'. *British Journal of Sociology*, 54(2): 155–75.

Urry, J. (2007). *Mobilities*. Cambridge: Polity Press.
Vasconcellos, E. (2001). *Transporte Urbano, Espaço e Equidade: Analise das Politicas Publicas*. Sao Paulo: Annablume.
Vigar, G. (2002). *The Policies of Mobility. Transport, the Environment and Public Policy*. London: Spon Press.
Webster, C., G. Glasze, and K. Frantz (2002). 'The global spread of gated communities'. *Environment and Planning B: Planning and Design*, 29(3): 315–20.

5

The *Vecino* as Citizen: Neighbourhood Organizations in El Alto and the Transformation of Bolivian Citizenship

Helene Risør

1 Introduction

On the morning of 25 June 2008, the neighbourhood, or *zona*, of Santiago Segundo was more sparkling than usual. Men, women, and schoolchildren had all gathered outside the community centre on the *Plaza del Minero* (Miner's Square), where the neighbourhood association (*junta de vecinos*) had its premises. St. Pedro's Day, the patron saint of Santiago Segundo, was only four days away and every year the local inhabitants, referred to generically as *vecinos*, celebrate it with speeches, games, and a carnival. 2008 was special because it marked the 25th anniversary of the founding of Santiago Segundo, which is one of several hundred poor neighbourhoods in the emergent city of El Alto, situated on the high plateau outside Bolivia's capital, La Paz. On this occasion, the members of the city council had agreed to hold an honorary meeting of the city council in Santiago Segundo, and their plenary session took the form of speeches celebrating both the neighbourhood and its inhabitants and their contribution to the city of El Alto. Diplomas and rewards were handed out to high-flying students and local dignitaries, and the *presidente* of the neighbourhood association gave a speech commemorating the history of Santiago Segundo.

He particularly emphasized the harsh living conditions in the neighbourhood, and described how many of the inhabitants were former miners who had been forced to move from mining centres to El Alto as a result of privatization and the economic crisis of the mid-1980s. He also highlighted the former miners' organizational capacities, and their courageous participation in the so-called 'gas war' of 2003, when then president, Gonzalo Sanchez de Lozada, sent the army against *los Alteños* (inhabitants of El Alto), and commemorated how 70 people had been killed, and many more injured, as a result. In doing so, the *presidente* clearly situated the inhabitants of Santiago Segundo as central actors in the history of El Alto and contemporary Bolivia. Yet his speech was entitled 'A forgotten but determinant actor in the fight for the city of El Alto', indicating how, most of the time, the inhabitants of neighbourhoods such as Santiago Segundo tend to be forgotten rather than celebrated by the authorities.

Drawing on 11 months of ethnographic fieldwork carried out between 2007 and 2008, this chapter explores the figure of the *vecino*, both in Santiago Segundo and El Alto more generally, as a forgotten and marginal subject but also as a central agent in the constitution of the modern Bolivian political landscape. This perspective differs from the assumption which emphasizes contemporary indigenous participation in Bolivian politics as a re-emergence of the 'deep' indigenous Bolivia. As Postero (2007a) has pointed out, the emergence of indigenous political actors (forcefully represented by the presidential election of Evo Morales) has allowed for an interpretation – among activists and academics alike – of Andean (indigenous) culture as historically coherent and enduring, thus interpreting today's insurgent struggle as a contemporary expression of an 'Andean culture of insurrection' (Hylton and Thomson 2007). Rather than focusing on an enduring indigenous (and insurrectional) culture, I emphasize the contradictory ways in which poor urban settings such as El Alto have allowed for the emergence of the inhabitants as actors articulating specific practices of citizenship, thereby becoming focal points for the new social movement politics that characterize contemporary Bolivia. Further, while I acknowledge an increased ethnic awareness among poor urban dwellers (Canessa 2000, 2007), my own ethnographic material suggests that *Alteños'* territorial identity resides in a creative and transformative combination of indigenous and non-indigenous forms of organization which have matured in the new urban settings of Bolivia, and that *Alteños* themselves recognize this plurality as the source of their political strength.

More specifically – in conversation with the recent works of Canessa (2006), Holston (2008), Lazar (2008), Postero (2007a, 2007b), Arbona (2007, 2008), and Goldstein (2004), among others – I argue that indigenous traditions of political organization in Bolivia have been re-articulated into a residence-based notion of urban citizenship, often referred to as the *vecino*. To this extent, the political mobilizations that characterize El Alto cannot solely be understood as a matter of 'indigenous' rebellion, but rather need to be seen as rooted in a specific form of urban territorialization from where people engage in broader collective struggles in order to be recognized as carriers of social, economic, and civil rights. This chapter begins with some general considerations about the relationship between indigeneity and citizenship in Bolivia. It then moves on to a characterization of El Alto and Santiago Segundo's respective urban development trajectories. On the basis of the latter in particular, I highlight how the primary nexus between the state and the citizenry in contemporary Bolivia is arguably the neighbourhood association; this is the institutional medium through which urban dwellers concretely engage with the state, and vice versa. I show how individuals tend to conceive of themselves first and foremost as inhabitants, and consequently sustain that the political strength gained by the poor and the indigenous in Bolivia during the past decade must ultimately be analysed in relation to the increasing urbanization of the population and the emergence of peri-urban cities such as El Alto, rather than through the lens of a static notion of indigeneity.

2 Indigeneity and citizenship in Bolivia

Despite its traditional connotations, the figure of the indigenous person is by no means a static one, and its meanings and associations have changed fundamentally over the course of the past century in Bolivia, in particular as the state-citizen relationship has evolved. The national revolution of 1952, for example, gave Bolivia's indigenous population the right to vote, while the Bolivian nation more generally was discursively transformed from a segregated to a unitary *mestizo* nation. Indeed, the *mestizo*, a category which refers to the urban assimilated and educated Indian or rural peasants, was in many ways promoted as the ideal-typical Bolivian citizen (Bigehno 2006). The election of Evo Morales as the country's first indigenous president in 2006 and the current transformation of Bolivian politics have been widely read as being the consequence of the failure of the promises of the national revolution and its project for the mestizo nation (see Grindle and Domingo 2003). Indeed, Canessa (2006) argues that an indigenous ideal citizen has now replaced the figure of the post-revolutionary ideal mestizo citizen. Writing about the 2003 'gas war' (ibid.: 254) he argues that:

> Not only have indigenous people gone from the margins to the centre of Bolivian politics; but, rather more interestingly, it appears that central political issues, national issues that affect everyone, are represented as indigenous issues – after all, there is nothing intrinsically indigenous about a gas pipe line. Indigeneity is becoming the language of protests over resources and the defense of the patria against the forces of globalization; it is breaking out of its specific concerns and offering a language of political engagement for a much broader public.

It is certainly tempting to analyse the election of the indigenous leader Evo Morales as President of Bolivia in 2006 as the return of the millenarian Indian onto the contemporary Bolivian political scene, following over five hundred years of oppression and exclusion. Yet, while there is no doubt that there has been an indigenization of Bolivian politics during the past few years, this process has been anything but straightforward, and the transformation of the relationship between indigeneity and citizenship has arguably been mediated by specific forms of urban social organization. More specifically, the ideal figure of the indigenous citizen does not necessarily bear reference to the daily life of the poor indigenous population of Bolivia, despite the fact that the greater part, if not all, of the Bolivian population tends to be discursively situated (and situate themselves) as indigenous – at least when asked about their ethnic affiliation. This was apparent in discussions with the people I interviewed during my fieldwork. When asked about their ethnicity, most replied that they were either Aymara or Quechua (despite not necessarily being able to speak either language). However, most of the time people simply referred to themselves as *Alteños*, *vecinos*, or, eventually, as workers or students, reflecting the fact that their identity was constituted principally through residence and occupation rather than ethnicity, even if they did not seem to consider these different vectors in any way contradictory.

Indeed, one could argue that to be indigenous in contemporary Bolivia is very much conflated with other subaltern positions, such as being a poor urban dweller. To this extent, there has arguably been a significant shift in Bolivian society, insofar as being indigenous and being *vecino* were historically considered mutually contradictory statuses, with the latter referring to the 'white' townsman, property owner, and citizen, while the former referred to the rural indigenous person lacking political and civil rights. In other words, as the notion of 'indigenous' increasingly becomes an all-encompassing notion of what it means to be Bolivian, the very category of the indigenous has undergone equally profound changes, and part of this transformation has taken place in everyday urban settings where being 'indigenous' – as a traditionally rural category – is negotiated alongside other identity markers such as being a 'worker', a 'student', or more significantly, a *vecino*. In this sense, as Lazar (2008: 34) points out, El Alto is perhaps similar to several other urban centres and neighbourhoods inhabited by Andean migrants who might belong in several contradictory categories and settings (see also Pærregaard 1997). At the same time, however, the city also has a number of unique particularities, as the next section outlines.

3 El Alto

The city centre of El Alto, *La Ceja*, is characterized by movement: people make their way via the infinite numbers of minibuses offering rides to areas in El Alto or down to the city of La Paz. Outside la *Alcaldia Quemada* (the 'burnt municipality'),[1] the meeting point of *La Ceja*, informal commerce has taken over the streets. People walk by the *cholitas*, as traditional street sellers are known, on their way into restaurants and galleries where everything from judicial assistance to architectural services and internet access is offered. This scene is overlooked by a seven-metre high statue of Che Guevara made of recycled scrap metal. He is holding a rifle, with one foot trampling an American eagle, and his head – complete with familiar beret – is raised and looking out towards the horizon. Yet there is something intriguing about the statue. While it is definitely Che Guevara, the structure of his face has become slightly indigenous. It is Che, but then again different – it is an *Alteño* Che. Further down the street, looking towards the Illimani Mountain and the city of La Paz, stands a statue of Christ the Redeemer. The statue is said to be placed upon the heart of the rebel Tupac Katari, who was tortured and killed by the Spaniards in 1781 after holding La Paz under siege for four months, almost succeeding in overturning Spanish colonial rule in the process.[2] The syncretistic character of the *Alteño* Che, the charred municipality, and the statue of Christ the Redeemer built on an indigenous rebel leader's heart are all paradigmatic reflections of the entangled character of El Alto, pointing to the city dwellers' common practice of drawing upon different traditions as they struggle to make ends meet.

3.1 The city

On 6 March 1985, El Alto was separated from La Paz and administratively became a city in its own right. Today the 8 urban and 3 rural districts of the city are divided into 436 neighbourhoods or zones (Albó 2006), and, according to the logic of continuous migration, the areas that yesterday constituted the city's periphery have today become yet another zone of El Alto. Today the city of El Alto has a larger population than La Paz, and 6 March each year sees *Alteños* proudly parading in honour of their city while the municipality shows off its latest cars or heavy machinery. At the same time, while life in La Paz is in many regards similar to that of El Alto (see Wildmark 2003), El Alto is much poorer. Except for a few commercial zones in the centre of El Alto, real estate prices are considerably higher in La Paz (Arbona and Kohl 2004), and in terms of material infrastructure such as pavements, tap water, and sewerage, El Alto suffers from serious insufficiencies. According to Duran et al. (2007) 85.2 per cent of households in El Alto have access to electricity, but just 63.3 per cent have access to sanitation systems[3] and only 34.9 per cent have running water.[4] It is important to note that access to these services varies according to the different districts and zones. In District 1, the wealthiest part of El Alto, which includes the central zones of *La Ceja* and *Ciudad Satélite*, coverage of these services is almost complete, while in the northern periphery of the city (Districts 7, 8, and 9) coverage is considerably lower. In District 2, where the neighbourhood of Santiago Segundo is, 90.7 per cent of households have electricity, 79.6 per cent have sanitation, and 32.9 have running water.

Between 1950 and 2002 the average annual growth rate of the city's population was 8.2 per cent (Arbona and Kohl 2004), and El Alto is now estimated to have a population of 960,767 inhabitants (INE 2010). The first migrants came to El Alto after the national revolution in 1952, when the peasants were freed from the semi-feudal *hacienda* system and allowed to move to cities. El Alto grew steadily, until the population swell of the 1980s which was caused by droughts in the countryside (due to the *el Niño* weather phenomenon in 1982–83), as well as the 1985 closure of state mines which forced miners to look for other work and living opportunities. At the same time, however, it is important to realize that not all *Alteños* are migrants. Indeed, by some measures up to 59 per cent of the population can be classified as non-migrants (Rossell and Rojas 2006: 11).[5] But, time and again, it was clear from the discussions and interviews that the category of 'migrant' and that of *Alteño* were not mutually exclusive, and indeed they were often considered to be almost synonymous. People periodically travelled back and forth between their rural home towns, mining areas, other urban (and foreign) areas, and El Alto. To this extent, the urban singularity of El Alto partly rested upon its status as a social, economic, and political mediator between rural and urban forms of life and economy.

Due to its recent urban status and because of its particular demographic distribution – 60 per cent of its inhabitants are under the age of 25 (Méndez and Pérez 2007) – El Alto is also known as the 'young city'. However, being young does not mean that the *Alteño*s have no past. Indeed, *Alteño*s pay careful attention to history – both to the migration history of their family and to the history of their current zones of residence, and they are also concerned with the way in which the history of El Alto forms part of the history of Bolivia. But this history is often an imagined and idealized past that says more about the current hopes and aspirations of *Alteño*s. For example, in a comic book version of the history of El Alto, the metropolis is introduced with a beautiful illustration of green grass and mountains. The accompanying text informs us that, in that mythic time, 'a long time ago, the city of El Alto was just a landscape where birds and other animals from Lake Titicaca passed by'.[6] Over the following pages the history of El Alto unfolds, with the appearance of the first human settlements and the arrival of the Incas in 1200, Tupac Katari's 1781 siege of La Paz, national independence in 1825, and the national revolution of 1952. In other words, the city is portrayed as if it had always existed, even if it only materialized in the past 50 years.[7] Similarly, when talking to *Alteños*, one often gets the impression that people are moving within an urban setting which is yet to come, as they often refer to dusty open spaces as *avenidas* and *plazas* when they can hardly be defined as such, yet. At the same time, it is in many ways precisely through this conflation of an idealized past and an imagined future that El Alto emerges as a radical city, as the following section, which focuses specifically on the neighbourhood of Santiago Segundo, highlights well.

4 Santiago Segundo

Santiago Segundo is a zone in the southern part of El Alto, situated about 15 minutes (by minibus) from the city centre's *Plaza del Minero*, the zone's geographical and social centre. In the middle of the plaza stands a statue of a miner with his fist raised and a female *palliri* (a female worker who extracts minerals from the rocks brought to the surface by the miners) sitting below. The miner stands on a split rock and inside one gets a glimpse of the devil-like figure of *el Tío* (literally, 'the uncle'), the underground spirit figure to whom the miners offer alcohol and coca leaves so that he will protect them when they enter the depths of the mines (Nash 1979; Taussig 1980). On the eastern side of the plaza are two market halls – one where meat is sold, and one with vegetables, spices, and flowers. On the western side of the plaza lie the church and the community centre where the neighbourhood association has its premises. The community centre also houses a small library, frequented by students, and a room used for workshops and meetings. Around the corner on 9th street is a small police station, where there are two police officers on duty at all times. Bringing together both clerical and local authorities, the plaza closely resembles the ideal central plaza of the colonial city, where different forms of social, cultural, and political power converged. Although Santiago Segundo is a more commercial zone than neighbouring Horizontes, Rosas Pampas, or Villa Bolivar, most of the commercial activity is quite concentrated and takes place on 9th and 10th streets, near the plaza. Twice a week an open street market is also held in Avenida Dos, north of the plaza.

4.1 Constructing the zone

Santiago Segundo is known as a *zona de mineros*, or miners' neighbourhood, with up to 85 per cent of households including a member originally from a mining area, according to the local neighbourhood president. Former miners initially came to Santiago Segundo in the late 1960s and early 1970s when their trade unions began forming housing co-operatives in urban areas to respond to their members' aspirations to become property owners. In the mining centres, companies provided housing for their employees, but once individuals stopped working in the mine they 'had to return to [their] community of origin', as a former miner put it. Some mining families moved to El Alto after retirement, but the major influx of miners occurred following the closure of mines in the mid-1980s, as Carlos, a retired miner in his sixties who came to El Alto in 1986 after the 'relocalization' of miners in 1985, recalled during an interview. He had owned a plot of land since 1971, bought through a trade union co-operative, when there had been 'nothing but pampas... there were two or three small houses [*casitas*] in 9th Street... and nothing else'. When I asked Carlos why he had decided to buy a plot in El Alto, he told me 'Well, I had children and I thought that they [one day] would like to study here, because [although]... there was a school [in the Corocoro mining area], but after finishing school they would not [want to] stay there. Therefore it was essential to get a plot of land, and for that reason I chose this plot.'

Construction of housing on the land was complicated, however, with the State National Housing Fund (FONVI, Fondo Nacional de la Vivienda) only offering facilities to do so over a 20-year period. As Carlos described: '[The FONVI representative] said: "In some 20 years we can deliver your house." But [we said] "Within 20 years we will have one foot in the cemetery already!" And so we decided to build our houses with our own money. We were 21 households, and we immediately organized ourselves.' Having bought the land was 'a [piece of] luck', as he puts it, since in 1986, due to the closure of the state mines, he was forced to leave the Corocoro mining area, and came to El Alto. Although the constructor hired by the group of 21 households to build their houses had not completed them, Carlos was able to finish his own house himself, and he described how, little by little, the *vecinos* of Santiago Segundo managed to secure electricity, water, and a sanitary system, and generally organized the neighbourhood. As the neighbourhood president put it, 'We did not even know which street was where...we walked wherever. Little by little we have been able to transform [the zone] and now the situation of the streets is a bit more organized.'

At the same time, however, according to Carlos, 'it was a martyrdom' to organize the neighbourhood. Not only did he build his own house, he and his wife also helped to carve out sidewalks, and made adobe bricks in order to construct the local school. Water was initially only accessible from public taps in the plaza, and the pressure was irregular. Many of those I interviewed who had been part of this process of self-organization told me how in the late 1970s very few houses had access to electricity, and newcomers often connected themselves illegally, trying to hide the cables from the company by burying them into the ground. Although accounts vary as to when the electricity situation was normalized, by 1988 most houses apparently had access to water and electricity.

Carlos' neighbours, Juan and Ursula, who identify as indigenous miners, put a different spin on what they experienced in order to organize the zone. Juan was a retired miner, and Ursula, a daughter of a mining family, worked as a teacher at the local school when I met them; they had met young in the mining centre of Viloco, where Juan worked in the mines and Ursula was starting out in her teaching career (having been lucky enough to receive a mine co-operative-sponsored scholarship to study in La Paz). Overcoming hardships, poverty, and the tragic deaths of family members, they married and lived in various mining centres until 1987, when they came to El Alto. Their small house and their three children, two of whom hold university degrees, were the tangible result of the struggle and hard work that their migration brought upon them, and Ursula often talked about what they had to endure:

> We have suffered a lot in order to obtain ... water and electricity. You had to pay a quota [to the neighbourhood association], you needed to give this and that amount, you had to work hard, you had to do whatever they told you. And then finally they brought the cables and we got electricity, but then there was the problem of the trámites [official bureaucracy] ... 'You need to have a certificate; you need to do this or that', was what they told us. It was a disaster, but thanks to God now we have water and power, and later on we will have piped gas too.

At the same time, both Ursula and Juan clearly felt that these sacrifices had been worth it as they watched their children go to university and engage in urban life. In this regard, they were similar to many other families who were also proud of the new opportunities that they had provided for their children. Juan and Ursula, however, also intimately associated the impetus to strive towards better conditions with the culture and tradition of unionism in the mines. For example, Juan recalled that: 'The miners organized in order to press their labour demands ... There were always marches ... we were always demanding better wages, more bread, more of everything', and clearly saw the neighbourhood association as a continuation of these collective forms of struggle, often pointing out that being an active neighbour was an organized form of engagement for better living conditions too. Tellingly, when I asked him about his family's involvement with the association, he replied: 'Of course we belong to the neighbourhood association ... we go and make suggestions so that the streets will improve, the lights, the water, the market ... We attend every meeting. We are still union members.' At the same time, although the unionized mining background of those who settled in Santiago Segundo clearly played an important role in its transformation into an urban settlement, this reorganization also transformed the figure of the miner into the *vecino*.

4.2 The zone and the state reforms

When I first met the *presidente* of the Santiago Segundo neighbourhood association in August 2007, he began telling me about the neighbourhood. Pointing to a map on the wall behind me, he said: 'We are more than 20,000 inhabitants; we are the biggest zone with only 150 vacant plots left.' He went on to explain that the zone covered 87 hectares, and was divided into 2460 plots of land, of which 2310 were occupied.[8] He also referred to a survey carried out by the local health centre which stated that the neighbourhood had 3500 primary school children, 3000 secondary school students, and 1000 university students, and that the average income of each household was US$100. As he rattled off these statistics, it slowly dawned on me that these data were not just useful for me, but also critical for the local authorities. The El Alto municipality assigned operational funds to neighbourhoods according to their number of inhabitants – the more residents, the more funds a neighbourhood would receive in order to carry out public works.

This system came into play as a consequence of the decentralization politics implemented by the Bolivian government during the 1990s, backed by international development agencies such as the IMF and the World Bank (McNeish 2006). Implemented in parallel with the neoliberal restructuring of the economy that privatized the state mines, this decentralization of the state led to a renewed focus on citizenship and, more specifically, to the participation of the country's marginalized and indigenous population in (local) decision-making. This initially translated into a new constitution in 1993,[9] which declared Bolivia to be a 'multi-ethnic and pluri-cultural nation', and legislated a renewal of the agrarian land reform that favoured collective titles to land (for indigenous communities). The subsequent Law of Popular Participation (*Ley de Participación Popular*, or LPP) provided for the decentralization of decision-making so that municipalities were empowered to draw up participatory budgets (Medeiros 2001; Postero 2007a). In her analysis of citizenship among the lowland Gurani population, Postero (2007b: 189) notes that, although troubled and often dysfunctional, the LPP served as an interpellation of the indigenous population as citizens, thereby developing new expectations about both their roles and their rights (ibid.). The participatory elements, however, were more formal than substantial, and the decentralization and popular participation allowed only certain groups to participate in public policymaking, and even this was on the state's own terms (McNeish 2006: 227). Thus, while people were allowed to participate in local decision-making there was no room for discussion regarding the government's neoliberal economic reforms with privatization by means of capitalization,[10] for example.

However, as Arbona (2007, 2008) and Postero (2007a, 2007b) demonstrate, the reforms had unexpected side-effects. Arbona's analysis of the neighbourhood networks in the city of El Alto, for example, is most convincing as he exposes how neoliberalization facilitated the rise of relatively autonomous local political organizations and networks (Arbona 2007: 130). In particular, he shows how collective memories of the struggle of the 'relocated' miners of Santiago Segundo were articulated in these local networks during the gas war of October 2003 (Arbona 2008). As such, the very reforms that aimed at making the population participate in neoliberal restructuring ended up fertilizing the ground for a very autonomous civil society with a strong organization, while the state suffered a loss of control.[11] Hence, while national indigenous leaders, neighbourhood associations, and workers' organizations were, at least partially, strengthened through institutions created by these reforms, they have equally questioned the ideological framework within which these reform were made (Postero 2007b: 17). As such, the surprising result of the neoliberal reforms promoting multicultural citizenship in Bolivia is that the poor indigenous population of the country today makes demands in terms of citizen's rights rather than in terms of class and race (ibid.: 222).

In accordance with the LPP, the neighbourhood association of Santiago Segundo was granted legal recognition in August 1996. The residents, however, have been organized since 1972 when the first houses were built, and the neighbourhood association has been in existence since 1977, fostering annual assemblies, elections, and the collective organization of public works in order to ensure basic services as well as the construction of the local school, market place, and central plaza. As such, the LPP basically systematized and recognized an already established form of local organization in El Alto and elsewhere. As such, though, the neighbourhood association effectively embodies a dual role as the neighbours' legitimate representative vis-à-vis the Bolivian state, but also constitutes the state's representative vis-à-vis the neighbours, to the point that it can sometimes be difficult to distinguish between the governing and the governed.

4.3 Being a *vecino* in the margins of the state

The political importance of the neighbourhood association helps us understand why the term *vecino*, or neighbour, must be considered as more than a simple reference to one's place of residence. As noted by Lazar (2008: 27), in El Alto the term *vecino* refers to a grounded, everyday notion of citizenship. This confluence between the terms *vecino* and *ciudadano* [citizen] has come about due to the specific history of El Alto (and other marginal urban areas), which in turn draws on historic notions of vicinity and citizenship. In colonial America, national citizenship was based upon residence in the cities. Hence a *vecino* was a townsman – normally a white, male property owner – with fully vested rights, and traditionally they would be non-indigenous. Indeed, in his ethnography of an Aymara highland community, Abercrombie (1998: 46–7) describes how the term *vecino*, from the perspective of the Indian community members, had profoundly negative connotations. In particular, he notes that the term *vecino*, like the term *criollo* (designating a white person of Spanish descent), can be 'stigmatized when pronounced with sarcasm or irony by a social critic from "below"' (ibid.: 46).

For the *Alteños*, however, *vecino* is very much a positive term, and they have universally adopted it to refer to themselves and their basic organizational unit, the neighbourhood association. A quick review of the foundational acts of the neighbourhood association in Santiago Segundo, however, reveals how the term is very much inscribed within a legal framework that draws upon historic notions of *vecindad*, or neighbourliness, that were very much alive during the colonial period. According to the principles of the neighbourhood association, in order to be considered a *vecino* of Santiago Segundo, one must: (a) be a property-owning resident; (b) have no pending (judicial) claims being made against oneself; (c) be an active participant in all the neighbourhood assemblies convened; and (d) respect all of the internal rules of the organization. Being recognized as a *vecino* of Santiago Segundo thus entails much more than just being resident in the zone; in particular, the reference to being a private property owner indicates how the *Alteño* notion of the *vecino* is very much built upon the colonial understanding of the term, in which ownership of private property was one of the prerequisites for citizenship.

At the same time, however, the *Alteño vecinos'* primary citizen relationship is not directly to the state, but rather to their local neighbourhood association. In this way, private property gives access to becoming a *vecino*, but unlike the liberal citizen who stands in an individual relationship with the state, the *Alteño vecino* accesses the neighbourhood association through collective social practices in which he or she must actively engage in order to maintain, or even gain, influence. It is through this collective action that the *vecino* citizen engages with the state, and it is through the actions of the collective that the state has presence in their everyday lives. As such, there are multiple layers of meaning attached to the term. The way in which the residents use their collective organization as *vecinos* to both call upon state recognition as rights-bearing citizens also modifies the nature of state-citizen relations in Bolivia. As they carry out state-like activities such as implementing basic services, drawing up budgets, and producing statistical data, they redefine the meaning of citizenship in terms of being a *vecino*. As Goldstein (2004: 24) notes with regard to the marginal urban dwellers of Cochabamba, while the Bolivian state recognizes formal electoral citizenship (cf. Caldeira and Holston 1999), to many in the country (including the *Alteños*) their social and civil rights have been neglected. For this reason they seek to provide for their necessities and engage with the state by turning a liberal and individual notion of citizenship into a kind of collective citizenship. They engage with private enterprises and state authorities by means of collective negotiations, and if these fail they turn to protests and strikes.

At the same time, the neighbourhood and the neighbourhood association are central political references. During the 2008 celebration of the neighbourhood's 25th anniversary described at the beginning of this chapter, this was very effectively stated. Later that day, the celebrations continued with a drilling competition among former miners at the plaza. After lunch, the annual parade took place, continuing late into the evening as different local dance companies danced their way through the streets, ending up at the Plaza del Minero, where the *dirigentes* of the neighbourhood association sat on the *palco* (literally a box, in reality a sort of balcony) alongside representatives from the municipality and the *Alteño* police force. On the one hand, as pointed out by Lazar (2008: 22), dance as movement is a very physical experience of belonging. On the other hand, as Goldstein (2004) describes, spectacles of this kind simultaneously constitute acts of belonging to a community as well as to a wider nation. Thus, state-citizen relations emerge from the zone of residence in a celebration organized by the *vecinos*.

The *vecinos'* form of organization and their hazy relationship with state authorities resonate with Das and Poole's (2004) notion of politics in the 'margins of the state'. State margins are located, and imagined as being, on the edge of what is accepted as the territory of unquestioned state control. These margins are not necessarily geographical sites but 'sites of practice on which law and other state practices are colonized by other forms of regulation that emanate from the pressing needs of populations to secure political and economic survival' (ibid.: 8). State margins are the zones and sites of practices where and through which the state constitutes itself by means of permanently re-establishing its modes of order and law-making. Hence, margins are not inert and they play a central role in state-making and in understanding the state; *Alteños*' creative ways of obliging the decentralized state to engage with them are clearly reshaping and reconstituting state-citizen relationships in Bolivia.

To a certain extent, one could also argue that these practices are akin to Holston's (2008) notion of 'insurgent citizenship'. This term refers to the ways in which marginal populations seek to expand the substantiation of their rights, often by means of illegal activities. Holston underscores the urban character of the enactment of insurgent citizenship, and in particular of the auto-constructed peripheries where 'the very same historical sites of differentiation – political rights, access to land, illegality, servility – fuelled the irruption of an insurgent citizenship that destabilizes the differentiated' (ibid.: 9). What is particular about the case presented here, however, is that the *Alteño* model of citizenship – which is also that of the indigenous movements and poor city dwellers in Bolivia in general – has, since the 2005 election of Evo Morales as president, been turned into the hegemonic form of citizenship. In Bolivia, the notion of the *vecino* thus embodies the notion of the citizen.

5 Conclusion: the *vecino* and the transformation of the Bolivian citizen

While the social and political weight of the figure of the *vecino* rests upon years of urban organization for survival and improvement, the *vecino* as political actor became particularly visible following Bolivia's infamous 'gas war' in October 2003. That year was marked by numerous strikes, protests, and road blockades, which came to a head during September and October as trade unions, neighbourhood associations, peasants, and indigenous organizations united in protest at the selling of Bolivian natural gas to the USA via Chilean ports.[12] Hundreds of thousands of people protested in El Alto and La Paz, and between 9–17 October (when President Sanchez de Lozada fled the country), the Bolivian army violently attempted to repress the protests, killing 70 persons in and around El Alto, and wounding around 500. This chapter is not the site for a detailed analysis of these events, nor of the lived experience of the *vecinos* of Santiago Segundo during these days of tension and suffering.[13] But the gas war marked the *Alteño vecinos* as both victims of state violence and as political actors, insofar as the protesters defined themselves first and foremost as *vecinos*, and their neighbourhood associations were the principle organizing vehicle for the protests. Thus, while the significance of what it means to be a *vecino* has been shaped over a period of many years, it was surely accentuated by the events of the gas war, and the visibility of the *vecino* as citizen and political actor was very much a consequence of said war.

At the same time, however, to a certain extent it could be argued that this was also because the gas war moved the central stage of political action from the capital La Paz to the urban periphery of the country – El Alto, a city yet to be – and therefore displaced the political lead away from traditional political parties and towards social movements organized through trade unions, peasant organizations, and local *juntas de vecinos*. This revolutionary shift in political action has been moulded upon a background of constructing neighbourhoods and cities despite meagre resources from a decentralized state, and by insisting upon the civil, social, and economic rights of the poor city dwellers in spite of the historic state neglect of their rights. In this sense, the frequent political actions of the *Alteño vecinos* (and other poor urban populations of Bolivia) should not be taken as a resistance to state power, but rather as continuous attempts to bring forth and give body to a state that takes their needs into account.

As such, the current configuration of the *Alteño vecino* constitutes both a continuation of earlier forms of popular struggle for the improvement of living conditions and a radical break from this tradition. The *vecino* is a citizen who engages collectively with the state through local collective organizations, and who, through these organizations, forces a presence of the state in the everyday. As a young city, El Alto itself constitutes a transformation of Bolivia's urban map. But life in El Alto is also a matter of transformation in which former elements and organizations are restructured as their significance is altered. Former traditions of organization are thus incorporated, but their signification is radically changed. Roughly stated, El Alto is a city inhabited by miners without mines, and indigenous peasants without land to farm. Through their attempts to create the city and become *Alteño*s, however, they have come to a radical new understanding of citizenship. This understanding resides in the fact that they situate their local social and political organizations as the central political platform of contemporary Bolivian social reality, thus forcing the neoliberal Bolivian state to be present in the everyday. In this sense they do not so much defy state sovereignty as enact 'stateness' themselves, and the first step towards an understanding of the reality of the so-called new, indigenous Bolivia and its transformations must therefore reside in taking into account these new expressions of citizenship and the context of everyday organizational struggle for survival and socioeconomic improvement among the poor city dwellers who have laid the ground for such expressions.

Notes

I am first and foremost grateful to friends and interlocutors from Santiago Segundo and El Alto for allowing me to glimpse into their lives, struggles, and concerns. I would also like to thank the staff at CEADL (*Centro de Estudios y Apoyo al Desarrollo Local* [Centre for Research and Support for Local Development]) in El Alto for lending institutional and emotional support during my time as a fieldworker in El Alto, and my field assistant Carmen Mamani for her dedicated involvement in the research as well as her transcription of the interviews. The analysis presented here has benefitted immensely from discussions with Alejandro Salinas, Pamela Calla, Steffen Jensen, Inger Sjørslev, Stine Krøijer, Regnar Kristensen, Henrik Rønsbo, and Lotte Buch, among others. Finally, this chapter has also benefited greatly from sharp comments and suggestions by Dennis Rodgers.

1. Protestors set the municipality on fire in February 2003 during a rally against a new tax system. Although municipal offices have been transferred to other zones of the city, the city council still meets in the *Alcaldia Quemada*, and the building now also houses the municipal theatre. During my fieldwork in 2008 one could still see marks from the fire on the building.
2. Tupac Katari is the name adopted by Julian Apaza, and refers to the Inca rebel Tupac Amaru in colonial Cuzco, Peru. In 1781 he and his partner Bartolina Sisa headed an army of 40,000 men and women who rebelled against Spanish rule and held the city of La Paz under siege for four months from the high plateau where the city of El Alto is situated today. Eventually the *criollos* and Spaniards of La Paz were rescued by troops coming in from Buenos Aires, and Tupac Katari was sentenced to death. He was tied to four horses by his arms and legs and torn apart. His head was taken to Kili Kili (today Villa Pablón in La Paz), his right arm to Ayo Ayo (recently known for the lynching of its mayor in 2004), his left arm to Achacachi (a village outside of El Alto), while his legs went to Chulumani and Caquiaviri, respectively. But his heart is said to rest in El Alto, where it overlooks the city of La Paz from the site of a statue of Christ.
3. Duran et al. (2007) base their data on information from the INE. As the authors note, the INE has a peculiar way of defining access to a sanitary system: within the 63.3 per cent in the category that have access to a sewerage system, it cannot be distinguished how many have access to a proper sewerage system and how many have homemade cisterns, or even access only to open fields or rivers. With river access included in the category, it is difficult to imagine the conditions of the remaining 37 per cent of the households that, according to the same census, lack a proper sanitary system.
4. The stated 34.9 per cent refers to households where people have access to drinking water inside the home. It is most likely that more families have access to drinking water from an outside tap in their yard.

5. Rossell and Rojas' numbers stem from a survey carried out in 2000. Interestingly, they note that of the remaining 41 per cent of the population that can be classified as 'migrants', 33 per cent have lived in El Alto for more than five years, and only eight per cent for less than five years. There is also evidence to suggest that recent migrants tend to be inter-urban rather than rural–urban migrants. It is also interesting to note that according to Rossell and Rojas, individuals are no longer considered as migrants after six years of residence.
6. The comic book is called *Historia en Imagenes: Ciudad de El Alto*, and was authored by Johnny Fernandez Rojas, but the year of publication is not known.
7. This idiosyncratic introduction to the history of El Alto is not unlike the preamble to Bolivia's new 2009 constitution: In immemorial times mountains arose, rivers flowed, lakes were formed. Our Amazonia, our Chaco, our Altiplano and our plains and valleys covered themselves with greenness and flowers. We populated this sacred Motherland with different faces, and we have understood since then the plurality of all things and our diversity as beings and cultures. So our peoples were formed, and we never understood the racism from which we suffered ever since the disastrous times of the colonization. We Bolivian people, of plural composition, from the depths of history, inspired by the struggles of the past, by the indigenous anti-colonial uprising, by our independence, by popular liberation struggles, by the indigenous, social and trade union marches, by the water wars and the war of October 2003, by the struggles for the land and for our territory, and with the memory of our martyrs, thus construct a new state. [My translation from Spanish.]
8. According to these numbers there would be an average of 8.6 members in each household of Santiago Segundo. I have no statistical information to back up these numbers, and it is my impression that the actual number is slightly lower because some buildings are up to three storeys, each inhabited by a different family. According to a small and non-representative survey I carried out among students of the local secondary school, Unión Europea, the average number of people per household is 6.1.
9. Bolivia has had 17 different constitutions since the foundation of the country in 1825, with the most recent having been promulgated in February 2009.
10. Capitalization is a Bolivian version of privatization, in which the state retains partial ownership of public utilities and national industries.
11. The fact that decentralization in Bolivia has led to strong local organizations that have increasingly defied the dominant political model (neoliberalism) that imposed the decentralization in the first place should not lead us to consider this as a universal consequence of so-called neoliberal reforms. In this respect, I fully agree with Dunkerley (2007: 15) when he reminds us that 'The notion of neoliberalism should not be deployed indiscriminately as a beast of self-evident characteristics that eventually will result in subaltern resistance.'
12. Natural resources are the object of intense political debate in Bolivia, and it is a central arena where the role of the state versus private capital and the rights of the citizenry is fought. The so-called 'water war' of 2000,

which affected the city of Cochabamba when peasants and city residents protested against high water bills due to privatization, marked a precedent (for an analysis of the water war see Olivera and Lewis 2004). The 'gas war' can be understood as yet another protest for the right of the citizenry to decide upon the country's national resources. However, the gas war marks a different kind of turning point due to the violent repression of the state against the protestors and its broader political effects (the resignation and flight of President Sanchez de Lozada and the subsequent election of Evo Morales).

13. For a more detailed analysis of the events of the gas war see Hylton and Thomson (2007) and Mamani Conde (2006). For an analysis of the lived experience of the events see Risør (2010). For an analysis of popular protests with regards to the broader political history of Bolivia see Dunkerley (2007).

References

Abercrombie, T.A. (1998). *Pathways of Memory and Power: Ethnography and History Among an Andean People*. Madison: University of Wisconsin Press.

Albó, X. 2006). 'El Alto, la vorágine de una ciudad única'. *Journal of Latin American Anthropology*, 11(2): 327–48.

Arbona, J.M. (2007). 'Neoliberal ruptures: local political entities and neighbourhood networks in El Alto, Bolivia'. *Geoforum*, 38(1): 127–37.

Arbona, J.M. (2008).'Sangre de minero, semilla de guerrillero'. Histories and Memories in the organization and struggles of the Santiago II neighbourhood of El Alto, Bolivia. *Bulletin of Latin American Research*, 27(1): 24–42.

Arbona, J.M., and B. Kohl (2004). 'City profile La Paz – El Alto'. *Cities*, 3: 255–65.

Bigehno, M. (2006). 'Embodied matters: bolivian fantasy and indigenismo'. *Journal of Latin American Anthropology*, 11(2): 267–93.

Caldeira, T.P.R., and J. Holston (1999). 'Democracy and violence in Brazil'. *Comparative Studies in Society and History*, 41(4): 691–729.

Canessa, A. (2000). 'Contesting hybridity: Evangelistas and Kataristas in highland Bolivia'. *Journal of Latin American Studies*, 32: 115–44.

Canessa, A. (2006). 'Todos somos indígenas. Towards a new language of national political identity'. *Bulletin of Latin American Research*, 25(2): 241–63.

Canessa, A. (2007). 'A postcolonial turn: social and political change in the new indigenous order of Bolivia'. *Urban Anthropology*, 36(3): 145–59.

Das, V., and D. Poole (2004). 'State and its margins: comparative ethnographies'. In V. Das and D. Poole (eds), *Anthropology in the Margins of the State*. Oxford: James Currey.

Dunkerley, J. (2007). *Bolivia: Revolution and the Power of History in the Present*. London: University of London, Institute for the Study of the Americas.

Duran, J., K. Arias, and M. Rodriguez (2007). *Casa. Aunque sea en la punta del cerro. Vivienda y desarrollo de la ciudad de El Alto*. La Paz: PIEB.

Goldstein, D. (2004). *The Spectacular City. Violence and Performance in Urban Bolivia*. Durham and London: Duke University Press.

Grindle, M.S., and P. Domingo (eds) (2003). *Proclaiming Revolution: Bolivia in Comparative Perspective*. London and Cambridge MA: Institute of Latin

American Studies, University of London, and David Rockefeller Center for Latin American Studies, Harvard University.
Holston, J. (2008). *Insurgent Citizenship. Disjunctions of Democracy and Modernity in Brazil*. Princeton and Oxford: Princeton University Press.
Hylton, F., and S. Thomson (2007). *Revolutionary Horizons. Past and Present in Bolivian Politics*. London: Verso.
INE (2010). Instituto Nacional de Estadística, Bolivia: http://www.ine.gob.bo/.
Lazar, S. (2008). *El Alto, Rebel City: Self and Citizenship in Andean Bolivia*. Durham: Duke University Press.
Mamani Conde, J. (2006). *Octubre. Memorias de dignidad y massacre*. El Alto: Centro de Estudios y Apoyo al Desarrollo Local (CEADL) and Agencia de Prensa Alteña.
McNeish, J-A. (2006). 'Stones on the road: the politics of participation and the generation of crisis in Bolivia'. *Bulletin of Latin American Research*, 25(2): 220–40.
Medeiros, C. (2001). 'Civilizing the popular? The law of popular participation and the design of a new civil society in 1990s Bolivia'. *Critique of Anthropology*, 21(4): 401–25.
Méndez, A., and R. Pérez (2007). *Organizaciones Juveniles en El Alto: Reconstrucción de identidades colectivas*. La Paz: PIEB.
Nash, J. (1979). *We Eat the Mines and the Mines Eat Us*. New York: Columbia University Press.
Postero, N. (2007a). 'Andean Utopias in Evo Morales's Bolivia'. *Latin American and Carribean Ethnic Studies*, 2(1): 1–28.
Postero, N. (2007b). *Now We are citizens: Indigenous Politics in Postmulticultural Bolivia*. Stanford: Stanford University Press.
Pærregaard, K. (1997). *Linking Separate Worlds: Urban Migrants and Rural Lives in Peru*. Oxford: Berg.
Risør, H. (2010). 'Violent Closures and New Openings. Civil insecurity, Citizens and State in El Alto, Bolivia'. PhD dissertation, Department of Anthropology, Faculty of Social Sciences, Copenhagen University.
Rossell, P., and B. Rojas (2006). *Destino Incierto. Esperanzas y realidades laborales de la juventud alteña*. La Paz: CEDLA.
Taussig, M. (1980). *The Devil and Commodity Fetishism in South America*. Chapel Hill: The University of North Carolina Press.
Wildmark, C. (2003). *To Make Do in the City: Social Identities and Cultural Transformation among Aymara Speakers in La Paz*. Uppsala: Uppsala University, Department of Cultural Anthropology and Ethnology.

6

Separate but Equal Democratization? Participation, Politics, and Urban Segregation in Latin America

Dennis Rodgers

1 Introduction

Many commentators have noted the existence of a historical correlation between cities and democratization (Dyson 2001: 83; Mumford 1995: 21). Whether implicitly or explicitly, this image of the city as an inherently civic space is fundamentally linked to the notion that the spatial concentration intrinsic to urban contexts promotes 'a democracy of proximity, of participation by all in the management of public affairs' (Borja and Castells 1997: 246). As Amin and Thrift (2004: 231) succinctly summarize:

> the city has very often been seen as a forcing ground for a politics of emancipation. Thus, the classical Graeco-Roman city is where the rule of democracy is supposed to have arisen, a democracy based upon the public deliberations of a supposedly 'free' citizenship ... The medieval city, and later, the Renaissance city are held responsible for such seminal events as the rise of guild politics, the forging of institutions of civic republicanism and the principle of sanctuary based around the rise of independent city states. The Enlightenment city – through its institutions of learning, intellectual exchange, and secular science – is associated with the rise of universalism and a cosmopolitan ethos. And so on.

Seen from this perspective, it is perhaps not surprising that the most urbanized region of the global south, Latin America, is also a heartland of vibrant and much applauded democratic innovation. Of particular note are the myriad local-level 'radical democracy' initiatives that have proliferated throughout the region's cities during the past two decades (see Van Cott 2008: 8). These are widely considered to have led to a fundamental 'reconfiguration of relationships and responsibilities' (Cornwall 2004: 1) in urban Latin America, devolving political decision-making to ordinary citizens through a process of decentralized public deliberation rather than the delegation of authority to elected agents that is characteristic of more conventional forms of representative democracy. Over two hundred and fifty cities in the region have implemented participatory forms of democratic governance (see Cabannes 2004: 27), and more are doing so every day. At the same time, however, it is a significant paradox that Latin American urban centres are amongst the most segregated in the world, something that is widely considered to have a significant fragmenting effect on public space (Pirez 2002), which undermines democracy and, more specifically, undermines the communicative processes upon which participatory democratic initiatives are founded.

This chapter explores the logic of this apparent disjuncture, seeking to understand how it is that participatory democracy can flourish, seemingly counter-intuitively, in contemporary Latin America's 'fractured cities' (Koonings and Kruijt 2007). It begins by considering the theory and practice of participatory democracy in a broad-brush manner, in order to highlight how such initiatives are not necessarily as inherently transformative as they are often thought to be, before then questioning the putative link that is often made between urban contexts and democratic practices. Drawing on Caldeira's (2008) recent research on 'neoliberal' participatory planning policies in São Paulo, Brazil, the chapter then goes on to show how participatory democratic initiatives can, in fact, actively promote urban segregation, to the extent that a heuristic parallel can be made with South African apartheid's notorious policy of 'separate but equal development'. What this dramatic comparison starkly highlights is how, in order to be truly encompassing, participatory democratic practices need to be implemented within the context of a unifying and integrating governance framework that is ultimately determined by broader political economy considerations. These, however, are particularly unfavourable in a contemporary Latin America characterized by extremely high levels of inequality and exclusion. The final section attempts to mitigate this rather depressing analysis by exploring how emancipatory democratic practices might nevertheless emerge in unpromising circumstances, drawing on the 'extraordinary events' framework recently proposed by Irazábal (2008), and illustrating it through a theoretical consideration of the contingent origins of the (at least initially) remarkable participatory budgeting process implemented in post-crisis Buenos Aires, Argentina.

2 Participatory democracy in theory and practice

In very general terms, participatory democratic initiatives can be said to concern an institutional model of governance that is based on a deliberative – as opposed to a representational – democratic framework. Rather than being organized around the delegation of decision-making to an elected agent, participatory democracy extends and enhances citizen participation in governance by devolving the exercise of authority through a process of bottom-up public deliberation. Intense personal interaction and collaboration generate mutual understanding and shared concerns, and consensual forms of governance are established through the persuasive transformation of preferences by force of communication and (the better) argument (see Avritzer 2002: 36–54). As such, it corresponds to 'a conception of the vitalization of democracy ... through popular participation' (Harriss et al. 2005: 1), and is seen to be radically different from representative democracy. It is widely considered to be not only fairer, more inclusive, and to lead to more efficient policies and decision-making, but is also widely thought to inherently transform individuals into better citizens, and enhance the quality of their life and government. At the same time, however, participatory democratic initiatives are not just bottom-up, voluntaristic forms of organization, insofar as they are fundamentally state-centred processes, with the state remaining the principal medium for the enactment of the consensually agreed-upon 'common good'. To this extent, they can be said to involve a potentially fundamental transformation of this all-important connection between state and society by creating 'a new relationship between government personnel and local citizens' (Abers 1998: 511).

The best-known form of deliberative democracy is undoubtedly participatory budgeting. The forms of participatory budgeting are highly diverse, but the process basically involves citizens participating in forums for discussion about budgetary concerns, generally at the municipal level, although participatory budgeting has also been experimented with at the provincial state level. The central goal of participatory budgeting is to hand over decisions about the allocation of municipal funds for basic urban infrastructural improvements – paving streets, extending drainage, building new schools and health centres, and so forth – to neighbourhood-level forums. The proportion of a municipal budget controlled by a participatory budgeting process can vary tremendously, from just a few per cent to the whole of the investment budget of a municipality; some participatory budgeting processes – such as the one implemented in Buenos Aires, for example – seek to determine an order of public work prioritization rather than a specific percentage of municipal spending (in some ways making them forms of participatory planning). Participatory budgeting has become extremely popular all over the world, and numerous cities in Africa, Asia, Europe, and North and South America, have implemented it, although undoubtedly the most paradigmatic instance is that of Porto Alegre in Brazil, where participatory budgeting was actually first applied in 1989 (see Abers 2000; Baiocchi 2005; Wampler 2007).

It is beyond the scope of this chapter to consider participatory democratic initiatives in anything other than a broad-brush manner.[1] But a striking element of the vast majority of studies about such processes is that few actually offer any concrete data regarding whether they make a difference in developmental terms. Although Abers (1998) argues that Porto Alegre enjoys better than average infrastructure, and better performing public services than any other Brazilian city of comparable size and socioeconomic profile that has not implemented participatory budgeting, it is striking to note that the Porto Alegre population voted out the Brazilian Workers' Party that implemented participatory budgeting, and elected a mayor, José Fogaça, who has explicitly criticized the process, and indeed, has been actively dismantling it (see Koonings 2009). What clearly emerges from even a cursory survey of the literature is that many contributions are imbued with a significant romantic – and sometimes even fanatical – idealism. There is a widespread (but not necessarily explicit) view that participatory democratic initiatives are inherently transformative and will, by the very force of their existence, sweep all before them. Suffice it to point out in this respect that Wright's (2003) preface to the overview volume that he co-edited with Archon Fung is entitled 'The Real Utopias Project', while a comparable tome in Spanish edited by the Argentinean political scientist Romero (2005) is entitled *Democracia Participativa: Una Utopía en Marcha* (Participatory Democracy: A Utopia on the March).

In both these cases, the term 'utopia' is used according to More's (2005 [1516]: 120) original coining of the expression, that is to say associating participatory democracy with 'the best in the world'. The word has also come to have a much more widespread second meaning, however, designating 'an impossibly ideal scheme'.[2] This second sense of the term probably best describes contemporary participatory democratic processes in Latin America, especially when one considers the practical pitfalls that they must surmount in order to be meaningfully implemented.

Evans (2002) outlines three basic problems. First, participatory democratic initiatives must be economically efficient. Second, there must be sustained participation. Finally, they have to overcome what he calls the 'political economy problem'. The first two issues we can take as given. Deliberative policymaking involving economic affairs will be subject to the same laws of accounting as non-deliberative forms of government, and without participants, there can be no process. The political economy problem is less straightforward, however. It can be approached in two ways: 'endogenously' and 'exogenously'. The 'endogenous' view focuses on the way that power relations play out between those participating within the deliberative process. As Baiocchi (2001) points out, inequality within participatory democratic processes can subvert public deliberation in a variety of different ways. For example, certain participants may be better-off citizens or dominant groups as a result of their privileged links to political parties or the state, and might use their superior resources to promote collective decisions that favour themselves. Other powerful participants may attempt to exclude or avoid issues that threaten their interests, to the extent that in cases where deliberative democratic arrangements challenge their power and privileges, they may actually seek to dismantle them. Ultimately, as Schönleitner (2006: 44) remarks, 'if powerful actors do not renounce their power over others as a means for shaping collective decisions, deliberation can hardly be sustained'.

This latter point relates directly to the 'exogenous' dimension of the political economy problem. It is difficult to imagine institutional innovations such as participatory democracy emerging in contexts where particular individuals and groups have a disproportionate amount of power as a result of the existing political framework, as they will obviously have an interest in perpetuating the current system. For the same reason, even the formal existence of an institutional framework for participation does not guarantee that a participatory process will occur, insofar as rules can be ignored or not respected. Although it is not completely implausible to imagine circumstances where traditionally dominant political actors might be prepared to spontaneously give up (at least part of) their power in favour of institutions that incorporate ordinary citizens, this is relatively unlikely except in very specific contexts and under particular circumstances; therefore, the critical question to ask concerning any participatory democratic initiative is clearly 'what political context is necessary to carry out such an experiment in the real world'? (Baiocchi 2001: 45).

The classic study which attempts to answer this question is Heller's ground-breaking comparative examination of participatory democratic initiatives in India, South Africa, and Brazil, where he underlines how such processes were 'given life ... because they were underwritten by ... the political initiative of a programmatic party', generally associated with a subaltern class (Heller 2001: 158).[3] A slightly different perspective is provided by Goldfrank (2007) in his recent comparison of the divergent experiences of participatory budgeting in Porto Alegre on the one hand, and Montevideo, Uruguay, and Caracas, Venezuela, on the other. In contrast to Heller, he argues that it was the weak political opposition to the promotion of participatory budgeting – rather than its strong promotion – that allowed its coherent implementation in the former city, while strong resistance in the latter two led to more 'restrictive designs ... in which citizen input was limited and subordinated within formal, party-dominated structures' (ibid.: 148). This leads Goldfrank (ibid.: 165) to conclude that 'in cities with strongly institutionalized parties, decentralization will likely result in elite capture and exclusionary politics. Even where new parties win office, established parties can debilitate institutional reforms. In cities with weakly institutionalized parties, however, decentralization's democracy-enhancing benefits are more likely to filter through'.[4]

The link that Goldfrank makes to the city is by no means fortuitous. His study highlights how participatory democratic initiatives require very specific enabling contexts in order to flourish, and he associates the particular configurations of party politics in the three cities with the varying natures of their urban contexts, including in particular differing levels of inequality, social mobility, and access to public services.[5] This concern with the nature of the city as a variable in its own right is one that implicitly or explicitly runs through all studies of participatory democracy. In his classic study of participatory processes in Brazil and Mexico, for example, Avritzer (2002) develops his notion of 'participatory publics' based on a very particular conception of the urban public sphere, the roots of which 'can be traced back to the Greek polis and the way it connected community and democracy' (ibid.: 36), or, in other words, the (perceived) specificity of urban contexts as inherently bringing otherwise disparate individuals into contact with each other.[6]

However, the problem with this vision of urban life is that it does not quite square with the observable reality of the overwhelming majority of contemporary Latin American cities. These are amongst the most segregated in the world, with high levels of violence (Moser and McIlwaine 2004), spatial inequality (Koonings and Kruijt 2007), the proliferation of gated communities (Caldeira 2000), and the growth of 'precarious peripheries' (Rolnik 2001) all widely reported to be primary features. As Jones (2004: 171) observes, such phenomena are clearly 'not...compatible with more inclusive notions of citizenship', in particular being fundamentally undermining of the communicative processes upon which participatory democratic initiatives are founded. Focusing in particular on the potential consequences of the proliferation of gated enclaves in Latin American cities, Jones (ibid.) asks 'how can norms be constructed where difference is defensive, diversity is mistrusted, and education, even if it had rarely ever meant learning *with* "others", now might not impress to learn about others either? What kind of radical or deeper democracy can emerge in societies in which a numerically small but economically significant group is physically isolated, socially less engaged and economically less dependent on the remainder of society?'

Yet the fact remains that participatory democratic initiatives *have* emerged – and continue to do so – in such extremely unlikely contexts, with the Brazilian city of São Paulo being a case in point, as Caldeira describes in recent work.

3 'Neoliberal' participatory planning in São Paulo, Brazil

Caldeira is of course well-known for her seminal work *City of Walls* (2000), which traces the way rising crime and insecurity changed the cityscape of São Paulo from the 1980s onwards, transforming it from a space of open circulation to a fragmented archipelago of isolated 'fortified enclaves'. She famously argued that this new urban morphology was most visible in the proliferation of self-sufficient gated communities and closed condominiums for the affluent, and contended that these significantly altered the character of urban public space in São Paulo, as those on the 'inside' of the enclaves no longer related to notions of spatial cohabitation with those on the 'outside', but rather to an ideal of separation from them. This in turn impacted on notions of citizenship and politics in Brazil, breeding exclusion, social differentiation, and inequality. It is largely due to Caldeira's work that the relationship between urban fragmentation, citizenship, and democracy has become a key concern of contemporary urban development scholarship on Latin America, as the many studies drawing on her ideas which have been published over the past decade attest well.[7] Caldeira's (2008) recent research has focused on the regulation of São Paulo's urban development, and more specifically on the rise of what she labels 'neoliberal' participatory planning policies, and their consequences for the city. The analysis that she puts forward in this regard offers certain helpful elements to understanding why it is that participatory democratic initiatives have emerged in such an unpromisingly fragmented and segregated context as São Paulo.

Broadly speaking, Caldeira (ibid.) presents the rise of participatory planning in Brazil as part of a new generation of urban policy that has developed since the country's return to democracy in the late 1980s. This has been underpinned by a new vision for the ordering of urban space, the nature of which is epitomized by the country's *Estatuto da Cidade*, or Law of the City, a federal piece of legislation mandated by Brazil's 1988 constitution and passed in 2001. This established the objective of urban policy to be the realization of 'the social functions of the city and urban property', through a 'just distribution of the benefits and costs of the urbanization process' (Caldeira and Holston 2005: 406). Brazilian municipalities were directed to formulate master plans based on the principles of 'popular participation' and 'democratic management', in order to guarantee 'the right to sustainable cities, understood as the right to urban land, housing, sanitation, infrastructure, transportation and public services, work, and leisure for present and future generations'. As such, the Law of the City establishes 'the production of social equality in urban space as a fundamental objective of urban planning and policy' and turns 'planning into a basic instrument for equalizing social disparities and securing social equality'. Over 1600 Brazilian municipalities have reformulated their master plans in line with this law since it was passed, including São Paulo.[8]

At first glance, this new urban policy would clearly seem to have the potential to promote a much more egalitarian ordering of urban space in Brazil, explicitly allowing for the empowerment of the excluded by placing them on an equal footing with those who have withdrawn into gated communities and closed condominiums. Caldeira (2008), however, contends that the new measures at best legalize existing spatial inequalities and, at worst, actually increase them, because far from constituting any sort of radical intervention, the new urban policies enshrined in the Law of the City – including participatory planning – constitute little more than an epiphenomena of the broader 'neoliberal' model that has been institutionalized in Brazil since the late 1980s. She points out, for example, how there exists a definite discursive coincidence between 'neoliberalism' and participatory democracy, insofar as the vocabulary of the Law of the City makes extensive use of 'neoliberal' terms such as 'participation', 'initiative', 'entrepreneurialism', 'autonomy', and, most of all, 'management'. More substantively, she also notes clear correlations between 'neoliberalism' and participatory democracy, insofar as both seek to promote grassroots social action and move away from top-down forms of governance. However, 'neoliberalism's primary concern lies with the dismantling of the interventionalist state', rather than the promotion of social justice inherent to participatory democracy, and it seeks to allow 'entrepreneurial citizens to organize themselves and formulate the initiatives that will implement their interests', which Caldeira suggests will effectively benefit those wielding the most power in society, since the dismantled 'neoliberal' state in contemporary Brazil is no longer able to act as an impartial and egalitarian arbitrator between various interests groups in the way the previous developmental state was.

Caldeira (ibid.) illustrates this through a detailed analysis of the 2002 São Paulo Master Plan. This ostensibly sought to address the issue of socio-spatial inequality in the city by promoting the densification of areas that were already legally provided with infrastructure, and slowing down the illegal expansion of the city towards new areas in the periphery. In line with the ideals of the Law of the City, the master plan stipulated that all planning, implementation, and control of urban policy was to be participatory, through active engagement and partnership with civil society, and the proposed plan was debated at a series of participatory public hearings that were held over the course of several months. These principally involved three coalition groups of *Paulista* citizens: the *Frente pela Cidadania* (Front for Citizenship), which was principally made up of real estate developers; the *Frente Popular pelo Plano Diretor* (Popular Front for the Master Plan), made up of popular movements, planners, consultants, and university-based researchers; and the *Movimento Defenda São Paulo* (Defend São Paulo Movement), which represented the interests of affluent upper-middle class neighbourhood associations.

All three groups actively sought to modify the content of the master plan proposal put forward by the São Paulo municipality, but did so in ways that would initially seem quite distinct. The real estate developers and affluent neighbourhood associations, for example, acted quite explicitly in line with their own parochial interest. The real estate developers' group sought to have the radical proposal of unifying land use regulations in the city and subjecting vertical construction to extra taxation abandoned, and successfully lobbied for a heterogeneous zoning regime that would allow for variable land utilization rates, albeit with higher construction standards for more intensely used land, thereby making city centre property more valuable. The affluent neighbourhood associations, for their part, successfully fought proposed changes in zoning regulations that would have affected the privileges of the exclusive residential areas they represented, spuriously justifying their endeavours by invoking concern for environmental issues, amongst other things. The *Frente Popular pelo Plano Diretor*, on the other hand, advocated for the establishment of *Zonas Especiais de Interesse Social* (Special Zones of Social Interest – ZEIS) that would identify currently illegal low-income areas for state intervention in the form of legalization and upgrading, while simultaneously protecting them from real estate speculation by formally establishing them as areas devoted to low-income housing.

On the face of things, this latter development would seem to be squarely in line with the basic principles theoretically underlying the master plan – that is to say, the promotion of social and spatial justice – and therefore very different to the more parochial proposals pushed through by the real estate-dominated Front for Citizenship or the Defend São Paulo Movement affluent neighbourhood association coalition. However, Caldeira (ibid.) points out that the ZEIS proposal effectively subjected low-income neighbourhoods to different land use rules than the rest of the city, thereby making it as parochial as the other proposals put forward. As a result, the new zoning regime adopted by the São Paulo Master Plan – following participatory democratic deliberation – ended up protecting richer areas of the city as exclusively residential or by making them more expensive to occupy, while institutionalizing low-standard ZEIS in poorer areas of the city, and thereby impeding any possible gentrification in these areas. The creation of these different urban standards constituted 'a clear reiteration of the legal distinctions between centre and periphery that the new rationality of planning was intended to extinguish', according to Caldeira (ibid.), and as such can be seen as a 'legalization of inequality' which contrasts strongly with the past, where inequality was intimately associated with illegality (see Earle 2009). In other words, a participatory democratic initiative intended to reverse pervasive urban inequality ended up institutionalizing it.[9]

4 Separate but equal democratization?

Bénit (2006) describes a highly analogous process to the *Paulista* one detailed by Caldeira in an insightful article on the relationship between participatory democracy and spatial justice in Johannesburg, the capital of South Africa. She focuses on the debates that surrounded attempts to implement participatory urban planning in the township of Alexandra, and contrasts them with those put in motion in the nearby rich business district of Sandton, highlighting in particular how different pressures in each location had an impact upon the debate over whether to keep the two areas segregated or to integrate them in view of their intimate economic links (i.e. Alexandra township providing much of the menial labour for Sandton). Bénit suggests that this debate points to a forgotten question concerning urban participatory democratic governance, namely the issue of scale, which she contends has important political implications. According to Bénit (ibid.: 58–9):

> participation is by definition local in scale, while a metropolitan vision can only be articulated from above. To expect local negotiations to lead to the emergence of coherent citywide governance (as most theorist of participation seem to expect) reduces – whether by default, convictions, or cynicism – what is a fundamentally political issue to a simple aggregation of preferences. Spatial justice cannot be built from the local level alone, and therefore participatory urbanism cannot exist coherently without explicit top-down urban planning.[10]

In other words, participatory planning in cities necessarily requires a unifying, integrating framework.

My invocation of Bénit's South African research in this respect is not fortuitous. In many ways, the differentiated participatory democracy that she describes bears an uncanny resemblance to the South African apartheid regime's notorious 'separate but equal development' policy.[11] Based on the spurious notion that the different racial groups of South Africa could only develop to their full potential if they were separated from one another, the idea of 'separate development' underpinned the apartheid regime, but the initial fiction of different races developing separately in their own 'homelands' quickly gave way to an unambiguous policy of white domination (see Posel 1991). It is only a small step to think of Caldeira's 'neoliberal' participatory planning in São Paulo as being based on an analogous form of 'separate but equal democratization', particularly in view of the way that it legitimizes and reinforces existing patterns of elite domination in the city, with its differentiated land use regulations and the creation of the ZEIS. The analogy is arguably all the more pertinent when one considers that the apartheid policy of 'separate but equal development' was originally a 'response to urbanization perceived to have run wild' (Jensen 2008: 16–17), a concern that the São Paulo Master Plan explicitly raises as a justification for instituting participatory planning practices.

Although the parallel may seem a little extreme, it is arguably a necessary one to make considering the way that participatory democratic initiatives often have a significant depoliticizing effect, as Pieterse (2008) points out. By advancing the ideal of a locally-built consensus over and above any systemic considerations, they obscure the real determinants of city governance, which are less the institutional mechanisms that are put in place (or not), but rather the systemic relations of power within urban society. It is this issue that I particularly want to highlight by drawing a parallel between participatory democratic initiatives and apartheid's 'separate but equal development' policy. In order to understand the dynamics of participatory democratic initiatives, we must consider the overarching urban political economy within which they are implemented. Arguably, this is particularly important to take into account in a contemporary Latin America where participatory democracy is flourishing despite exclusion, fragmentation, and segregation. The conventional view is that participatory democratic initiatives are proliferating because they will mitigate these phenomena. Caldeira's account of participatory planning in São Paulo, however, suggests that they can institutionalize them instead, and although she does not make the link explicitly, it can be contended that this is likely why such measures are being implemented. They serve the purposes of the elite in São Paulo, who can decide whether or not to implement them, and it is this, more than anything else, that explains the rise of participatory democracy in the seemingly unpromising circumstances of São Paulo, as well as other cities in Latin America.

5 Extraordinary events and contingent democratization

The above analysis is admittedly a rather depressing one, especially when considered in relation to the practical possibilities for promoting social justice in contemporary urban Latin America. A key question to consider, therefore, is how truly emancipatory democratic practices might nevertheless emerge in the face of overwhelmingly unfavourable socio-political circumstances. In this respect, it is worth remembering, as Jones (2004: 172) points out, that while urban public spaces inevitably reflect broader power relations, they are also 'the sites of the contestation of power. Spaces are made public when they inform others about the discourses of the groups that physically occupy them or symbolically invest them with meaning. Public space therefore is performative, where identities are exposed and communicated, interpreted, understood, and transformed.'

This is an insight that goes to the core of the 'extraordinary events' framework recently proposed by Irazábal (2008), which seeks to explain how urban spaces can come to be (re)configured in contemporary Latin America in ways that go beyond hegemonic relations of power within society. In particular, she argues that certain political and social events, which she labels 'extraordinary events', can actively (re)frame urban space in ways that challenge existing patterns of domination. Her edited volume details a range of such events, some mundane, others more obviously exceptional, but all of which involve a reshaping of the urban public sphere through the creation of often highly contingent alternative meanings and occupations.

A concrete example of the way an 'extraordinary event' led to meaningful social change that is particularly germane to the discussion of participatory democratic governance is the highly unlikely implementation of participatory budgeting in the city of Buenos Aires in 2002, which occurred in the face of significant opposition from the dominant urban political class, and within a context known for its particularly complex – and even byzantine – political dynamics (Levitsky 2001). This was a direct result of the crisis known as the *Argentinazo* which affected Argentina in December 2001, upsetting the political balance of power in the city of Buenos Aires, and leading to the crystallization of unique and temporary political circumstances that *contingently* created a space in which a truly emancipatory participatory budgeting process was able to emerge, at least for a while (see Rodgers 2010). The different actors involved interacted in particular ways that, first, produced a space within which a participatory budgeting process could be introduced, before, second, holding both top-down and bottom-up attempts to politically manipulate the process in check, thereby allowing a genuine sense of local autonomy and empowerment to flourish during the first few years of the process, as I have described in ethnographic detail elsewhere (see Rodgers 2007). Subsequent shifts in the Buenos Aires political field upset this delicate balancing act, and led to the gradual erosion of the city's participatory budgeting process, but it remains an important case to consider because it highlights how 'politics is an "instituted process", embedded in institutions political and non-political', which cannot 'be understood simply through the analysis of formal arrangements for representation, decision-making and policy implementation' (Lowndes 2001: 1960 and 1955).

In particular, the implementation of participatory budgeting in Buenos Aires highlights a critical but underestimated dimension of the politics of 'instituted processes', which is that they are frequently much less purposeful and directed than we often imagine them to be. Although most of the diverse actors involved in the Buenos Aires participatory budgeting process, whether acting top-down or bottom-up, had relatively clear aims and aspirations, the very fact of interacting with each other in the context of a 'moment of shock' such as the *Argentinazo* meant that their actions inevitably became imbued with a significant degree of 'contingency',[12] both intrinsically as well as in relation to the way they came together. This was true in a way that goes beyond the fact that social practices will inevitably have unanticipated consequences – as Merton (1936) classically pointed out over seventy years ago – or accepting that institutional arrangements will be imbued with 'a certain degree of opacity... that cannot easily be modelled, predicted or managed' (Cleaver 2000: 382). Rather, what the contingent implementation and execution of participatory budgeting in Buenos Aires illustrates very well is how institution-building can often occur less as the result of purposeful socio-political action and more as the consequence of contextually and temporally specific articulations of both conscious and unconscious intents and practices, which in turn have both intended and unintended meanings and consequences that are beyond the control of the actors involved.

6 Conclusion

Participatory forms of democratic interaction are widely considered to be one of the key governance innovations of the past twenty years or so. Their introduction in – generally urban – contexts all over the world has been hailed as a veritable revolution, poised to fundamentally transform relationships between governed and governing as a result of the emphasis on communicative rather than representative processes. Latin America, however, presents something of a paradox in this respect, insofar as its urban centres are amongst the most segregated in the world, something that is widely considered to critically undermine participatory democracy. A closer examination of both the underlying logic of participatory democratic initiatives, as well as their contextual application, suggests that they are not necessarily as inherently transformative as is generally thought to be the case, to the extent that they can in fact sometimes actively promote urban segregation, in ways that bear comparison with South African apartheid's notorious policy of 'separate but equal development'.

This is crucial when considering the fact that participatory democratic initiatives in Latin America have been introduced in contexts of extreme inequality, and suggests a very depressing reading of the underlying logic of such innovations. Under such conditions, instances of participatory governance often become little more than forms of 'separate but equal democratization' which legitimize and sustain highly unequal and iniquitous structures and systems of power and domination. The case of the introduction of participatory budgeting in Buenos Aires in the wake of the crisis of 2001, however, illustrates an alternative scenario whereby a truly emancipatory enabling environment can emerge contingently as a result of 'extraordinary events'. It is an example that highlights how participatory democratic governance does not necessarily have to stem from purposeful social action, to the extent that it can make sense to talk of processes of 'contingent democratization'.

Understanding and potentially harnessing these moments, however, requires a fine-grained understanding of the dynamics of urban contexts and the social actors that inhabit them, and therefore, as Robins et al. (2008: 1082) point out:

> any analysis of the limits and opportunities for participatory governance needs to start from particular places and issues on which citizens *act*, rather than with abstract notions of citizenship and participation. This requires narrating and situating stories of citizen action, and working back from these stories to explore what was going on in terms of relationships and positioning, and what understandings and analytical tools might make best sense of these forms of engagement (and whether the notion of citizenship has any place in this at all).

Only through this kind of detailed vision are we likely to be able to identify avenues through which to meaningfully promote measures to overcome the deep segregation of Latin American cities, and thereby uphold the civic benefits of urban life.

Notes

1. For wide-ranging collections of detailed studies, see the excellent special issues of *Politics and Society* on 'Empowered Participatory Governance' (2001, 29[1]), *Environment and Urbanization* on 'Participatory Governance' (2004, 16[2]), and the *IDS Bulletin* on 'New Democratic Spaces' (2004, 35[2]), as well as the volumes by Chavez and Goldfrank (2004), Cornwall and Coelho (2007), Fung and Wright (2003), and Harriss et al. (2005).
2. See 'utopia', *Oxford English Dictionary*, http://dictionary.oed.com/.
3. Other studies that have reached similar conclusions include Baiocchi (2003), Goldfrank and Schneider (2006), Van Cott (2008), and Wampler (2007).
4. Goldfrank's analysis is in fact quite complementary of Heller's, insofar as the existence of weakly institutionalized parties is no guarantor of the emergence of participatory democratic initiatives, and some programmatic impulse is inevitably needed to promote them, but conversely the latter is also not enough by itself to ensure their implementation.
5. To the extent that urban political morphology inevitably reflects the broader societal political economy, Goldfrank's observation is not necessarily surprising, and can in many ways be seen as a re-statement of Evans' 'political economy problem'.
6. Indeed, the main elements Avritzer (2002: 51) associates with the emergence of participatory publics, that is to say 'free expression and discussion, the formation of plural identities, and free association', can be directly linked to the vision outlined by Wirth (1938: 192) in his classic article 'Urbanism as a Way of Life', whereby 'the juxtaposition of divergent personalities and modes of life [in cities] tends to produce a relativistic perspective and a sense of toleration of difference which may be regarded as prerequisites for rationality and which lead toward the secularization of life'.
7. See, for example: Borsdorf (2002); Fischer et al. (2003); Rodgers (2004); Sabatini and Arenas (2000); Salcedo and Torres (2004); and Svampa (2001).
8. See Caldeira and Holston (2005), Earle (2009), and Fernandes (2007) for fuller discussions of the *Estatuto da Cidade*.
9. Although Caldeira (2008) also contends that the Law of the City and the master plans it has spawned – and even to a certain extent the idea of ZEIS – can be seen as potentially providing powerful instruments to help foster social justice and reduce spatial inequality if deployed in a slightly more enabling context, the reality is much more ambiguous. As the work of Earle (2009) on housing movements in São Paulo highlights well, the particular political conditions to which the provisions of the master plan have contributed mean that they end up making their claims through illegal acts of civil disobedience rather than the institutionalized channels of democratic participation.
10. I have taken some liberties with my translation. Original French: 'La participation est par essence d'échelle locale et quotidienne; il est au contraire du ressort des politiques de définir, de présenter et de soumettre au débat la vision d'un ou de plusieurs avenirs métropolitains possibles. Attendre du concert des négociations locales et localistes l'émergence d'une vision d'échelle métropolitaine (comme le préconisent la plupart des théories de la participation) conduit bien souvent à réduire le politique – par défaut,

conviction ou cynisme – à un simple accompagnement des dynamiques de marché. Pas d'urbanisme participatif sans urbanisme:...la justice spatiale...ne saurait se construire à la seule échelle locale'.

11. The parallel between apartheid and post-apartheid urban planning and development is something that also has also been noted in the work of Lemanski (2004, 2006a, 2006b, 2007).
12. I use the term in relation to 'the condition of being free from predetermining necessity in regard to existence or action' (see 'contingency', *Oxford English Dictionary*, http://dictionary.oed.com/).
13. This was subsequently published in substantially modified form as Evans (2004). 'Development as institutional change: the pitfalls of monocropping and the potentials of deliberation'. *Studies in Comparative International Development*, 38(4): 30–52.

References

Abers, R. (1998). 'From clientelism to cooperation: local government, participatory policy, and civic organizing in Porto Alegre, Brazil'. *Politics and Society*, 26(4): 511–37.

Abers, R. (2000). *Inventing Local Democracy: Grassroots Politics in Brazil*. Boulder: Lynne Rienner.

Amin, S., and N. Thrift (2004). 'The emancipatory city?'. In L. Lees (ed.), *The Emancipatory City? Paradoxes and Possibilities*. London: Sage.

Avritzer, L. (2002). *Democracy and the Public Space in Latin America*. Princeton: Princeton University Press.

Baiocchi, G. (2001). 'Participation, activism, and politics: the Porto Alegre experiment and deliberative democratic theory'. *Politics and Society*, 29(1): 43–72.

Baiocchi, G. (ed.) (2003). *Radicals in Power: The Workers' Party and Experiments with Urban Democracy in Brazil*. London: Zed.

Baiocchi, G. (2005). *Militants and Citizens: The Politics of Participatory Democracy in Porto Alegre*. Stanford: Stanford University Press.

Bénit, C. (2006). 'La Difficile Définition de la Justice Spatiale à Johannesburg: un Processus de Démocratie Participative'. *Les Annales de la Recherche Urbaine*, 99: 48–59.

Borja, J., and M. Castells (1997). *Local and Global: The Management of Cities in the Information Age*. London: Earthscan.

Borsdorf, A. (2002). 'Barrios cerrados en Santiago de Chile, Quito y Lima: tendencias de la Segregación Socio-Espacial en Capitales Andinas'. In L.F. Cabrales Barajas (ed.), *Latinoamérica: Países abiertos, ciudades cerradas*. Guadalajara: UNESCO and Universidad de Guadalajara.

Cabannes, Y. (2004). 'Participatory budgeting: a significant contribution to participatory democracy'. *Environment and Urbanization*, 16(1): 27–46.

Caldeira, T.P.R. (2000). *City of Walls: Crime, Segregation and Citizenship in Sao Paulo*. Berkeley: University of California Press.

Caldeira, T.P.R. (2008). 'Democracy, Neoliberalism, and the City: Remaking Urban Policy in Brazil'. Keynote presentation to the conference on 'Conflict, Fragmentation, and Hope in the Neoliberal City: Urban Space in Latin America'. NALACS-CEDLA. 6–7 November. Amsterdam.

Caldeira, T.P.R., and J. Holston (2005). 'State and urban space in Brazil: from modernist planning to democratic intervention'. In A. Ong and S.J. Collier (eds), *Global Assemblages: Technology, Politics and Ethics as an Anthropological Problem*. Oxford: Blackwell.

Chavez, D., and B. Goldfrank (eds) (2004). *The Left in the City: Participatory Local Governments in Latin America*. London: Latin American Bureau.

Cleaver, F. (2000). 'Moral ecological rationality, institutions and the management of common property resources'. *Development and Change*, 31(2): 361–83.

Cornwall, A. (2004). 'Introduction: new democratic spaces? The politics and dynamics of institutionalised participation'. *IDS Bulletin*, 35(2): 1–10.

Cornwall, A. and V.S.P. Coelho (eds) (2007). *Spaces for Change: The Politics of Participation in New Democratic Arenas*. London: Zed.

Dyson, T. (2001). 'A partial theory of world development: the neglected role of the demographic transition in the shaping of modern society'. *International Journal of Population Geography*, 7(2): 67–90.

Earle, L. (2009). 'Occupying the Illegal City: Urban Social Movements and Social Citizenship in Sao Paulo'. London: Development Studies Institute, London School of Economics and Political Science. Unpublished PhD dissertation.

Evans, P. (2002). 'Beyond "Institutional Monocropping": Institutions, Capabilities, and Deliberative Democracy'. Mimeo. Available at: www.sociology.berkeley.edu/ faculty/evans/workingpapers.htm.[13]

Fernandes, E. (2007). 'Constructing the "right to the city" in Brazil'. *Social and Legal Studies*, 16(2): 201–19.

Fischer, K., J. Jäger, and C. Parnreiter (2003). 'Transformación Económica, Políticas y Producción de la Segregación Social en Chile y México'. *Scripta Nova*, VII(146[127]). Available at: www.ub.es/geocrit/sn/sn-146(127).htm.

Fung, A., and E.O. Wright (eds) (2003). *Deepening Democracy: Institutional Innovations in Empowered Participatory Governance*. London: Verso.

Goldfrank, B. (2007). 'The politics of deepening local democracy: decentralization, party institutionalization, and participation'. *Comparative Politics*, 39(2): 147–68.

Goldfrank, B., and A. Schneider (2006). 'Competitive institution building: the PT and participatory budgeting in Rio Grande do Sul'. *Latin American Politics and Society*, 48(3): 1–31.

Harriss, J., K. Stokke, and O. Törnquist (eds) (2005). *Politicising Democracy: Local Politics and Democratisation in Developing Countries*. London: Palgrave.

Heller, P. (2001). 'Moving the state: the politics of democratic decentralization in Kerala, South Africa and Porto Alegre'. *Politics and Society*, 29(1): 131–63.

Irazábal, C. (ed.) (2008). *Ordinary Places, Extraordinary Events: Citizenship, Democracy, and Public Space in Latin America*. London: Routledge.

Jensen, S. (2008). *Gangs, Politics and Dignity in Cape Town*. Chicago: University of Chicago Press.

Jones, G.A. (2004). 'The geopolitics of democracy and citizenship in Latin America'. In C. Barnett and M. Low (eds), *Spaces of Democracy: Geographical Perspectives on Citizenship, Participation and Representation*. London: Sage.

Koonings, K. (2009). 'Surviving regime change? Participatory democracy and the politics of citizenship in Porto Alegre, Brazil'. In P. Silva and H. Cleuren (eds), *Widening Democracy: Citizens and Participatory Schemes in Brazil and Chile*. Leiden: Brill.

Koonings, K., and D. Kruijt (eds) (2007). *Fractured Cities: Social Exclusion, Urban Violence and Contested Spaces in Latin America*. London: Zed.
Lemanski, C. (2004). 'A new apartheid? The spatial implications of fear of crime in Cape Town, South Africa'. *Environment and Urbanization*, 16(2): 101–12.
Lemanski, C. (2006a). 'Spaces of exclusivity or connection: linkages between a gated community and its poorer neighbour in a Cape Town master-plan development'. *Urban Studies*, 43(2): 397–420.
Lemanski, C. (2006b). 'Residential responses to fear (of crime plus) in two Cape Town suburbs: implications for the post-apartheid city'. *Journal of International Development*, 18(6): 787–802.
Lemanski, C. (2007). 'Global cities in the south: deepening social and spatial polarisation in Cape Town'. *Cities*, 24(6): 448–61.
Levitsky, S. (2001). 'An 'organised disorganisation': informal organisation and the persistence of local party structures in Argentine peronism'. *Journal of Latin American Studies*, 33(1): 29–65.
Lowndes, V. (2001). 'Rescuing Aunt Sally: taking institutional theory seriously in urban politics'. *Urban Studies*, 38(11): 1953–71.
Merton, R. (1936). 'The unanticipated consequences of purposive social action'. *American Sociological Review*, 1(6): 894–904.
More, T. (2005 [1516]). *Utopia*. New York: Elibron.
Moser, C., and C. McIlwaine (2004). *Encounters with Violence in Latin America: Urban Poor Perceptions from Colombia and Guatemala*. London: Routledge.
Mumford, L. (1995). 'The culture of cities'. In P. Kasinitz (ed.), *Metropolis: Center and Symbol of Out Times*. New York: New York University Press.
Pieterse, E. (2008). *City Futures: Confronting the Crisis of Urban Development*. London: Zed.
Pirez, P. (2002). 'Fragmentation and privatization of the Buenos Aires metropolitan city'. *Environment and Urbanization*, 14(1): 145–58.
Posel, D. (1991). *The Making of Apartheid, 1948–1961: Conflict and Compromise*. Oxford: Clarendon Press.
Robins, S., A. Cornwall, and B. von Lieres (2008). 'Rethinking "citizenship" in the postcolony'. *Third World Quarterly*, 29(6): 1069–86.
Rodgers, D. (2004). 'Disembedding the city: crime, insecurity, and spatial organization in Managua, Nicaragua'. *Environment and Urbanization*, 16(2): 113–24.
Rodgers, D. (2007). 'Subverting the spaces of invitation? Local politics and participatory budgeting in post-crisis Buenos Aires'. In A. Cornwall and V.S.P. Coelho (eds), *Spaces for Change: The Politics of Participation in New Democratic Arenas*. London: Zed.
Rodgers, D. (2010). 'Contingent democratization? The rise and fall of participatory budgeting in Buenos Aires, Argentina'. *Journal of Latin American Studies*, 42(1): 1–27.
Rolnik, R. (2001). 'Territorial exclusion and violence: the case of the state of São Paulo, Brazil'. *Geoforum*, 32(4): 471–82.
Romero, R. (ed.) (2005). *Democracia Participativa: Una Utopía en Marcha*. Buenos Aires: Ediciones Cooperativas.
Sabatini, F., and F. Arenas (2000). 'Entre el Estado y el Mercado: Resonancias Geográficas y Sustentabilidad Social en Santiago de Chile'. *EURE*, 26(79): 95–113.
Salcedo, R., and A. Torres (2004). 'Gated communities in Santiago: wall or frontier?'. *International Journal of Urban and Regional Research*, 28(1): 27–44.

Schönleitner, G. (2006). 'Between liberal and participatory democracy: tensions and dilemmas of leftist politics in Brazil'. *Journal of Latin American Studies*, 38(1): 35–63.

Svampa, M. (2001). *Los que Ganaron: La Vida en los Countries y Barrios Privados*. Buenos Aires: Editorial Biblos.

Van Cott, D.L. (2008). *Radical Democracy in the Andes*. Cambridge: Cambridge University Press.

Wampler, B. (2007). *Participatory Budgeting in Brazil: Contestation, Cooperation, and Accountability*. Sage: University Park.

Wirth, L. (1938). 'Urbanism as a way of life: the city and contemporary civilization'. *American Journal of Sociology*, 44(1): 1–24.

Wright, E.O. (2003). 'Preface: The Real Utopias Project'. In A. Fung and E.O. Wright (eds), *Deepening Democracy: Institutional Innovations in Empowered Participatory Governance*. London: Verso.

Part III

Reconnecting the City

7

Irregular Urbanization as a Catalyst for Radical Social Mobilization: The Case of the Housing Movements of São Paulo

Lucy Earle

1 Introduction

This chapter focuses on the city of São Paulo, Brazil and examines the ways in which irregular and illegal growth, characteristic of much of the city, have influenced the collective action of social movements of the urban poor. Based on a year of ethnographic fieldwork with the Alliance of Housing Movements in São Paulo, or UMM, the chapter describes how, during the 20th century, São Paulo grew as a socially segregated city due to calculated neglect on the part of the municipal authorities. Highlighting the city's socio-spatial inequality, the degradation of the central districts and the widespread irregularity, it illustrates how these factors have both negatively affected the urban poor and provided a catalyst for social mobilization. In a recent examination of urban citizenship in São Paulo, Holston (2008) has shown how the irregularity of settlements on the peripheries of the city stimulated homeowners in lower-income neighbourhoods to use the law to assert their claims to land and to regularize tenure. However, beyond becoming *insurgent citizens* in Holston's terms, this chapter shows how social movements of the poor do more than simply use the law to protect home ownership: they are able to radically reinterpret constitutional law, so as to justify theoretically illegal acts of civil disobedience and promote a vision of a more just city.

2 The growth of the illegal city

Home to an estimated 19 million people, the greater São Paulo area is made up of 39 municipalities, the largest of which, the Município de São Paulo, has a population of nearly 11 million.[1] The city is Brazil's largest and richest, contributing approximately 18 per cent of the GDP. But São Paulo's size and significance for Brazil is a relatively recent phenomenon. At the end of the 19th century it was little more than a provincial backwater – a stop on the railway line between the coffee plantations of the interior of the state of São Paulo and the port of Santos. Its phenomenal demographic growth began with overseas immigration due to the coffee boom at the turn of the 20th century. This was later replaced by internal migration from the north and northeast of the country as Brazil began a programme of intensive industrialization in the 1930s. The city's population had steady growth rates of five to six per cent per year from 1940 until 1970.[2] Average rates for the city currently stand at about 1.5 per cent annually, but this figure belies significant differences between regions. While central districts have negative growth rates, new peri-urban settlements in environmentally sensitive zones in the furthest reaches of the municipality have recorded growth rates of 8.1 per cent (Torres et al. 2007).

Despite its wealth and, as a state capital at the centre of a huge regional economy, its status as the economic powerhouse of the country, São Paulo does not escape the problems of massive income inequality for which Brazil is notorious. Recent data show 22.4 per cent of the Brazilian population living on less than $2 a day, while the Gini coefficient measure of inequality stands at 0.564,[3] amongst the highest in the world. Frequently cited statistics point to the massive concentration of wealth in a very small segment of the population: the poorest ten per cent of the population account for 0.1 per cent of national income, while the richest ten per cent account for 47 per cent of national income (UNDP 2005). Levels of inequality in São Paulo have remained almost constant over the past decade despite reductions in the national average: the Gini coefficient for the Metropolitan Region was 0.543 in 2006.[4]

São Paulo is a bewildering large and sprawling city. It is architecturally diverse, if not muddled and seemingly unplanned. Its growth during the 20th century has been described by architects, planners, and social scientists as anarchic and chaotic. It has been dubbed the 'wild city' (Rolnik 1995) and much of the literature on the Brazilian urban experience posits the city as the 'new configuration of disorder' (Rizek 2003). São Paulo, along with other Brazilian metropolises, is also characterized as a divided city. It has enormous and extremely visible disparities between the residential areas of the rich and poor. Much of the impression of the chaos of the city must derive from the huge expanse of rambling low-rise, low-income, self-built peripheries. These are in marked contrast to the planned garden-city neighbourhoods, glitzy high-rises, and gated condominiums of the wealthier areas, giving rise to Santos's (1996: 231) evaluation that, 'The housing situation is a visual reflection of what is happening in the rest of São Paulo society'.

It is not just the huge disparity in income, lifestyle, and residential areas that fuels the depiction of São Paulo as a divided city. Alongside these highly visible markers of inequality, academics have established another division between the legal city and the illegal, clandestine, or 'non-city' (Santos 2002; Grostein 1987; Maricato 2000). Social scientists, planners, and architects differ in their interpretations of how and why these divisions arose, but they are driven by the reality that characterizes São Paulo today, where 50 to 65 per cent of land is illegally or irregularly occupied, or in some other way infringes on laws of planning, building, or zoning (Rolnik et al. 1991; Maricato 2000; Caldeira 2000). State absence is often posited as the cause of São Paulo's anarchic sprawl, particularly in the area of regulation for low-income settlements. However, research would suggest that this was a wilful absence that suited the state's interests in industrial expansion, and the elite's desire to maintain social segregation in the city. Far from lacking regulations and legislation, as Grostein (1987) points out, the state's planners and legislators were busy throughout the 20th century.

It was during the final decades of the 19th century, as São Paulo began to grow significantly, that questions of urban planning and the problem of low-income housing came to the fore. Separation of neighbourhoods by social status and function became a priority. This was motivated in part by epidemics of cholera and yellow fever that swept through the centre of the city where there were large populations of former slaves as well as high-income residences (Bonduki 1998). The elites began to move out of the centre in a southwesterly direction towards new, planned, garden-city neighbourhoods, an exodus that still continues today.[5] By contrast, the rural zone of the municipality, which was beyond the urban perimeter and far from the high-income neighbourhoods, became the principal zone reserved for the poor. Here land could be illegally occupied, or bought at low prices from a 'clandestine' sub-divider, who may, or may not, have had legal title to the land. The strategy of reserving the most distant of lands for the poor 'survived the century without significant change' (Rolnik 1995: 89).

The model of self-building on the periphery, outside the urban zone, accelerated with the advent of the diesel bus in the second half of the 1920s (Holston 2008). Once mass transport was easily and cheaply available, the expansion of low-income settlements on clandestine or irregular subdivisions in the peripheral rural zone exploded. *Favelas* were not a feature of the São Paulo landscape until the 1970s, since, up until that time, land on the peripheries was cheap enough for poor urban workers to purchase and then slowly build their homes (Kowarick 1979; Bonduki 1998). This has led to a situation in the city today whereby 80 per cent of residents of the peripheries are home owners, as compared to 69 per cent in other areas (Holston 2008: 183).[6] Grostein (1987) illustrates how and why the unserviced rural zone was reserved for the poor: while building within the urban perimeter was, in theory, subject to regulation, homes in the rural zone were not covered by urban legislation. This zone was reserved by the municipal authorities as the space where planning norms did not apply, the space where 'everything is allowed' (ibid.: 243). Thus, the state would not have to involve itself in approving plans, ensuring the quality of the built environment, or making sure public services were provided. As Rolnik notes, during the 1920s a pattern of building in low-income peripheral settlements was established that would become characteristic of São Paulo's metropolis, with 'a near total irregularity before the laws and codes that set the rules for land use and occupation in the city' (Rolnik 1995: 275).

Whilst low-income housing is concentrated on São Paulo's periphery, there are also pockets of extreme poverty and deprivation in the centre of the city. The central districts are where the majority of the city's slum tenements are located. Known as *cortiços*, these are generally large, formerly single-family residences given over to multiple occupancy. They are far less visible than São Paulo's *favelas* and self-built peripheries, but conditions are considered as bad, if not worse (Andrade 2001): families live in one room and share the use of bathrooms and laundry facilities. Rooms are small and poorly ventilated: a survey in the early 1990s recorded an average of 2.6 people living in one room, varying from 8 to 15 square metres (Santos 1996). Residents are routinely intimidated by the 'intermediary' who collects rent payments, and evictions are frequent. However, when weighing up the prospect of living on the periphery and travelling up to 4 hours a day to work in the centre, some families prefer the *cortiço* option. It is extremely difficult to obtain accurate figures on the numbers living in this type of accommodation. Some estimates put the number of *cortiço* residents in the city at 600,000.[7]

They constitute yet another space of illegality in the city and represent a type of peripheral marginality in the heart of the centre.

Thus, although many scholars of São Paulo refer to the dichotomy between the unplanned, poorly connected peripheries and the closely regulated upper-income areas of the centre of the city, São Paulo's historic centre is in fact badly run down. As noted above, the fear of contagion from the poor in the early 20th century provoked the exodus of upper-income residents from the city centre towards new exclusive residential areas such as Higienópolis and Jardins in the southwest (Simões 1991). At the same time, changes in the rental market in the centre meant that, with the exception of a room in a *cortiço*, the area was no longer an affordable option for the working classes. São Paulo Centro thus began its long decline. Today the area comprising the sub-prefectures of Sé and República is described as 'degraded'. Middle- and upper-income Paulistanos[8] consider it dangerous, dirty, and over-crowded. In other words, it has been taken over by the *classes populares* or 'popular classes' who swell the streets during the day but leave it almost empty by night, apart from the population of homeless rough-sleepers.

It is not just higher-income residents who have moved out of the centre. Businesses began to follow suit in the 1960s, as the first skyscrapers were put up along Avenida Paulista, the new 'chic' residential and corporate neighbourhood. Paulista, however, appears to have had its day, and elite business has followed the wealthy neighbourhoods further into the southwest of the city. Commerce does still exist in the centre: the huge numbers of people who still come into the centre to work (it is the area with the highest concentration of jobs in the city) means that it is still profitable to run a shop or restaurant in these areas, thus maintaining high property and land values (Comarú et al. 2005). However, the centre is now characterized by its empty buildings, illustrating its unpopularity as both a residential area and a hub for business. It is estimated that there are 400,000 empty residential units in São Paulo, of which 45,464 are to be found in the central districts. In these areas 17 per cent of homes are empty (Prefeitura Municipal de São Paulo 2004). There are also numerous abandoned hotels, factories, and office buildings. While many buildings are left empty for speculative purposes, they are also abandoned because of legal wrangles over ownership (often amongst heirs), because of problems of irregular documentation with the land registry (the registry offices have a notoriously corrupt past), or because of unpaid property taxes. The vast numbers of empty homes and buildings contrasts with the city's elevated housing deficit, estimated at 850,000 units.[9] This paradox is not lost on the housing movements, as will be shown below.

Despite its problems, the city centre is well-equipped with urban infrastructure. The streets are paved and lit, there is full connection to mains water and the sanitation system, and it is the public transport hub for the entire city. The gulf between the centre and the periphery, in terms of urban services and proximity to the workplace, and the fact that the only low-income housing option in the centre is the *cortiço*, further highlights the marginality of life for the poor in the city.

3 Irregularity as a catalyst for social mobilization

Along with the poor quality of their housing, residents of peripheral settlements and *cortiços* are affected by lower socioeconomic indicators, reduced life opportunities, and social stigma (Caldeira 2000; Marques and Torres 2005). These factors, combined with the problems of illegality and insecurity of tenure, have catalysed considerable mobilization amongst marginalized groups in São Paulo. The city has been dubbed the 'City of Resistance', and it was in its peripheries and industrial municipalities that protest against the military regime began in the late 1970s. In the vanguard were the new unionists, amongst them Luiz Inacio Lula da Silva, who organized a metal workers' strike in 1978. The protest spread from factories to the neighbourhoods of poor workers, where grassroots organization, supported by the Catholic church, had been growing during the 1970s. Over the course of the 1980s a discourse linking democratic freedoms with rights to basic goods and services began to emerge, and urban social movements are generally seen to have played an important role in the consolidation of democracy during the 1980s, culminating in their contribution to the drawing up of the new constitution promulgated in 1988.

In his examination of citizenship on the peripheries of São Paulo, *Insurgent Citizenship*, Holston (2008) argues that historically in Brazil, differences in education, occupation, race, gender, and access to property have been used to exclude certain groups from the political process, force them into 'segregated and often illegal conditions of residence', and funnel them into labour 'as servile workers' (ibid.: 7). What he labels 'differentiated citizenship' was also used to justify privileged treatment for certain social groups. However, with the transition to democracy, residents of the self-built peripheries of Brazil's large cities have begun to challenge differentiated citizenship and assert their rights to the legal ownership of property and urban services. He argues, therefore, that the city is not just the context of citizenship struggles, but also the substance of these struggles (ibid.: 8).

Holston's work on São Paulo's periphery has shown how irregularity of tenure spurred lower-middle class residents who had bought land or homes in good faith, but had been swindled by fraudulent sub-dividers, to organize themselves to claim title to the land on which they were living. He labels them 'insurgent citizens' and argues that, parallel to the democratization of the country, they began to challenge those social hierarchies so characteristic of Brazilian society. Holston's subjects organize and use the law – traditionally the preserve of the elite – to assert their claims to land and to resist eviction by property developers and speculators who contest their ownership. My research supports Holston's general claim that ambiguity of legal status surrounding a person's place of residence (whether the *favela*, *cortiço*, or, in Holston's case, land and property that has been bought in good faith) causes insecurity and has been a mobilizing factor for organized popular action in the city. It also supports, up to a point, Holston's general argument about the increasing use of the law to press for rights amongst members of lower-income groups. However, as will be shown below, there are some significant differences in the ways that the specific characteristics of São Paulo's growth have impacted on the housing movements of the city's lowest-income residents.

Much of the activity of São Paulo's housing movements over the past 20 years has been catalysed by the irregularity and illegality of the city. The vast majority of the movements' members' (estimated at 50,000 across São Paulo state) are amongst the poorest residents of urban areas, with household incomes equivalent to three minimum wages, who are generally living in *favelas*, *cortiços*, or other irregular accommodation. Similar to Holston's 'insurgent citizens', the movement's leaders organize resistance to evictions, demand for basic services, and seek to secure tenure for members. But the movement has also made creative use of federal and constitutional law to make claims on the Brazilian state. It has made repeated calls for all levels of the state – municipal, subnational, national – to uphold the right to housing and adhere to other articles of the constitution that deal with the urban environment. In particular, the movement challenges the model of growth in the city whereby the poor have little choice but to live in underserviced peripheries, either in self-built homes on illegally occupied marginal land, or in poor quality social housing in areas that are similarly distant from places of employment and bereft of transport, health services, and other facilities. The movement's leaders argue that this violates the constitutional right to adequate housing. But intriguingly, as well as evoking the law, the movement also theoretically breaks the law when it organizes occupations of empty buildings. These acts of civil disobedience seek to draw attention to the many thousands of empty buildings in the city's degraded central areas, and highlight the paradox of such a situation in the context of a massive housing deficit.

4 The right to the centre

Data gathered during the fieldwork phase of the research study, mainly through participant observation and semi-structured interviewing, revealed the importance of the law for members of the housing movement. A significant number of leaders who often had only basic or incomplete education when they joined the movement have since gone on to study at tertiary level, and the most popular choice of course is law. Currently, of the core group of twenty-five movement leaders, four have graduated in law and two are still studying, although only one, the UMM's leader in all but name, has passed the notoriously difficult bar exam. This interest in studying law reflects the significance that the movement places on effecting change through the legal system. In the early 1990s, the UMM took advantage of a provision in the 1988 constitution that permits organized groups to submit a 'popular initiative' to introduce a law and was the first entity to do so, collecting over 800,000 signatures in support of the creation of a fund for social interest housing. The UMM also contributes to legislative processes through the lobbying of Workers' Party politicians, and engages in litigation against the state over housing issues, through allies in legal NGOs, the legal aid provider, and the public prosecutor's office.

Two factors were of critical importance for the movement: the inclusion of housing as a social right in an amendment to the federal constitution in 2000, and the federal legislation passed in 2001 – known as the city statute – that regulates the articles of the constitution that deal with housing and urban services. The National Forum for Urban Reform (FNRU), a coalition of academics and representatives of NGOs and social movements, lobbied intensively for both pieces of legislation over more than a decade. The constitutional right to housing has guided much of the movement's strategy with regards to how it deals with the three levels of the state, all of which have competency for housing. Crucially, the fact that progress towards surmounting the housing deficit in São Paulo is almost negligible has allowed the movement to denounce the state's behaviour as illegal: the UMM accuses the state of denying the constitutional right to housing. In addition to this, the role the state has played in permitting the chaotic growth in São Paulo – which has left the city visibly segregated – leads the movement to claim that the population is being denied the right to the city.

The evocation of the 'right to the city' has developed out of the UMM's engagement with the city statute and the FNRU. The term was first popularized by the French philosopher Henri Lefebvre in his short work of the same name, *Le droit à la ville*, published in 1968. Concerned with the impact upon urban life of industrialization, suburbanization, and the concentration of power amongst small groups of the elite, Lefebvre's *Right to the city* further critiques the way in which architects' and planners' influence on the urban landscape leads to a homogenization of its residents. Technocratic approaches to the city and a prioritization of the logic of the market are seen to suppress the particular characteristics of urban areas, which Lefebvre sees as the places of encounter, and dynamic exchange. In Lefebvre's own words, the right to the city is the right 'to urban life, to renewed centrality, to places of encounter and exchange, to life, to life rhythms and time uses, enabling the full and complete usage of these moments and places' (Lefebvre 1996: 179). The importance of the use-value of the city is a recurring theme throughout the work, and is related to the idea of the *oeuvre* – implying that the city is a work of art that all residents should be involved in creating. 'The right to the city manifests itself as a superior form of rights: right to freedom, to individualization in socialization, to habitat and to inhabit. The right to the *oeuvre*, to participation and *appropriation* (clearly distinct from the right to property), are implied in the right to the city' (ibid.: 174, emphasis in the original).

Lefebvre's ideas influenced the members of the FNRU who worked on the city statute, and, to date, Brazil is the only country with national legislation that evokes the right to the city (Parnell and Pieterse 2010). However, Lefebvre's thoughts and writing style can be somewhat opaque, and his 'meandering' (Kipfer et al. 2008) has generated a number of different interpretations of the concept, ranging from the right to basic services in the city (Brown and Kristiansen 2009) to a call for the radical restructuring of social, political, and economic relations (Purcell 2002). Developing law based on this somewhat elusive idea is clearly a difficult task. In the case of Brazil, the city statute is guided by two of the central themes of Lefebvre's thesis: participation and appropriation/use-value. As Fernandes (2007a: 208) notes in his discussions of the Statute, 'The right to the city would basically consist of the right of all city dwellers to fully enjoy urban life with all of its services and advantages – the right to habitation – as well as taking direct part in the management of cities – the right to participation'.

The internationally acclaimed city statute provides the basis for a 'new legal-political paradigm for urban land use and development control' (Fernandes 2007b: 182). The opening passages of the law establish its intent to regulate urban property in order to contribute to the collective good, and the security and wellbeing of citizens. To this end, the Statute reinforces the role of municipal governments in controlling urban development, and seeks to ensure that land use policies recognize the 'social, cultural and environmental interests of other groups and the city as a whole' alongside those of landowners (ibid.). Although the Statute upholds the right to urban property, this is qualified by a clause which insists that property must serve a social function and it gives power to municipalities to 'interfere with, and possibly reverse to some extent, the pattern and dynamics of formal and informal urban land markets, especially those of a speculative nature, which have long brought about social exclusion and spatial segregation in Brazil' (Fernandes 2007a: 213). The city statute also introduces mechanisms which attempt to democratize local decision-making and ensure the participation of citizens and their associations in the management of the urban environment.

However, the enactment of the legislation has had other – perhaps unforeseen – consequences. The housing movements in São Paulo have made pragmatic use of the city statute to support their claims to housing in the central areas of the city. Of particular importance are its elaboration of the social function of property (thus buildings should not remain empty for a lengthy period of time) and the wording of the second article, which sets out the purpose of urban policy as follows:

> To guarantee the right to sustainable cities, understood as the right to urban land, housing, environmental sanitation, urban infrastructure, transportation and public services, to work and leisure for current and future generations. (Presidência da República 2001)

Because of the way the city developed during the 20th century, the only areas of São Paulo where these conditions are truly achieved are the more central districts of the city. But the UMM does not simply call for low-income housing provision in these areas: it has extrapolated from the city statute the idea of the *right to the centre*.

The idea of having a right to live in the centre has become an unquestioned element of the UMM's general struggle for housing in São Paulo, and it was fully endorsed by every single representative of the movement questioned on the issue for this research. The idea of the right to the centre is also current outside of the housing movement. In a letter to representatives of the executive at all three levels of the Brazilian state from the forced evictions group at UN-Habitat and the São Paulo research institute, Instituto Pólis, it was used as a defence against an impending eviction of the residents of an occupied building:

> The elements that make up the right to adequate housing are, legal security of tenure, habitable conditions, reasonable cost, general accessibility, cultural appropriateness, access to infrastructure and basic services and good localization. In this case, this means the right of the low-income population to live in the centre of the city, since it is equipped with infrastructure and services and is close to opportunities for work, leisure, health and education.[10]

Furthermore, the responses from my interview respondents outside the movement – politicians, academics, civil servants, and members of the executive – to the question 'is housing in the centre a right?' varied from indignant affirmation to cautious evasion, through reference to the general right to housing within the city. Only one of the respondents, a political appointee in the municipal housing company, emphatically refuted the notion, declaring that it was not a right but a 'preference' (*É gosto*). Of the three practising lawyers interviewed, only one responded directly that housing in the centre was not a right, although she qualified her answer with reference to the state's failure to plan adequately for the mixed usage of the city centre.[11] It should be emphasized here that the right to the centre is not specifically grounded in Brazilian legislation. As such, it could be dismissed as mere fantasy. However, as Freeden (1991) notes, people do assume that certain rights exist and behave accordingly. It therefore remains opportune to

> Devote analytical attention to the *fact* that the belief exists and discuss the impact of that fact on both theory and practice. Whether rights *exist*, or are figments of the human imagination, or are what lawyers call legal fictions, is thus analytically irrelevant. (ibid.: 5, emphasis in the original)

On first appraisal the right to the centre would appear to be, in Hohfeldian terms, a 'liberty right'[12] since it falls into the category of action that all people should be at liberty to undertake, there being no law specifically prohibiting this (Jones 2005). Consequently, movement members and leaders assert their right to live anywhere in the city. And yet the lack of adequate housing provision for lower-income groups in huge swathes of São Paulo allows them to argue that the state is denying them this freedom. On closer examination of the discourse of the movement and its supporters, it appears that the right to the centre is being asserted as a positive right, since it involves a demand for action from the state to provide adequate housing for the poor in these areas (Freeden 1991). In Hohfeldian terms this is a positive claim right, defined as 'rights to specific goods and services [that] are so called because they call for a positive response from those who bear the corresponding duties' (Jones 2005).

It could therefore be argued that São Paulo's irregularity and segregation has created the conditions for social mobilization around legality of tenure, but has also led to the creative interpretation of federal law by marginalized groups, who seek to alter patterns of city residence based on class and social segregation. In tandem with this type of legal argumentation, however, the UMM has also taken direct action to emphasize its claims on the state for the right to adequate housing and urban services.

5 Occupying the city

The failure of the state to develop and implement an adequate housing policy for the poor, particularly in the well-serviced, more central areas, leads to a perception that the state is violating the rights to housing, the city, and even the centre. In particular, the movement criticizes the local and national states for failing to reverse the pattern of city growth that was fuelled by low-income informal settlements on its peripheries, and further exacerbated by the building of social housing on the city's outermost limits. This policy is perceived as contributing to a type of 'social apartheid', and is also seen as paradoxical in light of the large numbers of empty buildings in better-serviced central areas of the city. Movement leaders also argue that renovation of these buildings would not require installation of sanitation, street paving, transport links, or other urban services. Whilst the movement frequently uses legal process to highlight these paradoxes, it also takes more direct action through the use of theoretically illegal occupations of empty building in the centre of the city. These occupations further serve to condemn the failure of the local and national states to both uphold the right to housing and ensure the social function of property.

The first organized building occupation in the centre of São Paulo took place in 1997. Several hundred families arranged to meet close to the chosen building, the Casarão Santos Dumont, at midnight, and then proceeded to break a hole in the door and enter. The families found themselves able to remain in the building and in a strong negotiating position with the São Paulo state government (the owner of the building), and subsequently a wave of organized occupations followed across the centre. These have become part of the core strategy of the housing movements over the past decade. The movements have occupied dozens of both privately and publicly owned abandoned buildings in order to force the relevant level of the state to negotiate housing solutions for its members. They either call for the building they are occupying to be renovated as social housing, or for the occupiers to be given adequate housing elsewhere. These occupations produce varied results. At times occupiers are only able to stay in the building for a few minutes before they are ejected by the police, or organizers choose to undertake a short-lived 'symbolic' or 'political' occupation. Other occupations have lasted for up to seven years.

The case of the Casarão Santos Dumont generated much media coverage, through which the UMM was able to broadcast its message to the city and country. The movement called for low-income housing to be provided in the centre of São Paulo, and criticized the general practice by municipal and state governments of building affordable housing only in the underserviced peripheries, despite the presence of many thousands of empty and abandoned buildings in consolidated areas of the city. As Pedro, a key movement leader, put it:

> The decision to occupy ... in the centre, was a decision that was about putting the question of living in the centre of São Paulo on the agenda. Because before that, there had always been a huge prejudice that people who were poor couldn't live [in adequate accommodation] in the centre.[13]

The occupation therefore contrasted the centre with the poor quality of life in the far-flung 'ghettos', from where workers had great difficulty in reaching their place of employment, and where social housing units have often been left for years in areas without street paving, schools, recreation facilities, transport, or street lighting. The centre is already equipped with infrastructure and services, which are, furthermore, seriously underutilized outside of office hours. The occupation was also a way of denouncing the existence of many thousands of empty buildings in the central areas of the city. This contrast between the centre and the periphery is ever-present in the rhetoric of the movement, and the transposition of a movement tactic used first on rural land (from the Rural Landless Workers, or MST), to urban peripheral land, and finally to centrally located buildings is also significant. The organized occupation of buildings shows that scarcity of land and inequality of tenure are not just rural phenomena, draws attention to the city's housing problem as a whole, and indicates that the city cannot rely on its peripheral areas to absorb the city's poorest populations forever.

Building occupations can be read as acts of civil disobedience, in that they purposefully break the law in order to highlight a legal injustice and communicate this to the wider public, but are not attempts to bring down the existing government or legal system.[14] In the case of building occupations in the centre of São Paulo, the movement aims to draw attention to the large number of empty buildings in the area that have been abandoned for many years and are not fulfilling a social function. They point out that this is in contravention of the constitution and contrast their emptiness with the significant housing deficit affecting the city. Frequently the movement chooses to occupy buildings where the private landlord has considerable property tax debts, or which flout zoning laws, so as to reinforce the message that the state is failing to ensure that its own laws are upheld. The central location is also key – occupations are a way of showing that there is potentially space for low-income families to be housed in areas that are well-provided with services and close to places of employment. Further, they broadcast to São Paulo and Brazilian society the fact that the state is not upholding the right to housing, again in contravention of the constitution. However, the way that the movement's members and leaders portray building occupations gives them a level of legitimacy beyond a standard act of civil disobedience. They argue that occupations are, in fact, legal. They may contravene the civil and penal codes (since they involve breaking into the building and assuming trespass) but the act of occupation is a way of ensuring that the constitutional right to housing is upheld. This is because an occupation will provide accommodation for members who do not have adequate housing, whilst also providing the empty building with a social function.

Building occupations are not guaranteed to succeed, in that they do not always result in permanent housing solutions for movement members.[15] However, my findings show that occupations as a movement strategy are now accepted as a legitimate form of protest by politicians, bureaucrats, and appointed advisors in housing departments from across the political spectrum. In the federal, state, and municipal governments, with their left-wing, centre, and centre-right ruling parties respectively, there is general consensus that occupations are justifiable. Indeed, not one of the 21 current and former public office holders interviewed (both political appointees and career civil servants) categorically opposed building occupations. But it was particularly remarkable that political appointees at the municipal level (under the Democratas, a centre-right political party) should take this line, and this perhaps points to a general acceptance of the UMM's tactics.

At the federal level, not surprisingly, the public servants appointed to the cities' ministry by the Workers' Party government were positively supportive of the UMM's activities. But even during the more conservative presidential administration of Fernando Henrique Cardoso (1995–2002) the UMM had managed to force concessions from federal bodies. In response to the occupation of an abandoned building owned by the federal savings bank (CEF) in the centre of São Paulo, the bank modified one of its building credit schemes, the Residential Leasing Programme or PAR, so as to be viable for a social movement.[16] The movement's departure from the building was negotiated through the promise that the occupiers would be housed in another empty federal building that would be renovated through the federal PAR scheme. Other movements in the centre of the city have since negotiated the renovation of six other buildings for its members through PAR funding. In four of these cases the building remained occupied until financing negotiations were concluded.

My research revealed that the principal reason for this somewhat surprising attitude towards housing occupations amongst representatives of the state was the almost complete absence of housing options for very poor residents of São Paulo, aside from self-building in *favelas* on the outskirts of the city or the *cortiço*. In a context where so much of the city is irregularly occupied and where there are such limited opportunities for low-income groups to find adequate accommodation in areas with urban services, few representatives of the state are willing to question the idea that low-income groups have an informal 'right to the centre' or that occupation is a legitimate form of protest. Beyond this, the fundamental illegality of so much of the city weakens the state's ability to respond aggressively to occupations. It is difficult for representatives of the state to criminalize the movement's occupations in a city where so much land is illegally occupied, and so much of the housing stock has been built in contravention of planning legislation.

As such, it could be argued that the way that the city grew during the 20th century has not only provided a catalyst for social mobilization, but has also created an enabling environment for radical, theoretically illegal, collective action. However, the extent to which municipal, state, and federal governments are willing to take steps to change patterns of settlement in São Paulo and to fund social housing in central areas varies considerably according to party politics. The current municipal administration is attempting to knock down empty buildings and create parks in central areas, whereas the federal government has been modifying legislation to make it easier for organized groups of the poor to buy abandoned buildings with credit and then convert them into low-income accommodation. Nevertheless, through its radical acts of occupation, the housing movement has, over the past decade, managed to place the issue of centrally located low-income housing onto the agenda of municipal, state, and federal governments.

6 Conclusion

To conclude, the way in which São Paulo grew over the course of the 20th century has resulted in a sprawling and highly segregated city where there are few options for low-income groups to live, other than on the furthest peripheries. The trend of reserving the non-regulated 'rural zone' for those who cannot afford to live elsewhere has been exacerbated by municipal and state housing programmes that also build on the city's outskirts. Further, the illegality of much of the city's residential accommodation – its irregular settlements, *cortiços*, and *favelas* – negatively impacts on the life chances of São Paulo's poorest residents. These factors, combined with the abandonment of thousands of buildings in the city centre and the state's inability to address the city's massive housing deficit, have acted as a stimulus for social mobilization amongst lower-income groups who have begun to use the law to support their denunciations and claims.

The city's housing movements assert that the failure of the three levels of the Brazilian state to provide adequate, well-located, low-income housing is a violation of the constitutional right to housing. They evoke federal legislation, in the form of the city statute, to assert a collective right to the city (understood as the right to participate in and benefit from all that the city has to offer) and even to the city centre. They further reinterpret the law so as to justify their building occupations, which are, theoretically, illegal acts of civil disobedience. These are instead presented as a way of implementing the right to housing and ensuring that empty buildings are fulfilling a social function. These strategies and rights claims have been accepted as legitimate by academics, policymakers, and politicians, and although building occupations have, in practice, had mixed results, they have been influential in putting forward a new model for the city that seeks to alter radically the segregated nature of the urban environment. The movement's dual strategy of legal reasoning and illegal action has led to a situation in which policymakers and politicians are forced to acknowledge the rights of all city residents to the use-value of the urban environment. They must now also, at the very least, debate the feasibility of social housing options for low-income groups in better-located and better-serviced areas of the city. The housing movements of São Paulo may not have the right to the centre guaranteed, but the very fact that this term is now in the vocabulary of policymakers, politicians and the academic community would suggest that a re-evaluation of the place of the poor in the city is taking place.

The case of the UMM demonstrates the importance of the law for social movements of the urban poor. Constitutional legislation is increasingly being used by marginal groups in the developing world to assert their rights to basic services and to demand that governments fulfil their commitments to all of their citizens. This is particularly notable in countries that have undergone democratic transitions in recent decades, accompanied by the promulgation of progressive constitutions. Alongside Brazil, South Africa provides several similar examples, including the Treatment Action Campaign which used the constitution to demand life-prolonging medication for people with HIV/AIDS. Whilst in Brazil – and beyond – the law has traditionally been seen as the preserve of the elite, and, where housing is concerned, as a way of protecting individual property rights (Holston 2008), the case of the UMM shows how the law can have 'emancipatory potential' (Santos 1995) for more marginalized social groups. Rather than perceiving the law as a limitation on collective action, reinterpretation of legislation can provide new avenues for social movement activism. Where the state is obviously flouting its own laws, the use of legal argument by a social movement can be extremely powerful. Movements can appeal to a general belief within society that the law should be upheld, not least by the government that introduced the law in the first place. Whilst some urban social theorists and commentators have dismissed the idea of enshrining the right to the city in law (Mayer 2009), in the case of Brazil it is precisely constitutional and federal legislation promoting the right to the city that has rendered the concept so useful for social movements, who are then able to draw on this legislation to promote their own vision of a more socially just city.

Notes

1. Source: SEADE 2006 Sistema Estadual de Analise de Dados.
2. Source: Prefeitura Municipal de São Paulo.
3. Where 1= perfect inequality.
4. Source: Instituto de Estudos do Trabalho e Sociedade.
5. The *Folha de São Paulo* 19/06/05, reports that between 1981 and 2000 the 13 central districts of the city showed negative growth rates. According to the paper it is principally the middle and upper classes who are leaving the centre.
6. The norm of property ownership, even amongst very low-income families, has significant implications for the work of the housing movements leaders today, who struggle to promote the concept of social rental to their members.
7. Source: O Estado de São Paulo 12 December 2006. This is probably based on an estimate of the *cortiço* population in São Paulo by FIPE in 1993 of 595 110.
8. Residents of São Paulo city.
9. Source: www.prefeitura.sp.gov.br
10. Source: Email reproduction of FNRU letter distributed to the Forum Centro Vivo web group, 22 February 2007.
11. Interview with Fernanda Leão 12 October 2007.
12. Hohfeld categorized rights as either claim rights or liberty rights. Each of these categories was further divided into positive and negative categories (Jones 2005).
13. Interview with Pedro 18 September 2007.
14. For discussion of the definition of civil disobedience see Rawls (1991) and Bedau (1991).
15. Measuring the 'success' of an occupation is problematic. At the time of the research, only approximately ten previously occupied abandoned buildings in central São Paulo had been renovated for social housing, with a further three undergoing renovation work. However, hundreds of families that have been involved in housing occupations have received subsidized credit from the state government to purchase homes on the open market. Others have been offered the opportunity to purchase subsidized public housing units.
16. The programme had to be modified to allow 'popular associations' to apply for this type of funding; in its original formulation this credit scheme was designed for building contractors.

References

Andrade, J. (2001). 'Da cultura da intervenção à intervenção da cultura: Consenso e gentrificação nas novas estrategias de revalorização do centro histórico de São Paulo'. São Paulo: Universidade de São Paulo. graduação.

Bedau, H. (ed.) (1991). *Civil Disobedience in Focus*. London: Routledge.
Bonduki, N. (1998). *Origens da habitação social no Brasil. Arquitetura moderna, lei do inquilinato e difusão da casa própria*. São Paulo: Estação Liberdade.
Brown, A., and A. Kristiansen (2009). *Urban policies and the Right to the City. Rights, Responsibilities and Citizenship*. Paris, UNESCO.
Caldeira, T.P.R. (2000). *City of Walls: Crime, Segregation and Citizenship in São Paulo*. Berkeley: University of California Press.
Comarú, F., R. Cymbalista, W. Sutti, and A.C. Teixeira (2005). 'Conflitos em torno do direito à moradia na região central de São Paulo'. *MAPAS: Monitoramento ativo da participação da sociedade*. Rio de Janeiro, Ibase/ActionAid/Ford Foundation.
Fernandes, E. (2007a). 'Constructing the "right to the city" in Brazil'. *Social and Legal Change*, 16(2): 201–19.
Fernandes, E. (2007b). 'Implementing the urban reform agenda in Brazil'. *Environment and Urbanization*, 19(1): 177–89.
Freeden, M. (1991). *Rights*. Milton Keynes: Open University Press.
Grostein, M. (1987). 'A cidade clandestina: Os ritos e os mitos. O papel da "irregularidade" na estruturação do espaço urbano no município de São Paulo. 1900–1987'. São Paulo: Universidade de São Paulo, Faculdade de Arquitetura e Urbanismo. PhD thesis.
Holston, J. (2008). *Insurgent Citizenship: Disjunctions of Democracy and Modernity in Brazil*. Princeton: Princeton University Press.
Jones, P. (2005). *Rights*. Basingstoke: Palgrave.
Kipfer, S., K. Goonewardena, C. Schmid, and R. Milgrom (2008). 'On the production of Henri Lefebvre'. In K. Goonewardena, S. Kipfer, R. Milgrom, and C. Schmid (eds), *Space, Difference, Everyday Life. Reading Henri Lefebvre*. New York: Routledge.
Kowarick, L. (1979). *A espoliação urbana*. São Paulo: Paz e terra.
Lefebvre, H. (1996). *Writings on Cities*. Translated by E. Kofman, and E. Lebas. Oxford: Blackwell.
Maricato, E. (2000). As idéais fora do lugar e o lugar fora das idéias'. In O. Arantes, C. Vainer and E. Maricato (eds), *A cidade do pensamento único: Desmanchando consensos*. São Paulo: Editora Vozes.
Marques, E., and H. Torres (2005). *São Paulo: Segregação, pobreza e desigualdades sociais*. São Paulo: SENAC.
Mayer, M. (2009). 'The right to the city in the context of shifting mottos of urban social movements'. *City*, 13(2): 362–74.
Parnell, S., and E. Pieterse (2010). 'The "right to the city": institutional imperatives of a developmental state'. *International journal of urban and regional research*, 34(1): 146–62.
Presidência da República (2001). Lei N. 10.257, de 10 de julho de 2001. Brasilia, Casa Civil – Subchefia para assuntos juridicos. www.cidades.gov.br, accessed 22 September 2008.
Purcell, M. (2002). 'Excavating Lefebvre: the right to the city and its urban politics of the inhabitant'. *GeoJournal*, 58: 99–108.
Rawls, J. (1991). *A Theory of Justice*. Oxford: Oxford University Press.
Rizek, C. (2003). 'Os sentidos da cidade brasileira: Figurações da ordem e de seus avessos'. *Espaço e debates. Revista de estudos regionais e urbanos*, 23(43–44): 79–91.

Rolnik, R. (1995). 'The City and the Law: Legislation, Urban Policy and Territories in the City of São Paulo (1886–1936)'. New York: New York University. PhD thesis.

Rolnik, R., L. Kowarick, and N. Somekh (eds) (1991). *São Paulo: Crise e Mudança*. São Paulo: Brasiliense.

Santos, A.L.T. (ed.) (2002). *Laboratório de projeto integrado e participativo para requalificação de cortiço*. São Paulo: FAUUSP.

Santos, B.d.S. (1995). *Toward a New Common Sense: Law, Science and Politics in the Paradigmatic Transition*. London: Routledge.

Santos, M. (1996). 'São Paulo: a growth process full of contradictions'. In A. Gilbert (ed.), *The Mega-City in Latin America*. Tokyo: United Nations University Press.

Simões, J. (1991). *Cortiços em São Paulo: O problema e alternativas*. São Paulo: Instituto Pólis.

Torres, H., H. Alves, and M. Aparecida De Oliveira (2007). 'São Paulo peri-urban dynamics: some social causes and environmental consequences'. *Environment and Urbanization*, 19(1): 207–23.

UNDP (2005). *Human Development Report: International Co-operation at a Crossroads: Aid, Trade and Security in an Unequal World*. New York: UNDP.

8
On-Street Upgrading? Assessing the Consequences of Allocation and Regulation Policy in Santiago de Chile's *Ferias Libres*

Lissette Aliaga-Linares

1 Introduction

Off-street relocation projects have become a common policy approach to upgrade the street trade of agricultural produce in Latin America, rendering many successful and unsuccessful attempts. In contract to this trend, in Santiago de Chile street vendors working in farmers' markets, known as *ferias libres,* achieved recognition as legitimate providers of agricultural produce in 1939 by plying their trade in the streets (Salazar 2003: 83). In a context of food supply scarcity, in *ferias* urban planners found an alternative, low-cost solution to building public markets in order to serve a growing city that demanded agricultural produce at affordable prices. Although most vendors were not necessarily farmers, as they traditionally had been, ferias remained steadfast through the 1980s within the upper-, middle- and lower-class residential areas.

Nevertheless, an expanding modern food retail sector and changes in the urban structure may question the utility of the service that ferias once provided. During the late 20th century, supermarkets benefited from the concentration of agricultural production fostered by free trade policies, and started to offer competitive prices to a wider clientele. Initially dominant in central areas and upper-class neighbourhoods, supermarkets began relocating into the densely populated working-class areas. Furthermore, the modernization of the city's transportation system and the gentrification of housing projects in the form of gated communities contributed to the accessibility of supermarkets, putting them within reach of those consumers traditionally served by *ferias*.

Therefore, even if the regulation of ferias contributed to their expansion across the city, new challenges emerged to jeopardise the sustainability of this economic practice. For instance, due to aggressive spatial competition, ferias may potentially be disadvantaged if the issue of location is not controlled. Legislation which gave legal recognition to the ferias empowered the *comunas* (local municipalities) to decide on the allocation of farmers' markets to specific streets in order to minimize their negative effects and to maximize consumer benefits.[1] However, the ferias are still marginalized in urban planning. None of the urban renewal projects related to Transantiago, the massive transportation system, has recognized the needs of the ferias in their designs. Instead, they have been relocated to backstreets far from their original, attractive commercial areas.

How does the current regulation affect the market opportunities of the ferias in the competitive environment? What are the consequences of the allocation practices for their image and competitiveness within the city? This document aims to answer these questions by providing a statistical analysis depicting the ferias' choice of location and disentangling the neighbourhood effects of residential segregation and gentrification on the populace of *feriantes* (licensed vendors) and *coleros* (unlicensed vendors). I start with a discussion of the role of regulation in open-air markets, and then I will review the overall nature of the regulations governing the ferias and discuss the implications of these for their market opportunity.

2 The regulation of open-air markets

Street trade can be considered one of the most typical images of the informal economy, regardless of whether it is a peddling occupation or a more stationary practice within a street market. This portrayal has permeated the majority of policymaking, especially since the informal economy debate became a subject of concern in fast-growing Latin American cities during the mid-20th century. However, this characterization, which has called much attention to the understanding of the rationale of small-scale economic activity, has often blurred the comprehension of the role of regulation towards street trade, particularly since the neoliberal approach to the informal economy became influential in the early 1990s.

Regulations have been imposed on open-air markets as long as they have existed. Initially, most cities enacted a licensing policy, discriminating zones in which street markets could operate, stipulating certain sanitary provisions, and, in some cases, banning the sale of certain products. At the heart of these regulations was the objective to reduce the negative effects associated with the economic use of public space. However, the level of enforcement of those policies has always been questionable as many downtown areas became encroached with more vendors than expected. On the one hand, the expedition of licences could be used to pay political favours, which would lower incentives for control. On the other hand, the collection of taxes, fees, or licences could also serve to increase local revenue and therefore encourage more street vending. Thus, even if street trade was portrayed as informal, it was usually a poorly regularized practice rather than an 'unregularized' economic activity.

The neoliberal approach to the informal economy has translated the lessons of Hernando de Soto to an off-street upgrading for street trade. De Soto (1989) popularized the idea that regulation of informal economic activities was the key to unleashing entrepreneurship potential. The regularization of economic activity focused on business registration to increase tax revenue and guarantee property rights. Using the case of Lima, his main propositions regarding street trade were that access to ownership by increasing access to credit for these activities may be beneficial to vendors. Since the organization of many vendors into street markets in the 1980s was able to save and build roofed markets, De Soto observed that a transition from itinerant vending to fixed post and then roofed market vending was likely, and even desirable, for the vendor. He argued that 'street vendors aspire to stability' (1989: 1132). However, this stability at that particular context meant being off-street rather than on-street.

Two issues, however, should be highlighted in order to set the Lima case in a comparative perspective and to evaluate if this approach can be extended to all types and forms of street trade. First, at the time in which De Soto studied Lima, there was little competition from the formal and modern retail sector. During the 1980s, malls and supermarkets only opened within predominantly middle- and upper-class neighbourhoods, usually located within central areas in the city. Nowadays, free market policies have promoted the inflow of cheap food and non-food imports which have increased the competitiveness of modern retail. In Lima, the number of supermarkets has increased considerably, and they are expanding toward peripheral neighbourhoods, exposing working-class residents to other forms of consumption different from traditional markets (Aliaga 2008). Second, the transition from itinerant to fixed post vendors was more attainable before given the regulation in place, in which vendors were taxed by their use of public space and the lower cost of land acquisition. Similar to other cities, Lima suspended the payment of *sisa* (the tax for the use of public space) prior to the massive eviction of vendors from downtown areas. Nowadays, few districts collect this tax, and many others have started to enforce group savings as mandatory in order to move vendors from the streets more quickly (Roever and Aliaga 2008). Also, similar to other cities in the region, Lima has become more consolidated in terms of provision of services and land ownership. With a rather weak market for second-hand housing, access to land for trade is expected to increase in cost, as vendors' associations become the only prospective buyers in those areas (Calderón 2004: 12–13). Moreover, even though titling has been granted to former street markets established between informal settlements, by 2008 only three out of fifteen markets which qualified for that regularization had attained ownership.[2] Therefore, in order to attain greater stability off-street, vendors might be more exposed to financial instability as relocation projects may become more costly, thus forcing them to acquire debt and not necessarily assuring higher returns given the greater competition they face from supermarkets and other retailers.

Assuming that this policy approach will fit every case of street vending has rendered many relocation attempts unsuccessful, not only in Lima but also in other cities across the region. In the case of Lima, part of the reason why the transition was possible was that, over time, street markets became channels of commerce which specialized in particular goods, such as agricultural produce or imported goods. The nature of the products sold contributed to attracting a continuing flow of buyers that could be retained even after relocation, given the reputation of the site. Bogota, for instance, has a form of predominantly itinerant vending which may have been rendered stationary, but which specializes in the sale of pedestrian-oriented products (such as candy bars, chopped fruits, cell phone calls, and so forth) rather than a specific product which may imply a more permanent use of space. The sudden transition from itinerant vendors to stall vendors was unsuccessful and costly for the city administration, which had to purchase the marketplaces and rent them to vendors, since the costs of building a market was beyond their reach. Only seven out of the twenty-nine projects constructed during the 1990s are still occupied (Castañeda and García 2007: 174–7). Even in

Lima, the continuity of this policy may need to be revised, particularly for those markets that specialize in agricultural produce and constitute a basic service for working-class settlements. Rushed relocations have been less successful since they require better leadership preparation and availability of suitable spots for sale (Guerrero 2001).

One consequence of this approach is that it has contributed to a perspective in which little urban design is implemented to accommodate street trade. Moreover, urban planning has failed to see this activity as a tool for urban renewal despite the fact that street trade has remained a popular practice within cities, and could also be valued as a cultural practice. Interestingly, in countries such as the United States, Canada, and the United Kingdom, street markets in the form of farmer's markets have increased in popularity, raising policy concerns mainly directed towards either improving quality of service and increasing accessibility to smaller towns (Schmit and Gómez 2011), or evaluating the cultural experience in terms of how they could strengthen local communities (Smithers and Joseph 2010), rather than removing them from the streets.

The neoliberal perspective has focused on relocation since the ownership of a stall in a market potentially increases the chances of control from the state, firstly because it becomes a place-binding economic practice, in which the actor becomes visible on records, and secondly, it increases opportunities for proposing policies to generate tax revenue, registration, and grant property rights. However, on-street regulation can also be used for these purposes. In other cities, such as Rio del Plata in Argentina and Santiago in Chile, street markets selling agricultural produce have persisted as a result of being regulated as open-air fairs or farmers' markets. On-street regulation may imply further legitimacy and could potentially increase provisions related to sanitary control and improved service, if controlled efficiently. Regulation can be a successful policymaking tool if the content of such regulation is oriented at the core of promoting economic growth, rather than assuming only one way to attain it. An effective policy may widen the market opportunities for vendors, if they include provisions for safety and sanitary control which could expand their popularity and attract more consumers. Therefore, it is important to understand cases in which different social and economic conditions have led to different ways of regulating food street trade and how these approaches have been affected by those current changes that are modifying modern food retail.

3 Ferias' regulation in Santiago de Chile

The regulations on ferias *libres* in Santiago de Chile not only govern the administration of the economic use of public space, but also supervise conditions to ensure consumer safety. The central components concern the choice of location, operating schedules, procedures for market access, and the norms and sanctions regarding customer service. While the 37 comunas of Metropolitan Santiago follow similar guidelines, each of them has political autonomy to modify certain components of the regulation.

3.1 Location and operating schedule

Each *comuna* defines the location and operating schedule within which the ferias may operate. Location, with due consideration for the opinion of neighbourhood associations, is established based on reports from the transportation department estimating how the *feria* would impact on the transit flow, and from the Secretary of Communal Planning, evaluating the suitability of zoning for economic activities. General criteria promote the selection of streets that are paved, low in traffic, furthest away from pollution sources, and unlikely to cause inconvenience to the resident population. The allocation of a *feria* site is renewable or may be changed by the *comuna* at any time; in some cases, a particular location is restricted to a time limit of one year. Each location can be used on a particular weekday (Tuesday to Sunday) from eight o'clock in the morning until three or four o' clock in the afternoon. *Feriantes*, or licensed vendors, are obligated to respect the regulations governing *feria* location and operating schedules, since a long and unjustified absence can count towards forfeit of licence.

3.2 Market access

The allocation of vending posts inside the ferias is governed by a licence – also known as *patente comercial* – granted by the local municipality which also determines costs and stipulations. The objective of the licence is to minimize the adverse effects associated with the increase of licensed vendors, such as noise, additional garbage, traffic jams, and even the possible increase in robberies due to the accumulation of people. Each *comuna* decides on the optimal size of the ferias based upon the maximum occupancy allowed by the street width. Most comunas establish a fee based on the land value assigned by the internal revenue service according to the law of public goods use. Some comunas also include a form of income tax in the price of the licence, which equals half of the current monthly tax unit for the given year. The fee may include payment for commercial rights, as well as other costs such as cleaning or security services. A number of comunas, however – particularly upper-class ones such as Providencia – consider each *feria* on a special-case basis and have established a 'social' cost for the license rather than calculating the cost in terms of land tax. In these cases, access is restricted to the current number of *feriantes*; in the case of death or abandonment, the license is not available to new applicants nor transferred to family members of former *feriantes*. To ease inspection, *feriantes* must have their licence clearly visible on operating days.

The main preconditions for obtaining a licence include the availability of posts at the site, the applicant having no prior involvement in a commercial business venture, and the applicant residing in the *comuna* in which the licence is being requested. Few municipalities require registration with the health insurance and social security authorities. They may ask the applicant to verify his residency by requesting additional documentation (such as utility bills), or (depending upon the type of product to be sold) request that the applicant obtain sanitary licenses. Inspectors can also make unannounced visits to the applicant. Comunas with a higher proportion of upper-class residents usually have licensed vendors who do not live within the actual municipality but whose operations were linked to producer activities at the time the *feria* was founded.

The department for commercial patents and inspection in each *comuna* is responsible for supervising the area size and the number of licences of the *feria* in order to ensure that they do not exceed the stipulations articulated in the founding decree. While most comunas try to restrict unlicensed vendors by confiscating their merchandise, some others (such Renca and La Granja) choose to issue partial licenses to this group, at half the fee of the actual permit (Aliaga 2006b: 61–2; Stillerman 2006: 518).

In some comunas, the applicant may need a letter of acceptance from the local *feria* organization. On inquiry, most municipalities generally deny the availability of licenses, and finding a spot is a matter of the individual's connections. At times, the mayor or a high-ranking public official may issue a special petition for a social case, and in many cases representatives of the ferias may provide letters of recommendation without prior consultation with the association. The licence is renewable each season, and can be terminated by the *comuna* at any time. It cannot be transferred to another person (unless they are working on the same stall), although some communities may give preference to relatives in the case of death or disability.

3.3 Customer service

Inspectors visit the ferias daily in order to supervise compliance with customer service requirements, as well as checking for absenteeism. The general terms establish that stalls must comply with the stated dimensions, prohibited or inferior quality products are not to be sold, working under the influence of alcohol is forbidden, as is the use of informal electric installations, weight value must not be falsified, and the authority of the inspectors must not be resisted. The penalties are graded according to the severity of the offence. There are four levels of penalty: a caution or ticket, a fine, confiscation, and cancellation of licence. Three warnings entail a fine in most comunas. Confiscation or termination of licence is mostly applied in cases of repeated offences or if the products sold are in dangerous or adulterated condition. Once confiscation occurs, the *feriante* is either banned from re-applying for a licence, or his licence is suspended for up to three years.

Comunas only allow certain types of products to be sold. These include agricultural produce, seafood, meat, groceries, and the like. Certain communities may allow the sale of clothing or other related articles. In some instances, the municipality may stipulate the percentage of non-food products that can be traded, while in others, any non-food product may be prohibited. Regulations stipulate that the delivery of perishable food products requires special provisions: a vendor must have an isothermal or refrigeration system for seafood and meat. All food vendors are required to have a sanitary certificate, while the regulations in some comunas even demand specific clothing (gloves, hats, aprons). A *feriante* is also obligated to take part in the expenses for mutual services maintained by the vendors' association, such as chemical bathrooms and private security.

4 Unintended consequences of ferias' regulation in Santiago

As described above, the regulation policy is concordant with the aim of keeping the streets safe and clean while guaranteeing sanitary conditions for food delivery. However, there are some key components of this regulation that merit further attention. Two distinctive trade-offs distinguish Santiago from the classical portrayal of the transition from itinerant-fixed post vendor to the market stall vendor, as described in De Soto's review of informal markets in Lima (1989). First, in contrast to

Lima where vendors gradually select their site of operation, Santiago de Chile's vendors are dependent upon allocation by the *comuna*. Second, the regulation of 'unfair' competition in Santiago, by limiting market access to new vendors, is delegated to public officials, in contrast to the case of Lima where market access usually depends on vendors' associations or the individuals' networks.

In Santiago, the comunas' choice of the site should increase the availability of food services in the city, but if supermarkets are expanding it is apparent that this function may decrease in importance and may unintentionally segment market opportunities for *feriantes*. In cities such as Lima, Mexico City, and Quito, where street markets are not strongly regulated, the site of the street market is up to the vendors, who tend to favour central areas in order to access a greater number of potential customers. Due to their informal nature, these vendors defend their 'gained' locations as their irrefutable right to pursue market opportunities, and often persist despite urban renewal or gentrification by supermarkets. In the case of Santiago, typically the willingness to incorporate the *feriantes* into the decision-making process is conditional on local politics. In many comunas, location decisions are neither term-binding nor contingent upon prior consultations with licensed vendors. The allocation criteria, as currently in effect, may intrinsically favour some neighbourhoods. It is easier to set-up ferias in neighbourhoods where private cars are not the main mode of transportation and thus residents would not be bothered by the installation of farmers' markets. Only 19 per cent of 364 ferias studied (out of a total number of 406 in Santiago) operate in areas such as plazas or parks instead of the street; only 17 per cent provide parking facilities for their customers (ODEPA–USACH 2008).

Ferias can serve a larger clientele by working in different locations. Each *feria* is generally located at one particular site in the *comuna* of the *feriante's* residency, operating either once (46 per cent) or twice (53 per cent) a week. Almost 70 per cent of Santiago de Chile's residents shop in the ferias at least once a week (ibid.: 4). As the customers are likely to be residents who live nearby, allocation may potentially segment ferias' clientele. According to a survey administered in July 2005, approximately 85 per cent of ferias' customers lived within a walking distance of 9–11 minute indicating that the possible area of influence of a feria is limited to a maximum one-kilometre radius (Aliaga 2006a: 18). An examination based on the mean travel time on Tuesdays to Sundays would indicate that approximately 6 per cent, 19 per cent and 75 per cent of the customers come from high, middle, and lower socioeconomic status households, respectively (ibid.: 26). As Map 8.1 shows, in comparison to supermarkets, ferias are more widespread throughout the city, but their locations differ as they tend to be closer to areas with a higher proportion of lower socioeconomic households.

As the ferias' sites bind market opportunities to specific areas, the balance between the needs and expectations of the area's residents not only affects the probability of allocation but also the performance of the farmers' markets themselves. For instance, in comunas where supermarkets have already opened, the ferias operating schedules may make them less accessible. The standard operational schedules for ferias

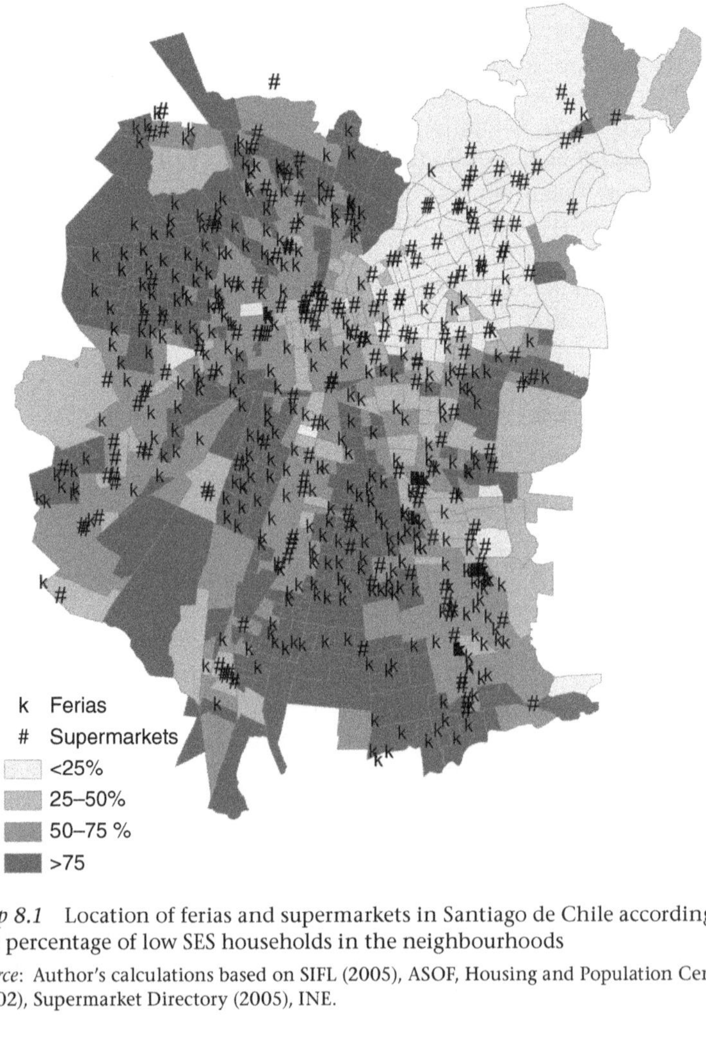

Map 8.1 Location of ferias and supermarkets in Santiago de Chile according to the percentage of low SES households in the neighbourhoods

Source: Author's calculations based on SIFL (2005), ASOF, Housing and Population Census (2002), Supermarket Directory (2005), INE.

restrict evening activities in order to avoid additional investments from the *comuna* for lighting or security. This limits the clientele to those who have the time to shop in the mornings, as opposed to supermarkets, which achieve their peak weekday sales between 6 and 9 pm (ODEPA–USACH 2008: 28). Based on a conservative perspective, this implies that those most likely to shop in the mornings are women who either do not work, or who work part-time. Even though female labour-force participation in Chile is low compared to other Latin American countries (World Bank 2005), younger women in Santiago are increasingly participating in the workforce (Contreras et al. 2005). In the long run, this may result in the operating schedules of the ferias becoming outdated and less competitive during weekdays.

A better allocation decision may further contribute to the efforts for improving customer service by providing different sets of clients who increase demand for higher quality products while, at the same time, demanding a fair price. Current regulation has encouraged *feriantes* to improve sanitary conditions, even within socially disadvantaged comunas. For instance, in 1992, the Food and Agricultural Organization (FAO) of the United Nations promoted a project for the improvement of temporary stalls selling fish and seafood products. Cerro Navia, one of the poorest comunas in Santiago, managed to have all licensed food, fish, and meat vendors using the updated stalls and registered for temporary sanitary checking. Moreover, a recent study reported that one-third of *feriantes* are increasing their security by contracting private guards and 72 per cent are developing marketing initiatives, such as *El cliente elige* (Let the client choose) which consists of letting customers select the products themselves, a practice particularly common in upper-class residential areas (ODEPA–USACH 2008). Despite the advances being made, in most impoverished comunas progress is sporadic and less evident. Pavez et al. (2004: 130) found that 85 per cent of neighbours living in the proximity of the ferias in the southwest communities, and with a higher proportion of working-class residents, claim that the markets attract sanitary hazards such street dogs, insects, and mice.

Regulation has entitled public officials to control access to ferias. The practice of licensing has recently been perceived by mayors in other cities as either increasing opportunities for political clientelism, which encouraged an increase in the number of vendors, as in Bogotá (Passoti 2009: 45–53), or granting extralegal property rights that promote more invasions on the streets, such as in Lima (De Soto 1989), consequentially advocating for their remission. Contrary to these cases, it can be stated that Santiago's policy enforcement succeeded by limiting the number of licences, rather than increasing them in pursuit of more revenue. However, this stricter practice has unintentionally encouraged another form of informality. The average number of licences among the younger ferias, if analysed according to the year of set-up, shows a decreasing or stagnant trend while the average number of *coleros* per *feria* is certainly on the rise (Figure 8.1). It could be argued that because the number of licences is increasingly restricted, many residents in the respective *comuna* are opting to operate as unlicensed *coleros*.[3] For instance, according to a study, 83 per cent of *coleros* work within their home municipality, and in 79 per cent of cases working at the ferias constitutes their main source of income (Pavez et al. 2004: 129).

Moreover, the practice of transferring licences to the close relatives of a disabled or deceased *feriante* may also have limited the access to newcomers who may need to work on the *feria* for only a few years. It has been estimated that almost half of the *feriantes* have worked as licensed vendors for at least 17 years (ODEPA–USACH 2008: 6), while 50 per cent of the *coleros* had less than 1 year of work experience, and 42 per cent had a maximum of 3 years.

Since the supervision of the *coleros* is the responsibility of the inspectors, the ferias' associations have little opportunity to block access to their market. Similar experiences of unemployment among the

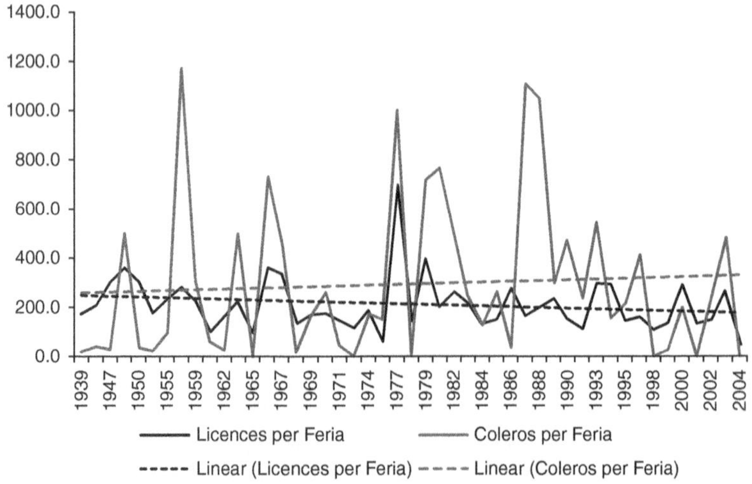

Figure 8.1 Number of licences and *Coleros* per *feria* according to the year of set-up, 1939–2004

Source: Author's calculations based on SIFL (2005), ASOF.

feriantes may trigger some sympathy towards the *coleros*. A recent study estimated that 39 per cent of licensed vendors had been unemployed before they obtained the necessary permits (ibid.: 6). While *feriantes* are bound by regulation in their spatial choices, *coleros* are not. Rather, they would benefit from a lack of effective control on a specific site. *Coleros* do not seem to be pedlars, as it is estimated that they work at the same location for 74 per cent of the time (Pavez et al. 2004: 129). Moreover, neighbourhoods with high unemployment rates may be more tolerant of the *coleros* as farmers' markets may offer an opportunity for other income-generating activities as well. Pavez et al. (ibid.) estimated that 12 per cent of neighbours provide some type of service – such as storage of merchandise or preparing breakfast – to either *feriantes* or *coleros*. Consequently, being unable to control the size of the ferias may be a response to the need for local sources of employment.

Allocation criteria and a stricter licensing policy seem to be distinguishing features of Santiago's regulation of farmers' markets. While in many other cities in Latin America, evictions and off-street relocation seem have led to increased operating costs for many food vendors, in Santiago de Chile an empirical question remains regarding how these features respond to a changing geography such as has been documented in many other cities in the region, that is, the expansion of supermarkets and gated communities in which the middle and upper classes started to move within working-class neighbourhoods.

5 Data and methods

I used the 2005 Information System of Ferias Libres (SIFL, Spanish acronym) produced by the Asociación Chilena de Ferias Libres (ASOF, Spanish acronym), which contains cartographic and attribute information on 401 ferias. Using the 1992 and 2002 population census, a household's socioeconomic status (SES) is computed with a score based on two variables: educational attainment of the head of the household and possession of goods.[4] Based on this score, the socioeconomic status groups are ranked from ABC1 (the highest) to C3, D, and E (the lower classes).[5] Throughout the chapter we define the lower socioeconomic status group as being composed of C3, D, and E. For computing residential segregation indexes, the number of households in each SES category is aggregated at the block and census tract level. The interaction or exposure index, applying the residential segregation indicators, measures the degree to which a lower SES household interacts with a higher status household within the neighbourhood. At the other end, the isolation index measures the degree to which the poorest SES households (D and E) interact with other similar SES households in the neighbourhood. The dissimilarity index is a measure of evenness. That is, it calculates the percentage of lower SES households that would need to move to achieve an even distribution within the residential blocks. In terms of gentrification, the model includes the percentage increase of high SES households from 1992 to 2002. It also includes an indicator of whether or not supermarkets were located in the area. Supermarket locations were geo-referenced using the 2005 Supermarket Directory for the Metropolitan Region of Santiago de Chile elaborated by the Chilean National Institute of Statistics (INE, Spanish acronym). The assembled dataset contains information on the 879 neighbourhoods approached using the census tract delimitations.

Using the ASOF dataset, a dummy variable indicating whether or not a *feria* has been located in a neighbourhood is computed as the dependent variable for the first test on probability of ferias' allocation. The approach chosen to perform the analysis is the logistic regression.

The 2005 SIFL dataset provides information on the estimated number of *coleros* and *feriantes* for 112 and 267 ferias, respectively. I used this information to analyse whether or not residential segregation in terms of the degree of interaction between the lower and higher SES households significantly affects both population groups, previously normalized using natural logs. In the OLS regression model, we introduced a dummy control variable corresponding to the downtown and northeast comunas, characterized by a higher capacity for enforcement such as that seen in central Santiago and the northeast, as well as to the neighbourhood unemployment rate, calculated from the 2002 population census.

6 Results

6.1 Effects of residential segregation, gentrification, and supermarket proximity on the probability of the allocation of ferias

Table 8.1 presents the results of the logistic regression, which predicts changes in the probability of a *feria* being established in a neighbourhood, according to the selected residential segregation and gentrification indicators. Compared to supermarkets, whose probability of allocation is 15 per cent, the probability for a *feria* is 44 per cent, and is considerably higher when the operating day of the week is ignored. However, if taken on the basis of a single weekday, the allocation

Table 8.1 Logistic regression for explaining ferias allocation

	Supermarkets	**Ferias**	**Sunday**	**Saturday**	**Friday**	**Thursday**	**Wednesday**	**Tuesday**
Probability, %	15.60	44.76	15.36	15.70	14.90	14.33	13.88	15.02
AIC	683.35	1123.50	727.26	736.42	720.81	685.62	684.97	708.50
Constant	1.38	1.88*	–0.24	0.94	0.25	0.72	0.07	0.95
	(0.699)	(0.738)	(0.701)	(0.707)	(0.716)	(0.717)	(0.702)	(0.718)
Interaction	–0.05	–2.68*	–3.22*	–2.47*	–2.50*	–3.27*	–2.78*	–2.76*
	(0.843)	(0.807)	(0.916)	(0.891)	(0.927)	(0.961)	(0.923)	(0.934)
Isolation	–5.16*	–1.68*	–0.93	–2.52*	–1.63	–1.82	–1.79	–2.05*
	(0.844)	(0.813)	(0.818)	(0.820)	(0.833)	(0.837)	(0.827)	(0.833)
Dissimilarity	1.83	0.03	–0.34	–0.12	–0.26	–1.11	0.48	–1.34
	(1.752)	(0.758)	(1.023)	(1.044)	(0.048)	(1.122)	(1.050)	(1.117)
% Increase high SES	–0.04*	–0.04*	–0.01	–0.05*	–0.03	–0.04	–0.04	–0.05*
	(0.014)	(0.014)	(0.021)	(0.022)	(0.022)	(0.027)	(0.023)	(0.025)
Presence supermarkets		0.02	0.42	0.16	–0.43	–0.21	0.40	–0.25
		(0.218)	(0.284)	(0.286)	(0.335)	(0.336)	(0.291)	(0.327)

Note: * p-value <0.05, standard errors given in parentheses.

Source: Author's calculations.

probability for the *feria* is very close to that observed for the supermarkets. Supermarkets are the city's only providers on Mondays, while ferias operate Tuesdays to Sundays in almost 15 per cent of the neighbourhoods. According to our analysis, if other parameters are held constant, the odds of a *feria* serving a neighbourhood on any given day of the week is higher than for supermarkets, but lower for each working day, even for Sundays.

Contrary to supermarkets, the interaction of lower SES with higher SES households decreases the probability of *feria* services more consistently for all days of the week. While the presence of both supermarkets and ferias is negatively associated with the isolation of poor households, it causes a weak reduction in the probability of service from the ferias on any day of the week, and on Saturdays and Tuesdays. Consequently, the existence of ferias is not as strongly related to the segregation of the urban poor as it is sensitive to the degree to which lower SES households interact with families of higher SES households. The dissimilarity index shows no significant relationship either for the presence of ferias or supermarkets, which corroborates the observation that the overrepresentation of the poor is not related to the location of ferias but rather to their exposure to middle-class or upper-class households. This implies that existence of the ferias is dependent on a consensus achieved in balancing the needs of various socioeconomic groups.

In terms of gentrification, while the presence of a supermarket has no effect on the presence of ferias in a neighbourhood, an increase in high SES households is weakly and negatively associated with the existence of ferias on any weekday, or on Saturday and on Tuesday. As the spread of supermarkets shows a similar relationship, it can be stated that the presence of wealthier families is related to commerce-free residential areas.

Overall, the fact that in certain zones of the city the presence of ferias is associated with forms of residential segregation points to the observation that the current regulation practice is, perhaps unintentionally, restricting the market opportunities of the ferias to the lower SES households.

6.2 Effects of residential segregation and local unemployment on licence enforcement

Table 8.2 summarizes the results of the OLS model predicting the number of licensed (*feriantes*) and unlicensed (*coleros*) vendors. A unit increase of the interaction of lower SES households reduces the number of *feriantes* and *coleros* by 0.31 and 0.54, respectively. Interaction noticeably reduces the number of *coleros* even when factors such as comunas with better

Table 8.2 OLS regression coefficients for the estimated effects of segregation, local unemployment rates on the number of licensed vendors (*feriantes*), and unlicensed vendors (*coleros*)

	Licensed vendors *feriantes*		Unlicensed vendors *coleros*	
Interaction	−0.31* (0.05)	−0.18* (0.06)	−0.54* (0.13)	−0.39* (0.16)
Comunas (downtown-northeast = 1)		−0.42* (0.12)		−0.60 (0.37)
Unemployment rate		0.10 (0.05)		0.09 (0.13)
Constant	4.42* (0.11)	4.15* (0.26)	3.70* (0.31)	3.63* (0.77)
N	267	267	112	112
R^2	15.0	20.1	14.2	16.4
Adjusted R^2	14.7	19.2	13.4	14.1

Note: *p-value < 0.001, standard errors given in parentheses.

Source: Author's calculations.

enforcement and the unemployment rates of the neighbourhoods are controlled for. It can be stated with 99 per cent confidence that, other than those at downtown and in the northeast, comunas are expected to have 3.33 more *coleros*, when controlling for neighbourhood differences in residential segregation and unemployment rates. The persistent suppressant residential segregation overpowers the anticipated effect of increasing neighbourhood unemployment, suggesting that a more integrated community could benefit from a balance between the need for employment and expectations from supervising the ferias.

7 Discussion: Working towards a legislation to increase competitiveness

Unlike other Latin American cities where policy attempts to relocate vendors from the streets have had limited success (Guerrero 2001; Lawrence and Castro 2006), the regulation of ferias in Santiago de Chile has shown that street markets can be regulated and promoted. However, as observed, the current regulations – and particularly the allocation practice – can also become a tool in segmenting their markets, thus intensifying social exclusion.

Recently, organized efforts by *feriantes* to update the law have been documented, but have not merited prompt attention. One key issue is assuring their stability as legitimate workers on the streets. A legislative project has been proposed to congress, which considers outsourcing streets for a ten-year period, favouring the *feriantes*. Hector Tejada, President of ASOF, defends his position by asserting:

> We want legislation that can be a tool which allows us to compete, and this is a responsibility because as a distribution channel, we support 300,000 small farmers throughout the whole sector, assisting to distribute their products throughout the city. Thus, we are talking about one million jobs. Nowadays, although we control 80 per cent of the sales in fruit and vegetables, there is aggressive competition with the supermarkets, which are essaying new ways to compete with small trade, and this directly affects our market. In this sense, we need to improve legislation and the system of property of public space, we need an outsourcing of the streets. (22 July 2005, Parliamentary Meeting, author's translation.)

The discussion and approval of this legislation has been delayed since 2005. The updated 2008 version of SIFL reports that *feria* locations are still the same (ODEPA–USACH 2008). Outsourcing the streets for ferias seeks to promote more investment for the provision of lighting, parking, and restrooms in their market space. Thus, a more detailed analysis of current locations is needed. A case study on Macul, a community located near downtown southern Santiago, advocated increasing centrality in the decision-making process for establishing ferias as this could increase potential benefits for consumers and may also promote investment in public areas with a better agglomeration of services (Troncoso Melo 2009).

Ferias are competitive not only because they offer affordable prices and connect the traditional agricultural chains of small farming in the city, but also because they produce a unique cultural experience which integrates social groups within their market practices. Sabatini finds that, in Chile, micro-scale residential segregation of the urban poor was subsequently more strongly associated with social exclusion indicators such as teenage pregnancy, youth inactivity, or higher unemployment rates (Sabatini et al. 2001). Moreover, some scholars have hypothesized that some of the segregation mechanisms could be related to the stigmatization of certain poor neighbourhoods (Katzman 1999). Evidence showing that ferias' allocation is significantly sensitive to the observed residential segregation patterns should be an issue of concern. As ferias are more likely to exist in neighbourhoods where poor households have less interaction with the higher SES households, these locations segregate their clientele, with potentially negative effects on competitiveness. Segregated locations may increase the stigma that ferias offer an inferior form of consumption and consequently may reduce incentives to improve services. Moreover, as greater unemployment rates are prevalent among the lower SES neighbourhoods, the need for employment opportunities may indirectly promote unfair competition for the *feriantes* as well as limit the capacity of the *comuna* to enforce supervision.

Consequently, it can be suggested that a more cautious location policy which promotes greater interaction between different socio-economic households could balance the need to shop and work, and could support those interests necessary to adequately manage the use of public space. From a market perspective, ferias in more attractive locations could encourage a more competitive attitude, and improve their quality of service. This outcome could materialize in Santiago de Chile, since legal recognition of the *feria* implies a social contract that is based on acceptance by the neighbourhood and *feriantes* are responsive to customers' demands. Moreover, the successful regulation of ferias could set an example for other cities across the region in order to avoid unsuccessful and costly attempts at off-street relocation projects.

Notes

The author would like to acknowledge Sally Roever for her support in the editing of this text.

1. Throughout this chapter, ferias and farmers' markets are used interchangeably.
2. Calculations based on the 2008 informal settlements shapefile provided to the author by COFOPRI.
3. *Coleros* or unlicensed vendors are used interchangeably in this chapter.
4. The author of this classification is Claudio Contreras, a professional geographer, who calculated it in the context of a project oriented to elaborate the socioeconomic map of Chile, co-ordinated by ADIMARK, a marketing agency operating in Santiago de Chile.
5. The breakdown of the SES groups:

		1992 (%)	2002 (%)
Highest	ABC1	7.1	10.9
Middle class	C2	10.5	23.3
Low-middle class	C3	29.8	33.5
Lower class	D	23.7	29.3
Lower class	E	12.4	19.6

References

Aliaga, L. (2006a). 'Feeding the Poor? Spatial Patterns and Neighbourhood Demographics in Metropolitan Santiago Informal Food System'. Paper presented at the Population Association of America 2006 Annual Meeting.

Aliaga, L. (2006b). *Street Markets in Santiago de Chile: An Assessment of their Locational and Regulation Policy*. Austin, Texas: University of Texas at Austin.

Aliaga, L. (2008). 'La consommation ambulante face aux supermarchés: production spatiale, concurrence et résistance à Lima'. *Espacés et Societés*, 135(4): 117–38.

ASOF (Asociación Chilena de Organizaciones de Ferias Libres) (2005). Sistema de Información Feria Libre – SIFL.

Calderón, J. (2004). 'La formalización de la propiedad en el Perú. Efectos económicos y socio culturales'. Paper presented at IV Seminario Internacional Innovando los procesos de acceso al suelo urbano. México: UNAM-PUEC-Lincoln Institute.

Castañeda, A., and J. García (2007). *Hábitat y espacio público. El caso de los vendedores informales en el espacio público físico de Bogotá*. Bogotá: Alcaldía Mayor de Bogotá, Secretaría de Gobierno, Instituto para la Economía Social, PNUD, ONU-Hábitat.

Contreras, D., E. Puentes, and D. Bravo (2005). 'Female labour force participation in greater Santiago, Chile: 1957–1997. *Journal of International Development*, 17(2): 169–86.

De Soto, H. (1989). *The Other Path: The Economic Answer to Terrorism*. (Digital edition) New York: Basic Books.

Guerrero, E. (2001). *De Ambulantes a Empresarios? Reubicación y Ordenamiento del Comercio Ambulatorio en Lima Metropolitana*. Lima: Alternativa-DESCO.

INE (Instituto Nacional de Estadísticas de Chile [National Statistics Institute of Chile]) (2002). Housing and Population Census.

INE (2005) Supermarket Directory.

Katzman, R. (ed.) (1999). *Activos y Estructura de Oportunidades. Estudios Sobre las Raíces de la Vulnerabilidad Social en Uruguay*. Montevideo: PNUD/CEPAL, LC/MVD/R.180.

Lawrence, P.G., and S. Castro (2006). 'Government intervention in street vending activities in Guayaquil, Ecuador: a case study of vendors in the municipal markets'. *Problemas del Desarrollo: Revista Latinoamericana de Economía*, 37(144): 145–70.

ODEPA–USACH (2008). *Estudio para la caracterización del canal feria para la distribución de productos hortofrutícolas en la Región Metropolitana*. Santiago de Chile.

Passoti, E. (2009). *Political Branding in Cities: The Decline of Machine Politics in Bogotá, Naples, and Chicago*. Cambridge Studies in Comparative Politics. New York: Cambridge University Press.

Pavez, L., H. Rautenberg, and J. Lee Mira (2004). 'Estudio y Catastro de las ferias libres del Gran Santiago'. Paper presented at the Camara Nacional de Comercio, Servicios y Turismo de Chile.

Roever, S., and L. Aliaga (2008). 'Case Report on Lima – Peru'. Paper prepared for the ILO In-Focus Initiative on the Informal Economy. Promoting Decent Work for Street Vendors New Delhi: ILO-India.

Sabatini, F., G. Cáceres, and J. Cerda (2001). 'Segregación Residencial en las Principales Ciudades Chilenas: Tendencias de las Tres Últimas Décadas y Posibles Cursos de Acción. *EURE*, 27(82).

Salazar, G. (2003). *Ferias Libres: Espacio Residual de Soberanía Ciudadana*. Santiago de Chile: Ediciones Sur.

Schmit, T., and M. Gómez. (2011). 'Developing viable farmers markets in rural communities: An investigation of vendor performance using objective and subjective valuations'. *Food Policy*, 36: 119–27.

Smithers, J., and A. Joseph. (2010). 'The trouble with authenticity: separating ideology from practice at the farmers' market'. *Journal of Agriculture, Food and Human Values Society*, 27: 239–47.

Stillerman, J. (2006). 'The politics of space and culture in Santiago: Chile's street markets'. *Qualitative Sociology*, 29(4): 507–30.

Troncoso Melo, C.G. (2009). *La Feria Libre Como Fenómeno de Centralidad Transitoria. Desafíos del Diseño Urbano ante las Transformaciones de la Actividad Comercial Ferial en Santiago. El Caso de una Comuna Mediterránea Macul*. Santiago de Chile: Pontificia Universidad Católica de Chile.

World Bank (2005). *Household Risk Management and Social Protection in Chile*. Washington, DC: World Bank.

9

Of Guns, Ideas, and Taxes: Understanding the Political Logic of Violence-Reducing Policy Innovation in Three Colombian Cities

Francisco Gutiérrez Sanín, María Teresa Gutiérrez, Tania Guzmán Pardo, Juan Carlos Arenas Gómez, and María Teresa Pinto

1 Introduction

Latin America is notorious for its persistently high levels of urban crime. Homicide rates in most of the region's major metropolises are extremely high, despite constant efforts to counter the phenomenon (Rico and Chinchilla 2002: 30). A major socio-spatial consequence of this widespread violence has been the ghettoization of Latin American cities, which has triggered a spiral whereby exclusion buttresses violence, which in turn produces more exclusion and more violence (Auyero 2007; Briceño-Leon and Zubillaga 2002). At the same time, this violence is constantly evolving, making it ever more difficult to engage with. In Central America, for example, the ubiquitous youth gang phenomenon of the 1990s has been widely reported to have made the proverbial leap to more organized forms of criminality in the 2000s (Rodgers 2009).

Colombia is widely regarded to constitute a case in point with regard to such trends. Certainly, the country has regularly been in the top three most violent of the continent during recent decades (Briceño-Leon and Zubillaga 2002), partly because the country has not been able to extricate itself from the Latin American cycle of peasant revolutionary wars (Crowley 1992), but also because it is one of the few peasant wars where genuine urban violence structures have developed due to the specificities of some of the country's cities, an idiosyncratic set of strategic decisions, and a literally explosive conjunction of political and criminal motivations and structures (Gutiérrez and Jaramillo 2004). The neoliberal roll-back of the state during the past two decades and the growth of already extraordinarily high levels of inequality have also been widely described as making urban violence both endemic and ineradicable (de Ferranti et al. 2003; Hoffman and Centeno 2003: 363).[1]

At the same time, Colombia has been the theatre for significant and successful violence-reducing policy innovations, and this chapter considers the dynamics underlying their emergence in the cities of Bogotá, Medellín, and Cali. In the first two cases, the new policies introduced have been associated with huge successes, including a radical reduction in homicide rates, improved taxation, and the strengthening of key government bureaucracies, to the extent that they have been labelled urban or metropolitan 'miracles' (Gutiérrez et al. 2009). This term partly relates to the fact that the transformative processes that resulted from the new policies were both rapid and large-scale. More importantly, however, it also underlines how they were also – quasi-universally – considered extremely unlikely, whether by academics, policymakers, or the general public. In the case of Cali, new policies have only half-heartedly been introduced and, moreover, have not worked.

This chapter does not seek to explore the reasons underlying the successful violence reduction of the 'miracles'. Rather, it aims to explore why and how such policies were implemented in Bogotá and Medellín against why and how they were not in Cali. Currently, there are two conflicting and rather unhelpful answers. The first contends that the 'miracles' are simply an illusion, and are nothing more than epiphenomena of broader societal trends within Colombian society, which has seen increasing securitization over the past decade (Sánchez, Espinosa, and Rivas 2003; Formisano 2002). According to the second view, the 'miracles' triggered local cultural revolutions, which fundamentally changed the nature of urban life and improved the quality of life in cities (Peñalosa 2003; Mockus 1994; Acero and Baracaldo 2007). In this chapter, we propose a third option, based on the premise that any proper interpretation of the 'miracles' has to include their underlying politics.

There arguably exists a significant effort to depoliticize the understanding of the 'miracles' (Delgado Uribe 2007), which is both conceptually and empirically wrong. Neither of the standard explanations can explain the fact that the 'miracles' anticipated, rather than followed, national trends, nor can they explain the rapid pace of change (the transformation of values and social mores is typically slow). But most importantly, they cannot explain why the 'miracles' occurred in Bogotá and Medellín, but not in Cali or other smaller municipalities. In this regard, our basic argument is that the successful implementation of the 'miracles' in Bogotá and Medellín was the consequence of the opening of a unique window of opportunity for new political actors and the concomitant development of a new 'government formula' – see Mosca (1939) on this latter concept – that did not occur in Cali. In short, the key explanatory dimension underpinning the so-called 'miracles' was the emergence of a new type of politics in some Colombian metropolitan contexts but not in others.

To explore the underlying dynamics of this new politics, this chapter analyses how the individuals who advocated the policy innovations associated with the 'miracles' came to be elected, and how and why they were able to translate their discourses into concrete policies in Bogotá and Medellín, but fell short of inducing significant change in Cali. The Section 1 reflects generally on the nature of ideological and policy innovation, an issue that is often forgotten or assumed *prima facie*. The Section 2 considers the basic nature of the new politics, while the Section 3 examines the 'signalling' processes that underpins this, and how this impacts upon governance. The Section 4 focuses specifically on the concrete example of taxation in order to illustrate how the new politics translated into policy determination. In each section, we show how ideas interacted with interests and constraints, and how this interaction produced specific policy outcomes. Our conclusions are somewhat apprehensive, highlighting in particular how the very condition that allowed for the emergence of the 'miracles' may in fact block their sustainability.

2 Understanding policy innovation

Successful policy innovation takes place because of the convergence of ideas and strategic demands (Hall 1997). This convergence fixes public notions and alliances onto a small set of focal points, and offers cues that allow collective actors to orient themselves and operate according to a new, freshly introduced set of verbal formulae, skills, and routines. With respect to ideas and the role they play, they are important for at least three reasons. First of all, they are often the avenue through which actors can concretely express, take hold of, and negotiate their interests. 'Politics is not only a contest for power. It is also a struggle for the interpretation of interests' (ibid.: 174). Public discourse has to be proffered in universal terms, even if it is produced to fulfil particular interests (Elster 2007), and it is the translation of a diverse constellation of interests, aversions, and fears into compact, articulate, and universalistic formulae that allows the process of collective action and discovery.

Second, ideas give origin to policy paradigms (Weir 1992). They offer blueprints and focal points for identifying and prioritizing problems, the toolkits to engage with them, and the yardsticks for evaluating and publicly negotiating the outcomes. They not only constrain policy choices, but also regulate access to decision-making, as only specific groups of individuals and networks have the skills to resolve the problem once the guidelines and evaluation criteria have been fixed. Last, but not least, ideas allow actors to discover actual or potential allies, and interact with them with respect to focal points. Innovation in the terrain of ideas is associated with the identification of privileged arenas of conflict enunciation and resolution, in order to expand the horizon of political imagination, and to push new agendas forward.

Ideas can be successfully translated into operational policies only if the 'stars are aligned' – that is, if they are able to match a series of 'objective' factors, and overcome the constraints that come from technological restrictions and strategic demands made by relevant agents, networks, and groups. In what follows, we show that such an 'alignment of stars' occurred in some major Colombian cities. Due to a deep national (urban) crisis, a demand for innovation existed. Thus, all political players were vying to demonstrate their innovativeness. This involved a game of signalling. Candidates had to show that they were new, and yet at the same time had to be able to win elections. However, once in power, they needed to implement genuinely transformative policies, which depended on having not only a broad margin of manoeuvre, but also on access to specific skills. This double set of contradictions – building credibility (and coalitions) and implementing new policies (but having to coordinate different interests) – defined the 'space of possibility' for the urban innovators.

The Colombian metropolises were burdened with both high rates of homicide and other crime, and the perception of disorder and anomie. There existed a widespread sense that traditional political parties were to blame for allowing the crisis to develop, which led to a self-reinforcing demand for a different type of politics. In concrete terms, this translated into a new political discourse which rejected all types of particularism, and 'business as usual'. At first glance, this might appear to be a rather standard political approach: a universalistic dialogue in terms of the nation, the people, the city, and the community, rather than interest groups. But this anti-particularistic discourse had an idiosyncratic twist to it, claiming to be disentangled from representation. 'Not to represent anybody', 'not to be in debt with anybody', and being able to demonstrate this type of purity, became the magic formula of the new politics that were associated with the Colombian metropolitan 'miracles'. All class or group interests that did not coincide with the interests of the whole city were to be exposed and castigated. Instead of the classical liberal definition of public space as a clash of diverse interests that limit each other, anti-particularism emphasized change in order to transcend such confrontation.

To a certain extent, such an approach can be associated, at least conceptually, with the neoliberal ideological paradigm that has been hegemonic in the Latin American context since the 1990s. A major difference, however, is that Latin American neoliberalism was furiously anti-statist (Roberts 1998). The anti-particularist discourse associated with the Colombian metropolitan 'miracles' evolved towards a clear state-building programme instead. Although, analogous to 'standard' Latin American neoliberalism, the decision-making associated with the miracle-inducing policy innovations was made in the name of a government of the most knowledgeable – the morally superior, the most efficacious manager, the ultimate technocrat; interest-based bargaining was shunned, and specific social and economic sectors were not privileged. Indeed, the discourse implied a strong pedagogy from above, emphasizing re-education, and the build-up of the state capacity. To this extent, the miraculous metropolitan experiences that we discuss here must be seen very much as outliers, going against the general hemispheric contextual grain.

3 A new form of politics?

In 1994, the mainstream Colombian newspaper *El Tiempo* published the following despondent description of Bogotá: 'The city is the incoherent sum of thousands of interests that have nothing in common. The proud towers of the emergent bourgeoisie coexist with enormous gulfs of misery, where the poisonous fungi of desperation are being cultivated. There is no communication or mutual understanding between both worlds' (*El Tiempo* 1994a). The city was affected by a narcotics war, high levels of violence, and a very tight budgetary situation. This urban crisis provided the backdrop for major political change, with the 1994 mayoral elections constituting a watershed in this respect.[2]

The few previous elections – subnational authorities have been directly elected in Colombia since 1988 – had generally been bipartisan, pitting a Liberal party candidate against a Conservative party candidate. The 1994 elections, however, were notable for the involvement of an independent candidate, Antanas Mockus. Mockus was an unconventional character who had previously been Professor of Philosophy and Mathematics and rector of Bogotá's National University – he was locally famous for having once bared his backside at students who were booing him – but his campaign rapidly caught the imagination of the city's population, as well as the support of various sectors of the media, NGOs, and social movements. His campaign emphasized its 'young', 'technical', and 'non-political' character (*El Tiempo* 1994b). It was designed to be low cost, to rely heavily on the media, and focused on a small number of iconic messages which converged around a central aspiration: 'everybody contributes, everybody wins'.

The fact that Mockus was a philosopher and mathematician who spoke and 'looked' very different to conventional politicians clearly motivated voters. In particular, Mockus benefitted from a bandwagon effect among the most affluent and educated.[3] Although not all – and indeed, not even a majority of – those belonging to the socioeconomic elites lined up behind Mockus, many of those who did were linked to the media and had access to power and communication resources, so their switching to the Mockus option influenced a lot of traditional Liberal and Conservative voters.[4] Mockus won the mayoral elections with almost two-thirds of the vote.

Mockus' victory signalled the end of traditional bipartisan politics in Bogotá. The two main political parties disappeared from city life as credible power alternatives, and this triggered an adaptation process by city politicians, who rapidly understood that in order to be elected, they needed to demonstrate their 'independence' to the voters. The most spectacular case of this adaptation was that of Enrique Peñalosa, previously a rising star of the Liberal party, and a losing candidate in the 1994 elections, who reinvented himself as an 'independent' for the 1997 mayoral elections, actively seeking the 'anti-political vote', and completely changing his campaigning style, for example personally distributing his propaganda in the streets, and, most significantly, stressing the 'civic', 'non-partisan' nature of his campaign. Peñalosa was duly elected as mayor of Bogotá, and subsequent elections have similarly seen independent candidates win. Mockus was re-elected following Peñalosa's term in office, and subsequently candidates of the newly-created Leftist Alternative/Democratic Pole (*Polo Democrático Independiente* and *Polo Democrático Alternativo*, PDI/PDA) won twice in a row.[5]

The situation in Medellín was initially much less favourable to the emergence of alternative independent politicians. The city was much more violent than Bogotá, and was in the grips of drug trafficking, guerrilla, and paramilitary violence. Moreover, the city was a Catholic and Conservative stronghold, and its traditional politicians were intent on maintaining and developing their networks and the assets intimately associated with the old, clientelist way of doing things. At the same time, however, they recognized the need to overcome the wear and tear of their political manoeuvres, and they also had a long history of innovation and compromise, not least due to the need to interact with the various violent actors controlling large swathes of the city. As a result, from the early 2000s onwards, taking a cue from Bogotá, traditional politicians strove to continue their political 'business as usual', but concealed it by representing themselves as 'managers' rather than politicians, and focusing their campaigns on new, one-shot, 'civic' undertakings.

For example, Luis Pérez, a member of the Liberal party who was elected mayor between 2001–03, portrayed himself as the ultimate manager (*El Tiempo* 1997a), and organized his campaign around an anti-corruption programme that specifically targeted the private sector (*El Tiempo* 2004a). However, partly because of his deep involvement in traditional clientelist politics, Perez was unable (or unwilling) to implement either his purported anti-corruption policies or any that might in fact have been associated with the promulgation of an 'urban miracle'; subsequently, the 2003 elections saw the emergence of a proper independent candidate in the shape of Sergio Fajardo, a university Professor of Mathematics whose campaign also gained traction due to the communication skills he demonstrated on television, which played a greater role than usual in the election campaign.

Fajardo was particularly adept at conveying simple yet powerful messages in television interviews, debates, and adverts. His catchword was 'trust', and in the name of 'trust' he was effectively able to mobilize a veritable rebellion against the traditional political practices. Contrary to Bogotá, Fajardo did not portray himself as 'something different' from politics, but rather as an alternative form of politics, focusing on the core message that 'decent' people had to 're-conquer' public life (*El Tiempo* 2003a). He won resoundingly, which provided him with a mandate to initiate a widespread programme of policy innovations, some inspired by the Bogotá experience, others specific to Medellín, and forged his own 'miracle' in the city.

Fajardo did not run for mayor again. The independent innovator template, however, was clearly established in Medellín. When Fajardo's anointed successor, Alonso Salazar, a journalist and researcher, was challenged by traditional politicians during the 2007 elections, he was vigorously defended by intellectuals and other local public figures who explicitly argued that the alternative to Salazar was a return to old, corrupt, anti-'miracle' politics of the past, and that they deserved to be defeated (*El Tiempo* 2007b). Salazar beat Luis Pérez, and continued to implement the policies associated with the Medellín 'miracle'.

Colombia's third city, Cali, has not benefitted from a 'miracle' in the way that Bogotá and Medellín have. To a large extent this is because although modalities of 'new politics' akin to those that emerged in Bogotá and Medellín did appear in Cali, they never did so in the 'pure' form incarnated by Mockus and Fajardo. Instead they were simply mixed and blended with traditional clientelist politics, producing a hybrid.[6] This gave a completely different twist to the 'signalling' game in which Mockus and Fajardo had been involved. To a certain extent this occurred because Cali has long been conversant with independent politics, flirting with non-traditional politicians as early as 1980 (Vasquez 2001), and the traditional political machinery has been able to co-opt them quite effectively. Consequently, potential policy innovators have generally had to draw on established political channels in order to get elected, something which has both limited their possibilities to 'signal' themselves as 'different', as well as their ability to actually implement universalistic policies. For example, Rodrigo Guerrero, who is in many ways the originator of many of the key policy innovations that inspired the Colombian urban 'miracles', was elected mayor of Cali as the Conservative party candidate, and his administration therefore had to include representatives of the party's different factions (*El Tiempo* 1992a). Not only did this have a powerful symbolic effect for the public, but it also empowered different claimants to defend their specific interests *from within* the innovative experience whenever the need arose. As a result, it was not easy to differentiate innovators from other political agents, and the hybridization of the Cali innovators not only diminished the opportunities to signal difference, but also allowed interest groups to neutralize proposed solutions.

To sum up, in Bogotá the breakdown of the bipartisan party system meant that candidates had to show voters that they were of the 'correct', independent type in order to be elected. Voters wanted to support independent candidates who would be able to overcome the old way of doing things; this forced candidates to publicly highlight that they did not belong to the traditional parties, and to exhibit their separation from traditional political clientelist networks. In Medellín, traditional politicians initially copied the independents, creating 'civic' brands and so forth, but eventually were out-signalled by a genuine independent who could exhibit irrefutable non-traditional credentials and, once in power, was able to draw on non-traditional networks to implement a range of policy innovations. In Cali, the innovators came from the old political personnel and gained power based on the support from these networks, and thus voters lacked clear criteria to make a distinction between the different types of politicians.

4 Governance and the politics of signalling

The contrasting examples of Bogotá and Medellín on the one hand, and Cali on the other, clearly suggest that a key issue to consider with regard to the Colombian urban 'miracles' is how their founders were able to push through their policy innovations in the face of opposition from traditional politicians and much of broader society. In Bogotá, the first years of the Mockus and Peñalosa administrations were quite turbulent, and their level of support was low (Gaitan and Parra 2008). Neither had strong representation on the municipal council and their initiatives were frequently defeated there. They were attacked by the political parties, traditional and new, and by special interests, but nevertheless ultimately found the clout to uphold their main policies, and later to defend the results of these policies.

There are a number of key factors involved here. First and foremost, the wave of reforms associated with the 1991 national constitution, specifically including the provision for the popular election of mayors, greater autonomy to municipalities, and the professionalizing of municipal employment (e.g. paying councillors, but excluding them from the management of public utilities), are all significant institutional innovations which constituted preconditions for the 'miracles'. At the same time, it is important to realize that this window of opportunity was not activated in all contexts, and depended on pre-existing power structures and social and cultural resources (Gutiérrez 2007).

What allowed them to do so was the fact that the new politics which emerged in the early 1990s interacted directly with the media, and especially television. The innovators' bent for differentiating themselves – both symbolically and pedagogically – from traditional politics coincided with the insatiable quest of television for the colourful and the bizarre, and the combination of political outsiders offering an alternative discourse through electronic media was a powerful one, which allowed breakthroughs in Bogotá and Medellín. In the case of Cali, these resources could only be utilized within a hybrid political dynamic where new voices were rapidly co-opted into the traditional system, making it difficult for voters to differentiate between genuine innovators and other political agents. While innovators in Bogotá and Medellín could easily speak against the poor nature of traditional politics, this was more difficult for their counterparts in Cali.

A similar issue affected governance by innovators once they were elected. In Bogotá and Medellín, governance was not portrayed as being about distributive issues, but rather about solving collective action problems. City actors had to be re-educated in order to be able to cooperate for the benefit of all. This vision was supported and promoted by an eclectic coalition of media, intellectuals, and technocrats, but was also one that many in the traditional urban elite could adhere to. The new discourse was based on guaranteed stability of property rights and reduced corruption, and was even presented as potentially reducing costs for the rich, insofar as the toll (read: bribes) generally extracted by the old-style politics in order to guarantee services was quite high. In effect, the trade-off faced by the urban elites was to surrender direct access to decision-making through clientelist links to individual traditional politicians versus lower transaction costs, better infrastructure, and increased predictability, as well as a sense of contributing to the public good.

This latter issue became one of the discursive battlegrounds of the new innovating styles. For example, under the old political system, the specific interests of different sectors of the economy were dealt with by clientelist intermediaries, who ensured that they would receive benefits, both legislative and material. This created huge collective action problems, as the example of public transport in Bogotá highlights well. Until the 1990s, public transport was fragmented, with different routes and forms of transport controlled by a range of specific interest groups who were all intimately connected to specific politicians who ensured that rules favourable to each of these interest groups were maintained at the expense of a coherent collective urban transportation system. Bypassing them in the decision-making process generated loud protests, and indeed could have triggered the formation of an anti-governmental coalition of different elite interest groups, but what in fact happened was that there was an almost unanimous reaction against particularist demands, to which enough interest groups eventually rallied (*El Tiempo* 2007c). Different interest groups could tolerate being stripped of their particularistic perks if they believed that others would suffer a similar fate and there would be no favouritism. To this extent, the trade-off separated the rich from immediate decision-making, but *at the same time* incorporated them much more strongly into the new municipal government.

In this respect, 'signalling' by the innovating regime was crucial, and it is striking that they all adopted a strong managerial turn and were made up of technocrats and intellectuals rather than politicians (*El Tiempo* 2007e).[7] The innovating mayors adopted a discourse stressing the role of the market, the importance of productivity, and fair competition (*El Tiempo* 2007d). In a broader context where neoliberalism – both nationally and internationally – was a major reference point, this managerial turn coincided well with dominant political agendas, and added a legitimacy to the new innovating regimes. This allowed them to overcome the fact that they did not have access to the clientelistic networks of traditional politics, and also that they often lacked any relevant governance experience. The next section explores how reforms were concretely achieved through a politics of signalling, focusing specifically on the issue of taxation.

5 Taxation without representation?

Municipal authorities have long been charged with collecting public utility payments in Colombia, but since national-level reforms – including in particular the 1991 Constitution – they can also levy taxes on industry, commerce, real estate, and the sale of gasoline. Having said this, evaluations by the Colombian National Department of Planning have shown that the fiscal trajectories of municipalities since the 1990s have varied tremendously (DNP 2005). Although certain municipalities have significantly developed their taxation regimes, others have not. Bogotá, Medellín, and Cali illustrate these different trajectories very well. Certainly, in all three cities, tributary issues played a major role in debates surrounding both elections and the implementation of new 'government formulae' by policy innovators. These particularly revolved around the need to strengthen the taxing capacity of the state in order to fund new violence-reducing policies. However, the way in which such outcomes were achieved (or not) was very different in each of the three cities under discussion.

Efforts to overhaul Bogotá's fiscal regime were initiated by Jaime Castro, the city's first elected mayor (1992–94), who sought to increase both gasoline and real estate taxes to fund a mega plan of public works (*El Tiempo* 1992c). Although he himself was a traditional politician, his proposals were very much technocratic and non-particularistic in nature. They were – not surprisingly – rejected by a broad swathe of interest groups in the city, including his own (Liberal) party (Castro 2001), as well as public figures and intellectuals, and they were one of the main reasons for his subsequent political discredit (*El Tiempo* 1993a). Interestingly, the only public figure to openly support Castro's proposals was Antanas Mockus, who was effectively running against him (or rather, his political party). Mockus openly advocated increasing taxation for everyone, and after winning the 1994 elections, he revived Castro's gasoline tax proposals and pushed for an 'integral' tax reform. The way he did so was to present a bill to the municipal council, which he publically and vocally insisted could not be changed. Although he was accused of arm-twisting by councillors of all political shades – and not unreasonably so, it must be said – his savvy media campaign in support of his proposals, and the support they enjoyed from a broad swathe of intellectuals and other public figures, meant that he was able to successfully implement his package.[8]

Mockus' second mayorship was even more pro-taxation (*El Tiempo* 2002), and was associated with a large-scale campaign to persuade people to pay more taxes than their obligatory share. What is surprising about this 'initiative of voluntary taxation' is that it garnered more than marginal support. In the 2003 fiscal year, the city collected 110 per cent of the amount of taxation it would have collected had contributors simply paid up what they owed. Some of the groundwork for this surprising development likely derived from Peñalosa's administration, which continually asserted how taxation was visibly transforming the city, emphasizing that the policy innovations associated with the urban 'miracle' in the city constituted proof that citizens' taxes were being spent properly, barraging these simple messages energetically and repeatedly in the media.[9]

Medellín has long enjoyed a reputation for fiscal probity in the Colombian context (Lopez Gonzalez and Mesa Callejas 2008). This is partly due to the efficiency of its public utilities firm, the *Empresas Públicas de Medellín*, or EPM, which is widely seen to incarnate the city's public managerial capacity. Towards the end of the Luis Pérez administration (2001–04), however, the EPM was affected by a major corruption scandal (*El Tiempo* 2003b). Furthermore, the city suffered a major debt crisis as a result of the construction of its subway system (in the 1980s), which the Colombian central authorities refused to help with (*El Tiempo* 2003c). Both of these factors contributed significantly to the loss of faith in traditional politics, and facilitated the rise of the innovator Fajardo.

Fajardo seized on the crisis in order to implement significant fiscal changes, albeit in a way that signalled powerfully that the new regime would foster transparency and accountability. He began by requesting special powers from the Medellín Municipal Council to change the EPM board, publicly declaring that its members would be selected purely via a meritocratic process (*El Tiempo* 2003d). However, Fajardo also used these special powers to put the EPM's telecommunication activities up for sale in order to balance the organization's books. Although this triggered a huge debate (*El Tiempo* 2005a), Fajardo was able to push the measure through, which brought the EPM back into the black (*El Tiempo* 2005b). Other fiscal innovations brought in by the Fajardo administration included increasing the real estate tax to fund housing projects in El Poblado, Medellín's iconic rich neighbourhood (*El Tiempo* 2004b).

The Cali fiscal trajectory is more tortuous. The first elected mayor of the city, a Conservative party politician called Germán Villegas, did propose an increase in real estate tax, but only for the poorest sectors of the city. Such blatant unfairness generated significant protest, including some from municipal councillors belonging to his party (*El Tiempo* 1991), and contributed to the election of a more independent figure, Rodrigo Guerrero (albeit still on a Conservative party ticket). Guerrero tried to increase and introduce progressive elements in key forms of taxation, including real estate, but faced resistance from entrepreneurs who were well-connected in the Cali political system. Because Guerrero had not been elected as an independent, he ended up beholden to particularist pressures.

Instead of promulgating fiscal reform, the Cali municipal council announced a tax amnesty that cost the city 37 billion pesos (2.9 billion USD) (*El Tiempo* 1995), and also promoted a tax exemption scheme for industrialists who invested in the city. At the same time, there was a steep increase in water and energy tariffs, which punished the poor more than the rich. As the manager of the city's public utilities enterprise, EMCALI, explained: 'it was convenient not to punish the high and high middle classes more than the rest of the population, and it was therefore decided to set a similar (proportionally) increase in the tariff' (*El Tiempo* 1996). The inability to promote a more equitable taxation regime has persisted in Cali. For example, Guerrero's successor, Mauricio Guzmán, was unable to push through a taxation increase, despite threatening to publish a list of rich individuals who opposed the payment of taxes (*El Tiempo* 1997c). The president of the regional industrialists' association publically denounced the 'wave of taxation' that he contended Guzmán was threatening, and argued that instead of taking money away from the entrepreneurs, the municipality needed to become more efficient.[10] Guzmán ended up conceding, just before being jailed on charges of complicity with narco-trafficking.[11]

The subsequent acting mayor, Julio César Martínez, froze the real estate tax, despite the fact the deficitary budgetary situation of the city. This led to the national government intervening and setting strict fiscal objectives for the city's municipal authorities, who had to commit to reporting regularly on tax collection, as well as naming debtors (*El Tiempo* 1997e). In exchange, the central Colombian government promised to partially finance Cali's proposed mass transport system – inspired by the Bogotá plan implemented by Peñalosa. In this way, Cali has seen some policy innovations, but they have been externally imposed. The city's private sector strongly criticized the agreement on several points, including on the grounds that it 'lacked community participation' (*El Tiempo* 1998), and it was notable that all the candidates in the 1997 mayorship campaign tried to attract voters – and campaign contributions – with the promise of a tax freeze. Despite the agreement with the central government, the Cali municipal council subsequently decided to revise the entire collection system for real estate taxes. Several (downwards) tax readjustments took place, and the city ultimately suffered a major fiscal crash at the turn of the century. It had to sign a new agreement with the central government, but on much worse terms, which caused the elimination of several municipal agencies and massive redundancies (*El Tiempo* 2001a). An austerity plan was initiated by mayor John Maro Rodríguez (*El Tiempo* 2001b). His successor, Apolinar Salcedo, actually increased taxation, but also decided to privatize collection, claiming this was part of a 'modernizing' plan. However, the outsourcing of the collection of taxes generated continuous scandals as rich Cali families were able to bribe collectors. One of these scandals ended in Salcedo's impeachment on 8 May 2007, and he was replaced by Ramiro Díaz Tafur, who had until then been the president of the Society of Agriculturalists and Cattle Ranchers of el Valle, a local elite private sector organization.

6 Conclusions

This chapter has explored how and why the policy innovations famously responsible for the Colombian urban 'miracles' were implemented – or not – in the cities of Bogotá, Medellín, and Cali. In particular, we have suggested that policy innovation has certain prerequisites, and cannot be fully understood without taking into account the crucial role of ideas and the ways – and conditions – in which they become a social force. We have particularly highlighted how the post-1991 Colombian political context – where mayors became directly elected and were granted greater powers, and where new media began to play an increasingly important role – facilitated the election of independent candidates who were able to resist becoming beholden to particularistic vested interests. They adopted technocratic, universalistic discourses, focused on security concerns in particular, which were effective as they appealed to a broad swathe of society. This type of discourse became the cement which held together heterogeneous coalitions that allowed large-scale urban transformation, and tamed the opposition of elite vested interests because it presented itself as the basis for solving their (and everyone else's) collective action problems. Crucially, although in many ways the discourse called for significant state-based action, it also sat well with the broader, hegemonic neoliberal discourse.

This approach allowed independent candidates to emerge and successfully neutralize traditional political parties in Bogotá and Medellín, and offer public goods and services, such as improved security, that past governance formulae had been unable to deliver. It was also a good 'signalling' resource which made it possible for voters and key audiences to tell the authentic, genuine innovators apart from the hybrids and imitators. In the case of Cali, such hybrids dominated and were unable to implement meaningful policy innovations, whether purposefully or because they remained beholden to vested interests. At the same time, although citizens and analysts alike concur that Bogotá and Medellín have undergone significant positive transformations during the period under discussion here as a result of the new policy innovations, it can also be argued that that such transformations have not been as universal in scope as the innovators' discourse itself suggests them to be. For example, the United Nations Development Programme's evaluation of Bogotá's fiscal regime reveals that although tax collection has improved substantially, it remains flat – that is to say, the 'commons' resources have increased, but inequality has not shrunk (PNUD 2008). Similarly, the reasons for the improvements in Medellín's security situation remain ambiguous, as the policy innovations associated with the city's 'miracle' also coexisted with a critical restructuring and strategic evolution of major criminal agencies in the city, including in particular the paramilitary and their successors, which changed patterns of violence (although it must be stressed that it would be inaccurate to attribute *all* of Medellín security improvements to this restructuring). In other words, there is still much to be learnt from the Colombian urban 'miracles', particularly – especially? – regarding their limits.

Notes

1. It should be noted that non-neoliberal models have been no more successful in curtailing urban crime, as the Venezuelan experience shows (Caldeira 2000).
2. A similar process also happened more generally in Colombia ten years later (see Gutiérrez 2007).
3. For quantitative evidence, see Gutiérrez (1995); for the positions of the representatives of the private sector, see, for example, the declarations of the Chamber of Commerce in *El Tiempo* (1994c), and the Corona Foundation in *El Tiempo* (1994d).
4. At the same time, many of the self-identified Liberals and Conservatives who supported Mockus did so without relinquishing their self-affiliation. Voters who considered themselves Liberals or Conservatives probably supported their party at the national level, but at the municipal one they placed their bet on the individual able to signal his 'otherness' (see the opinion poll published in *El Tiempo* 1994e).
5. Although we are not aware of any systematic study of the issue, evidence from the opinion polls suggests that PDI/PDA voters were the same who had previously voted for Mockus (twice) and (the reinvented) Peñalosa, rather than the radicalized popular sectors, as is often contended (Gutiérrez 2007). Part of the reason for this, at least with regard to the first of the two PDI/PDA victories, is that the candidate, Luis Eduardo Garzón, was able to present himself as 'different', running a low-budget and idiosyncratic campaign. The second PDI/PDA victory, however, seems to have been due to the fact that the party was identified less as a source of change, and more as the best option to maintain and develop the policies that were associated with the so-called 'miracle' in the city (*El Tiempo* 2007a).
6. This is rather ironic, since many of the key policy ideas that have underpinned the Bogotá and Medellín 'miracles' were actually hatched by individuals working in Cali, including Rodrigo Guerrerro in particular.
7. This was also the case of the Leftist municipal governments in Bogotá (*El Tiempo* 1997b).
8. It is interesting to note that Castro also attempted to appeal directly to public opinion in the form of an open letter published in the media, in which he promised that his reforms would not lead to a 'tributary cascade', and that the 'fiscal sacrifice' would be 'a demonstration of love for the city' (*El Tiempo* 1993b), but that this failed to mobilize support, most likely

because he was associated with traditional politics. Indeed, his bypassing of traditional channels for political horse-trading was likely a further reason why he was repudiated by his political party.

9. Ironically, Bogotá's fiscal passion cooled down somewhat when the left gained power. Despite a very ambitious social programme, Garzón pledged a freeze on taxes, but the citizens apparently did not believe him. An opinion poll concluded that 'what the Bogotanos do not believe [of Garzón's campaign] is his promise of not exacting new taxes...'. When asked if they thought that Garzón would fulfil his promise of not increasing tributes, 19.3 per cent said that they did, and 74.3 per cent said that they did not. Later, the elected mayor recognized that in some areas this promise [of not raising taxes] was not possible (*El Tiempo* 2004c). In the end, Garzón backed away from reducing taxes (Guzmán 2008).
10. There is some evidence that the anti-tax stance of the Cali private sector had broad citizen support. For example, an opinion poll concerning a possible gasoline tax increase found that 79.25 per cent of those interviewed were against it, while only 15.25 per cent supported it (*El Tiempo* 1992b).
11. He was already facing other corruption scandals (*El Tiempo* 1997d).

References

Acero, H., and E. Baracaldo (2007). 'Una Policía Mejor, Una Mejor Seguridad y Convivencia: Un Proyecto Conjunto Entre Autoridades Civiles, Policía y Ciudadanía'. Paper presented at First International Seminar Reforma policial en México y América Latina: principios de un proceso exitoso. 12–13 March. México City.

Auyero, J. (2007). *Routine Politics and Violence in Argentina: The Gray Zone of State*. Cambridge: Cambridge University Press.

Briceño-Leon, R., and V. Zubillaga (2002). 'Violence and globalization in Latin America'. *Current Sociology*, 50: 19–37.

Caldeira, T. (2000). *Cidade de Muros: Crime, Segregação e Cidadania em Sao Paulo*. São Paulo: Editora 34.

Castro, J. (2001). 'Déficit Galopante'. Presentation made to the Foro sobre el Plan de Desarrollo 'Bogotá para vivir todos del mismo lado' organized by the Cámara de Comercio de Bogotá, 23 May, http://www.redbogota.com/univerciudad/bajar-pdf/deficitgalopante.pdf.

Crowley, T.W. (1992). *Guerillas and Revolution in Latin America*. New Jersey: Princeton University Press.

De Ferranti, D., G. Perry, F.H.G. Ferreira, and M. Walton (2003). *Inequality in Latin America and the Caribbean: Breaking with history?* Washington, DC: World Bank.

Delgado Uribe, M. (2007). 'Propuesta Pedagógica Para una Nueva Forma de Hacer Política en el Contexto Colombiano'. Undergraduate thesis, Department of Governance and Political Science, Universidad Mayor del Rosario, Bogotá.

DNP (2005). *Capacidad Fiscal de los Gobiernos Territoriales Colombianos*. Bogotá: DDTS, http://www.dnp.gov.co.

Elster, J. (2007). *Explaining Social Behaviour: More Nuts and Bolts for the Social Sciences*. Cambridge: Cambridge University Press.

Formisano, M. (2002). 'Econometría Especial: Características de la Violencia Homicidas en Bogotá'. CEDE Working Paper 2002–10. Bogotá: CEDE.

Gaitan, L., and A. Parra (2008). 'Políticas de Seguridad y Convivencia Ciudadana. Caracterización del Rediseño del Espacio Público en Bogotá 1993–2007'. Undergraduate thesis, Department of Political Science, Universidad de los Andes, Bogotá.

Gutiérrez, F. (1995). *Curso y discurso del movimiento plebeyo*. Bogotá: IEPRI-Áncora Editores.

Gutiérrez, F. (2007). *Lo Que el Viento se llevó? Los Partidos Políticos y la Democracia en Colombia 1958–2002*. Bogotá: Norma.

Gutiérrez, F., and A.M. Jaramillo (2004). 'Crime, [counter] insurgency and the privatisation of security: the case of Medellín, Colombia'. *Environment and Urbanisation*, 16(2): 1–14.

Gutiérrez, F., M.T. Pinto, J.C. Arenas, T. Guzmán, and M.T. Gutiérrez (2009). 'Politics and security in three colombian cities'. *Crisis States Working Papers*, 44(2). London: CSRC.

Guzmán, T. (2008). 'El Deterioro de los Partidos Políticos en Bogotá Como vía de Transformación de las Élites Políticas en el Concejo entre 1970 y 2000: El Proceso de la "Destrucción Creadora"'. Master's thesis, Instituto de Estudios Politicos (IEPRI), Universidad Nacional de Colombia, Bogotá.

Hall, P. (1997). 'The role of interests, institutions and ideas in the comparative political economy of the industrialized nations'. In M. Lichbach and A. Zuckerman (eds), *Comparative Politics: Rationality, Culture and Structure*. Cambridge: Cambridge University Press: 174–207.

Hoffman, K., and M. Centeno (2003). 'The lopsided continent: inequality in Latin America'. *Annual Review of Sociology*, 29: 363–90.

Lopez Gonzalez, M., and R.J. Mesa Callejas (2008). 'Improved local public finance: the case of the municipality of Medellín, 2002–2005'. *Cuadernos Administrativos*, 21(35): 327–51, http://www.scielo.org.co/scielo.php?script=sci_arttext&pid=S0120-35922008000100014&lng=en&nrm=iso>.

Mockus, A. (1994). 'Anfibios Culturales y Divorcio entre Ley, Moral y Cultura'. *Revista Análisis Político*, 21, http://www.lablaa.org/blaavirtual/revistas/analisispolitico/anfibios.htm.

Mosca, G. (1939). *The Ruling Class*. New York and London: McGraw-Hill Book Company.

Peñalosa, E. (2003). 'La Ciudad y la Igualdad'. *El Malpensante*, 45: 12–34.

PNUD (2008). *Informe de desarrollo humano para Bogotá: Bogotá con desarrollo humano*. Bogotá: PNUD, http://www.pnud.org.co/sitio.shtml?apc=jEa-2 – &x=18684.

Rico, J.M., and L. Chinchilla (2002). *Seguridad Ciudadana en América Latina*. Mexico City: Siglo XXI.

Roberts, K. (1998). *Deepening Democracy? The Modern Left and Social Movements in Chile and Peru*. Palo Alto: Stanford University Press.

Rodgers, D. (2009). 'Slum wars of the 21st century: gangs, *Mano Dura*, and the new geography of conflict in Central America'. *Development and Change*, 40(5): 949–76.

Sánchez, F., S. Espinosa, and Á. Rivas (2003). 'Garrote o Zanahoria? Factores Asociados a la Disminución de la Violencia Homicida y el Crimen en Bogotá, 1993–2002'. *CEDE Working Paper* 2002–27. Bogotá: CEDE.

Vasquez, E. (2001). *Historia de Cali en el Siglo 20: Sociedad, Economía, Cultura y Espacio.* Cali: Universidad del Valle.
Weir, M. (1992). *Politics and Jobs.* Princeton, NJ: Princeton University Press.

Newspaper articles

NB/ All articles online at: http://www.eltiempo.com/archivo/.
El Tiempo (1991). 'Impuestos Injustos y Escándalosos'. 25 November.
El Tiempo (1992a). 'Guerrero: Rojo o Verde'. 25 February.
El Tiempo (1992b). 'Guerrero En Contravía'. 10 December.
El Tiempo (1992c). 'Bogotá: Castro dirá si a la Valorización'. 8 October.
El Tiempo (1993a). 'Una Inversión que no duro un año'. 18 December.
El Tiempo (1993b). 'El Alcalde Justifica la Valorización'. 30 July.
El Tiempo (1994a). 'La Ciudad Desvertebrada'. 23 March.
El Tiempo (1994b). 'Mockus, Rector de Bogotá'. 5 February.
El Tiempo (1994c). 'Primer Reves de Mockus'. 25 November.
El Tiempo (1994d). 'El Fenomeno Mockus'. 3 March.
El Tiempo (1994e). 'Puntean Mockus y Peñalosa'. 2 August.
El Tiempo (1995). 'Amnistía Para Morosos En Cali'. 20 December.
El Tiempo (1996). 'Incrementan las Tarifas de los Teléfonos'. 20 December.
El Tiempo (1997a). 'Luis Perez Gutierrez'. 11 October.
El Tiempo (1997b). 'Que va a Hacer en los Proximos Tres Años'. 9 November.
El Tiempo (1997c). 'Ni Condonación Ni Amnistía en Predial'. 5 March.
El Tiempo (1997d). 'Conmoción En La Torre De La Alcaldía'. 27 August.
El Tiempo (1997e). 'Gobierno Obliga a Cali a Cumplir Meta de Impuestos'. 20 December.
El Tiempo (1998). 'Industriales Critican Plan de Desempeño'. 4 May.
El Tiempo (2001a). 'Aval de $ 650.000 millones para Cali'. 14 June.
El Tiempo (2001b). 'Luna de Hiel a Los Cien Días'. 5 April.
El Tiempo (2002). 'Mockus va por Mas Impuestos'. 14 January.
El Tiempo (2003a). 'Sergio Fajardo en El Tiempo'. 27 October.
El Tiempo (2003b). 'EPM: una Joya Que Pierde Brillo'. 16 November.
El Tiempo (2003c). 'La Ciudad que Recibe Fajardo'. 29 December.
El Tiempo (2003d). 'Cambio de Estilo en Empresa Publicas de Medellín'. 20 December.
El Tiempo (2004a). 'Los Traspiés de Luis Perez'. 8 March.
El Tiempo (2004b). 'Aprobado Pago por El Poblado'. 16 December.
El Tiempo (2004c). 'Garzon, Buena Imagen, Pero Mal en Impuestos'. 10 March.
El Tiempo (2005a). 'EPM Separa Telecomunicaciones del Resto de Negocios'. 24 February.
El Tiempo (2005b). 'Fajardo y Gaviria Consiguieron Escindir a Empresas Publicas'. 29 December.
El Tiempo (2007a). 'Bogota no va por Buen Camino: Peñalosa'. 1 February.
El Tiempo (2007b). 'Juanes Respalda a Alonso Salazar'. 26 September.
El Tiempo (2007c). 'Pagar Impuestos en Bogotá Paga, y Bien'. 8 July.
El Tiempo (2007d). 'Bogotá, Alcaldia, Caos y Gerencia'. 24 October.
El Tiempo (2007e). 'Alonso Recibe Respaldo de las ONG de Medellin'. 17 October.

10

Public–Private Co-operation for Gas Provision in Poor Neighbourhoods of Buenos Aires: Assessing the Impact on Housing Improvements and Health

Cynthia Goytia, Ricardo A. Pasquini, and Pablo Sanguinetti

1 Introduction

Among the interventions aimed at reducing poverty, the improvement of infrastructure is certainly one of the most relevant. For example, the attainment of almost all of the Millennium Development Goals (MDGs) depends, at least in part, on improvements in infrastructure services (Willoughby 2004). The reason for this is the impact of these services upon the quality of life and the sanitary conditions of the population (Amis 2001). Despite the significance of a dwelling's characteristics and infrastructure as crucial factors for the general wellbeing of its inhabitants, little work has been done to assess the causal impact of infrastructure and housing improvement programmes on the formalization, health, and welfare of the very poor.

In this chapter, we examine one particular aspect of housing infrastructure: the impact of the provision of pipelined natural gas services on the health and satisfaction of dwellers in informal settlements. Specifically, we analyse a programme for a network, pipelined gas supply in the Greater Buenos Aires area (GBA) and identify its impact upon the formalization of the dwellings, and the households' happiness and health (flu, fever, respiratory, and gastrointestinal diseases in particular).

The programme *Redes Solidarias* (solidarity networks) was implemented in the locality of Moreno in the GBA area, through a novel institutional project that included strong community participation. A non-governmental organization (NGO), Fundación Pro Vivienda Social (FPVS), in co-operation with the licensee company for the distribution of natural gas services, the local municipality, and neighbourhood organizations, were involved in its implementation. It provided access to the gas network for low-income households living in the informal settlements of a relatively poor neighbourhood in the area called 'Cuartel V'. This area comprises 2.5 square kilometres or 200 blocks, in which 4100 families (approximately 17,000 people) live (Goytia 2009).

In order to identify the causal impact of the intervention, we took advantage of a geographical discontinuity in the programme's allocation. Because of technical constraints, the programme had to be implemented in the group of neighbourhoods that were closer to the existent pipeline, leaving other, similar neighbourhoods for a future stage. The allocation mechanism can be considered exogenous and permits evaluation, avoiding possible self-selection biases. We test the hypothesis that access to a gas programme induces home improvements (such as better quality wall or floor construction), which is related to a forced housing formalization process and other related outcomes such as connection to a water network inside the dwelling. In terms of health indicators, we examine the occurrence of flu, fever, and other respiratory and gastrointestinal diseases.

The contemporary literature on the provision of infrastructure services in Latin America has, in part, been concerned with the competing approaches to service provision that cities have experienced during recent decades. Efficiency concerns prevailed over equity or affordability when the reforms of the 1990s were implemented (Estache and Fay 2007). Central to this debate have been the roles that the state and the private sector should have in delivering infrastructure services (Spiller and Savedoff 1999; Budds and McGranahan 2003; Kessides 2005; and Gilbert 2007, among others). The main arguments that characterize this debate have been caught between the notions of social equity and basic rights to resources (for example, the United Nations declared access to adequate amounts of clean water for personal use to be a human right), to market-based approaches that focus on the financial sustainability of service supply, relying on principles of efficiency and effectiveness (Cook and Kirkpatrick 1988; World Bank 1994). Adding to this controversy, Ostrom (1996) supports the concept of coproduction, which implies that citizens can play an active role in producing public goods and services of consequence to them, exploding potential synergies while dismissing the divide between sectors. The case analysed here presents some evidence in this direction.

It is in relation to basic services that urban inequalities are often most evident. Coverage levels for most infrastructure services have improved only slightly over the last two decades. However, one constant observation valid for many Latin American cities is that the households that lag behind in achieving access to infrastructure services are always poor (Fay and Morrison 2007). There are marked intra-regional disparities. In particular, half the region's poor (around 113 million people, according to World Bank estimates[2004]) live in urban or peri-urban areas, many of them in informally settled areas that lack basic services. For example, in the Metropolitan Region of Buenos Aires (MRBA), some municipalities have almost universal provision of services, whereas in others the deficit is almost absolute, especially with regard to water, sewerage, and natural gas services (Goytia and Lanfranchi 2009). In other words, it is possible to conclude that great imbalances persist and neither the access, nor the quality, is distributed evenly among different income groups of the population (Goytia 2009).

The provision of infrastructure is very important for upgrading and housing improvements. On examining these issues empirically, there was evidence that once the initial infrastructure was installed, particularly water and sewer systems, the more rapidly other improvements followed (Strassman 1984; Hirschman 1984).

Furthermore, access to basic infrastructure services has a direct effect on the economic equation of households, since such services represent a significant portion of their monthly expenses. In particular, families living in informal settlements or peri-urban areas have to pay relatively high prices to purchase low-quality substitutes for these services (Estache et al. 2002; Briceño-Garmendia et al. 2004). Therefore, the provision of infrastructure services may have a very high social return.

The literature examining infrastructure interventions also shows that they produce direct and indirect effects on the physical and mental health of the population, as well as on their welfare (Shaw 2004). For example, the goal of the programme Piso Firme de México was to replace earthen floors with cement ones in low-income dwellings. This intervention had significant effects for children, since their health improved and so did their cognitive development. Adults were happier and their mental health also improved, although there was no change in the household income indicators for the dwellings that were part of the programme (Cattaneo et al. 2007).

In relation to health outcomes, some articles in the literature show that the lack of heating or hot water, the use of certain alternative fuels, the existence of excessive humidity, and insufficient home ventilation are risk factors for the respiratory health of household members (Dasgupta et al. 2004; Duflo et al. 2008). The medical literature, in particular, remarks that the quality of the fuel and the kind of devices used to cook and provide heating inside the dwelling may affect the respiratory health of its inhabitants, especially for children (Triche et al. 2002). In dwellings with building deficiencies and bad ventilation, the frequent use of fuel to cook in the same room that the household members sleep is a risk factor that increases the likelihood of suffering respiratory diseases (D'Souza 1997). The presence of particles in the air within the dwelling generated by domestic combustion processes that use solid fuels, such as biomass or wood-fuel, is associated with the prevalence of respiratory diseases and allergies (EPA 2006; WHO 2002). Similarly, in order to have acceptable levels of air quality within the dwelling, it is necessary to maintain proper ventilation. However, proper ventilation facilities within low-income households mean a rise or fall in room temperature, which generates additional costs in heating or cooling that these households cannot face (Engvall et al. 2003; D'Souza 1997; Cappelletty 1998).

The rest of the chapter is organized as follows. Section 2 describes the programme and its expected effects. Section 3 describes the conditions for a 'natural experiment' that allows an evaluation to be carried out in order to analyse the impact of the programme, as well as describing the other methodological steps. Section 4 shows the results, including the pre-intervention and post-intervention analysis of the data. The chapter ends with our main conclusions.

2 Conceptual framework: the gas programme and its expected effects

Households living in informal neighbourhoods of the MRBA lack access to infrastructure services and formal tenure. These characteristics are typical of this type of neighbourhood in many other Latin American cities. In Buenos Aires, the utilities concession contracts that regulate the provision of pipelined gas services state that the network expansion must be financed by the customers, hence the driving idea behind the programme was to induce households to finance their connection to the gas network with savings generated by substituting the new, lower-cost network gas for tube gas. Households were offered a financing mechanism that charged a monthly amount about equal to the monthly gas tank expenses that households had paid before the provision of the network service. The NGO also made individual micro-credits available, which allowed families to finance other related improvements inside their dwellings (Goytia 2009).

A key dimension of the programme was the induced participation and interaction of the community, which helped to build social capital and trust among its members. With that purpose, the programme fostered the involvement of local social organizations to help promote it. An essential requirement was that over 70 per cent of the households on each block had to express their interest in receiving the service in order for that block to be incorporated into the gas network. This guaranteed the necessary economies of scale to make the scheme profitable for the commercial firm (ibid.). To meet this requirement, many inclusion-related activities took place among neighbours, raising a significant level of social capital between all of the families living on the block and in the neighbourhood.

2.1 Infrastructure improvements

A key aspect of the gas programme was that it induced a process of formalization in the dwellings. We must recall that these dwellings had been progressively constructed over time, without professional help, and depending upon the households' savings (ibid.).

One of the major limitations to the incorporation of households as public service customers was the need for housing formalization, since in many cases dwellings did not meet the minimum habitability requirements (such as dimensions or ventilation) set by municipal ordinances for the authorization of services. In particular, a gas service connection within a dwelling has to comply with strict safety-related measures, which are set by the authority that regulates the services. Therefore, families may have needed to undertake improvements in the infrastructure of their dwellings in order to obtain the gas company's authorization and have access to the gas connection, including the construction of and improvements to walls and floors (ibid.).

The informal tenure of the lot and the lack of finance to afford the improvements necessary for connection constituted further significant constraints. A major achievement of the programme was that it managed to connect to the network households without 'formal' legal rights to their lot, overcoming the standard constraint (namely, the service provision company's requirements) for services connection. We argue that this formalization process has reinforced the (self and third party) perception of ownership, providing new incentives to invest in the improvement of the dwelling.

A third factor that might have induced improvements in the dwellings' infrastructure is related to the savings generated by the programme. Families that were part of the programme saved a significant amount of money on gas consumption. According to FPVS estimates, the cost of gas represented 1.9 per cent of the total household income of families connected to piped gas, whereas for families that were not part of the programme, the cost represented 5.2 per cent. This effect is even more significant in those households that developed a work-related activity in their dwelling. These savings may have been used for improvements.

The availability of hot water in the bathroom might also have been a consequence of the new opportunities offered by the gas connection. In particular, the connection might have made it possible to have hot water inside the house at a low cost, creating an incentive to build water installations for dwellings in neighbourhoods where only a low proportion of the households had running water. Due to the substitution of tube gas for the new low-cost network gas, the savings in fuel expenses allowed for new resources that might have been used to finance indoor water installation in dwellings.

2.2 Disease reduction and satisfaction

The gas programme may have had an impact upon health in several ways. The gas connection allowed families to enjoy several improvements in their standard of living: heating and an enhanced regulation of room temperature, hot water in the kitchen and in the bathroom, improved personal and food hygiene, and faster and better quality of food preparation. All of this is reinforced by the aforementioned improvements in infrastructure. For example, properly finished walls and floors may have also helped to regulate the temperature of houses.

All of these factors have clear implications for the probability of acquiring certain diseases, in particular respiratory and gastrointestinal diseases. As previously mentioned, the substitution of gas for solid fuels to cook or provide heating has a beneficial effect on health thanks to a decreased carbon dioxide concentration. Therefore, a reduction in respiratory diseases and allergies is expected. Diseases in the upper respiratory tract have also been associated with defective housing. Improvements in food hygiene and quality of cooking facilities are also expected to reduce gastrointestinal diseases.

Finally, the programme and its associated improvements in the standard of living may well be related to families' perceived satisfaction regarding their homes.

3 Methodology

A 'natural experiment' created the possibility of evaluating the impact of the gas programme in Moreno. This section describes those characteristics of the programme which allowed the application of an impact evaluation methodology, and then presents the econometric models that were estimated to measure the effects.

3.1 Identification strategy

With the aim of isolating the causality effect of the gas programme from other changes that occurred in the region, the evaluation consists of estimating a counterfactual scenario to reconstruct the hypothetical situation regarding what could have happened with those households if they had not been beneficiaries of the programme. In this vein, the difference between what would have happened and what effectively did happen would be the impact of the gas programme. Although it is impossible to observe the hypothetical situation, it is possible to approximate it by establishing a comparison group (control group) composed of households that did not receive the programme, which should be as similar as possible to the group that benefited from the intervention (treatment group).

The allocation mechanism of the gas programme made it possible to establish a treatment and a control group from neighbourhoods with similar characteristics. For technical reasons related to the geographical location of the main gas pipe, the gas distribution company decided to extend the network to a particular group of neighbourhoods during the first stage.[1] The treatment group was defined as the group of neighbourhoods that were connected in August 2005, while the control group consisted of bordering neighbourhoods which would be connected at a future stage. The mechanism used to select neighbourhoods can be considered exogenous and therefore permits the evaluation, avoiding possible self-selection biases.

3.2 Characteristics of the groups prior to the intervention

In order to corroborate the degree of similarity of the selected groups (treatment and control), we analysed information that was available prior to the intervention. Data from the area was provided by INDEC

(2001). This data is publicly available in census-range level statistics; it allowed the comparison of both groups in terms of several socioeconomic and infrastructure-related variables and tested their differences. In the case of the area under analysis, the data represents approximately 17,000 individuals in the treatment group (4170 dwellings) and 15,100 individuals in the control group (3800 dwellings).

3.3 The issue of partial compliance

Although the programme was open to all of the families living in the region, not all of them wanted to participate. Hence, if the treatment group for the analysis only included the families that entered the programme, the results would potentially reflect self-selection bias since the decision of each household to join could be considered an endogenous component (in other words, self-selection). We dealt with this potential endogeneity in the following way: first, the treatment group was created from a random selection of a sample of households in the region where the programme was offered, whether or not they had joined the programme. For the control group there was, again, a random selection of households from the region where the programme was not offered. Thus, this estimation is based on the *intention-to-treat* sample.

Second, we measured the impact of the programme *per se* by estimating its effect on only those who actually entered it, and instrumented this potentially endogenous variable with the *intention-to-treat* variable. Finally, we can compare the results arising from both specifications (namely, the *intention-to-treat* estimation and the instrumental variable (IV) estimations) and check the consistency of the estimated effects.

3.4 Data

Two surveys were carried out in the neighbourhoods by specialized staff, in November 2006 and November 2007. They collected information about the households' demographic structure, socioeconomic status, expenses and income, housing and infrastructure – detailing the construction materials of the dwelling – health-related indicators, and subjective indicators of satisfaction with their housing and quality of life.

The first survey, carried out in 2006, was delivered to a total of 450 households; 250 households were randomly selected from the group of neighbourhoods where the gas network expansion programme was offered, which included households that became clients of the service as well as those that did not. In order to ensure that the control group sample was representative the 200 households in the neighbourhoods that had not yet benefited from the intervention were surveyed. They were selected at random from amongst those households that declared their intention to access the gas service.[2] Both samples were prepared using administrative records kept by FPVS.

3.5 Econometric model

As suggested in the previous section, some of the expected effects of the programme are: (i) improvements in the infrastructure of the dwelling; (ii) reduction in the occurrence of diseases among family members; (iii) happiness with respect to the dwelling. We obtained a measure of the programme's effects on these potential outcomes (Y) by estimating econometric models of the variables related to each of these outcomes. With regard to materials, finishing, and other infrastructure improvements, we considered: (1) walls with cement plastering; (2) hot water installation; (3) ceramic tiles on the floor. The second group of variables accounts for illnesses that family members had within a period of two months before the survey: (1) flu or fever; (2) respiratory diseases; (3) gastrointestinal diseases. Finally, we evaluated the effects of the programme on the satisfaction of individuals in relation to their households. We used scores of 0–10, as given by the individuals regarding the level of satisfaction they felt with their respective dwellings, as the satisfaction indicator.

Several variables were incorporated as controls on the estimations: socioeconomic variables (per capita family income, head of household's age and level of education, overcrowding, number of children under ten years of age), tenancy-related variables (formal owner of the house and the plot), and others that are unrelated (at least, theoretically speaking) to the expected results of the intervention. As discussed in Section 2, water quality is an important factor in the occurrence of gastrointestinal diseases, and therefore we added a dummy variable for the existence of water connection. Another important factor, as explained in the following section, is the existence of prior differences in the access to water connection between the treatment and the control group. As a consequence, we cannot omit this variable for a proper identification of the causality of the programme. In the case of flu, fever, and respiratory diseases models, the use of heating origins dummy variables were also incorporated.

Summing up, the *intention-to-treat* specification of the econometric model is defined as follows:

$$Y = \alpha + \gamma\, sample\_dummy + \beta X + \varepsilon \quad (1)$$

where Y is one of the potential outcome variables (a dummy variable for all infrastructure-related and health-related variables, and a variable that ranges from 1 to 10 for the level of satisfaction); γ is the parameter of interest, which captures the effect of the programme; *sample_dummy* is the dummy variable with value 1 for observations in the treatment group (that is, households in the region where the programme was offered regardless of their participation, also called *intention-to-treat* variable) and 0 for observations in the control group (that is, households in the region where the programme was not offered); X is the vector of control variables; and ε is the error term.

The estimated models are robust Probit models in the cases of infrastructure- and health-related variables, and an Ordinal Probit for the happiness indicator. For all of these models, we computed average marginal effects and elasticities.

Finally, the treatment on the treated effect (that is, the effect on those who actually got connected) was computed using a standard instrumental variables approach, using the *intention-to-treat* variable (the offer of the programme) as the instrument of those who were connected.

4 Results

4.1 Characteristics of the groups before the intervention (2001)

Table 10.1 presents the pretreatment information from the 2001 Census. The aim of this comparison is to confirm that the main characteristics of the treatment and control groups are similar and, if differences emerge, to properly define the post-intervention comparison. Table 10.1 presents a summary of the results of tests of difference of means calculated on each variable. As can be seen, socioeconomic, housing, and infrastructure service variables are reasonably well-balanced for both groups, displaying no differences in most indicators, and small differences where significant differences emerge. For example, in terms of socioeconomic characteristics, there are no significant differences as regards household welfare, as measured by the Unsatisfied Basic Needs (UBN) indicators (including the housing, sanitary, education, and subsistence characteristics).[3] Again, there are no significant differences in the head of household education level.

Table 10.1 Evaluation of the differences between the treatment and control groups for selected variables (2001 Census)

Variable	Diagnosis*	Mean, %
Socioeconomic characteristics		
Born in Argentina	Higher in treatment group	96 in treatment group,95 in control group
Incomplete primary school	No difference between groups	42
Rate of children aged less than 14 years	No difference between groups	37
Rate of households with UBN	No difference between groups	27
Other goods/labour status		
Computer	No difference between groups	5
Fridge with freezer compartment	No difference between groups	40
Unemployed head of household	Higher in treatment group	24
Characteristics of the dwellings		
Overcrowding in rooms	Higher in treatment group	11 in treatment group,9 in control group
Dwelling and landowners	Higher in treatment group	69 in treatment group,65 in control group
Rate of precarious housing units	No difference between groups	9
Dwellingswith UBN	No difference between groups	10
Rate of dwellings with ceramic floor tiles	Higher in control group	30 in treatment group,32 in control group
Rate of dwellings with plasterwork walls	No difference between groups	57
Infrastructure services		
Connection to a water network	Higher in treatment group	22 in treatment group,6 in control group
Gas cylinder or bottle gas	No difference between groups	90

Notes: The complete output of the difference in means tests is available in Goytia (2009). *A difference between groups is reported when there is a rejection of the equality of means null at one per cent error level.

The difference in the mean values of the variables corresponding to household appliances (refrigerator with freezer, computer) – which we use as another indicator of household income, since the census gives no information about this – is not significant.

The proportion of households with an unemployed head is one per cent; the mean value is 0.24 and 0.17 in the treatment and control group, respectively. Although the difference is small, it suggests greater employment precariousness in the treatment group. As a function of this difference, the incorporation of the variable of per capita income in the regressions shown below might be necessary.[4] Finally, the demographic variables of children under 14 years of age, and the proportion of Argentines, display differences that seem not quite relevant – 0.372 and 0.363 in the first case and 0.958 and 0.947 in the second, for the treatment and control groups, respectively.

In terms of the housing and living conditions variables in general, there do not seem to be important differences except for the connection to water. The variable measuring overcrowding – associated with the number of people per room in the dwelling – shows a slightly higher difference in the treatment group (11 per cent) than the control group (9 per cent). This variable can have a direct incidence on some diseases (especially on respiratory diseases) and as a consequence it should be included as a control in disease model regressions.[5] Another slight difference may also be seen in the proportion of households with formal tenure of the house and the plot, which is higher in the treatment group (68.5 per cent and 65.1 per cent respectively). This characteristic may directly influence some of the result variables analysed later. In particular, the literature on this subject has shown how informality affects investment in home improvements, as noted by Besley (1995), Brasselle et al. (2002), and Field (2005). In particular, this situation would affect the incentive to improve housing and would also have an impact on the estimated health and satisfaction outcomes.

There are no differences in the variable of plaster walls, which is one of the possible programme outcomes that we examine. This data is relevant since it is one of the variables that could be affected by the intervention and could become one of the channels through which housing formalization may affect household health. Instead, the difference in the variable of floor quality is significant (1 per cent), being higher in the control group.

Finally, differences are found in the proportion of dwellings with access to the water network (22 per cent and 6 per cent respectively).[6] The difference in this indicator is largely explained by the existence of one particular neighbourhood within the control group, Alem, which is part of the treatment group where precarious community water and sanitation networks are located. In order to control the impact that the aforementioned difference could have on the variable of access to a water network, we have decided to include this variable as a control in the regressions. At the same time, as a robustness check, the observations from Alem are excluded.[7] Nevertheless, the census data also show that there are no differences in the variable of water of good bacteriological quality. This variable is built by adding the households that get water from a well. This water is located at a considerable depth and has to be extracted with a motorized pump.

4.2 Characteristics of the groups after the intervention (2006–07)

Table 10.2 compares a selection of variables for the treatment and control groups using data obtained in the post-intervention surveys of 2006 and 2007. As in Table 10.1, the summary of mean difference tests between control and treatment groups is presented.

Most socioeconomic variables do not show any significant statistical differences, a result that is consistent with our hypothesis that the intervention had, at the time of the survey, no effect on socioeconomic variables. This is the case for the head of household's educational level; the proportion with completed primary or secondary school is similar on average (61 per cent and 8 per cent respectively). Household income per capita in both groups is also similar (247 pesos on average). Other demographical characteristics such as the number of household members are similar on average. The exception is number of children, which seems to be slightly higher in the control group (0.58 children aged between 0–5 years in the control group compared to 0.3 in the treatment group). In addition, the components of UBN variables do not show differences between groups. The minimum standard of living conditions that are set by this indicator (such as basic sanitary conditions, overcrowding, minimum education level) remain similar between groups.

Summing up, many of the observable characteristics in the treatment and control groups remain similar after the intervention. However, this is not the case with many of the key variables that are related to the aforementioned expected outcomes from the gas programme.

4.3 Impact of the programme on housing improvements

Table 10.3 reports a summary of the econometric results of the impact evaluation. The outcomes examined are listed together with the effect that can be attributed to the gas programme, and the range of effects

Table 10.2 Evaluation of the differences between the treatment and control groups for selected variables: post-treatment survey data (2006–07)

Variable	Diagnosis*	Mean
Socioeconomic characteristics		
Number of household members	No difference between groups	4.8
Head of household age	No difference between groups	47.5
Complete primary school	No difference between groups	0.62
Complete secondary school	No difference between groups	0.08
Total household income per capita	No difference between groups	247.5
Number of children in the house	Higher in control group	0.31 in treatment and 0.58 in control group
aged 0–5		
Number of children in the house	Higher in control group	0.61 in treatment and 1.2 in control group
aged 0–10		
Characteristics of the dwelling		
Age of the house	No difference between groups	21.05
Number of rooms	No difference between groups	2.24
People per room	No difference between groups	2.37
Water origin		
Tube connection	No difference between groups	0.14
Well	No difference between groups	0.75
Other source outside the house		0.11
Basic needs		
Unsatisfied Basic Needs (UBN)	No difference between groups	
UBN people per room	No difference between groups	0.18
UBN house	No difference between groups	0.09
UBN sanitary conditions	No difference between groups	0.02
UBN education	No difference between groups	0.01
UBN survival	No difference between groups	0.18

Notes: The complete output of the difference in means tests is available in Goytia (2009).
*A difference between groups is reported when there is a rejection of the equality of means null at one per cent error level.

Table 10.3 Summary of econometric results: intention-to-treat estimator*

Dependent variable	Sign of the intention-to-treat coefficient	Estimated size of the effect**	Control variables and sign of the coefficient (between brackets)***
Dwelling infrastructure			
Plasterwork walls	Positive	12–15%	Income per capita (positive), age of the head of household (positive)
Ceramic floor tiles	Positive	12–16%	Income per capita (positive)
Hot water in the bathroom	Positive	22–28%	Age of the head of household (positive), head of household with complete secondary school (positive), overcrowding in rooms (negative)
Occurrence of diseases in people			
Fever or flu	Positive	18–45%	Income per capita (negative), overcrowding in rooms (positive)
Respiratory diseases	Negative	4–18%	Income per capita (negative), age of the head of household (negative), number of minors (negative)
Gastrointestinal diseases	Negative	37–130%	
Satisfaction			
Satisfaction with the dwelling (0–10 scale)	Positive	0.26–0.45 points	

Notes: *The complete output of regressions is available in Goytia et al. (2009). **Range of elasticities obtained from the estimation of Probit models. ***Statistically significant variables (one per cent error) that were found in the estimated models.

that was estimated according to the different specifications of the econometric models;[8] finally, a list of the control variables that were found to be statistically significant is detailed. Table 10.4 adds a summary comparison of the results obtained from both the standard estimation of the model and the alternative incorporating instrumental variables.

In the case of infrastructure variables, the results suggest that the gas programme caused an increase in the three variables that were analysed: the proportion of dwellings with plasterwork on the walls, ceramic tiles on the floors, and hot water installation in the bathroom.

In the case of the availability of hot water in the bathroom, an increase of 22 per cent to 28 per cent in the proportion of households with this type of improvement is attributable to the programme.[9] Despite the fact that the actual proportion of dwellings with this kind of connection is small, the effect is still statistically significant. In the case of the proportion of dwellings with plasterwork on the walls, an increase in proportion from 12 per cent to 15 per cent is attributable to the gas programme, whereas an increase from 12 per cent to 16 per cent is found for the proportion of dwellings with ceramic tiles on the floors.

Table 10.4 Summary of the results on the instrumented treatment estimator

	Range of treatment coefficient	**Diagnostic**
Infrastructure improvements		
Plasterworkwalls	0.94–1.07	Robust
Ceramic tiles in floors	0.42	The effect might disappear when incorporating tenure controls
Hot water in the bathroom	0.46–0.64	Robust
Occurrence of diseases		
Cases of flu or fever	–0.55	The effects are stronger when incorporating heating variables
Respiratorydiseases	–0.43	The effects are stronger when incorporating heating variables
Gastrointestinal diseases	–	Not robust. The effects do not appear in some specifications

Notes: The complete output of regressions in available in Goytia et al. (2009). *Range of significant coefficients at one per cent obtained from the specification of treatment model using the intention-to-treat variable as the instrument.

The instrumental variables (IV) estimation of the treatment effect suggests similar conclusions, but with higher estimated coefficients. This finding is quite reasonable since the IV model estimates the effect of the treatment on those actually treated, while the *intention-to-treat* estimator incorporates households that rejected the programme.[10] All of the significant effects are confirmed under the IV model, with the exception of ceramic tiles on the floors, which disappears when incorporating the tenure condition as a control. In other words, the difference in this item that is observed between groups might be due to a higher proportion of households with formal tenure in the treatment group (instead of being a consequence of the programme).

The results on infrastructure seem consistent with our hypothesis that the formalization induced by participation in the programme fostered these kinds of improvements. Also, as explained above, the results may have arisen because of the savings generated by the substitution of the energy source.

Regarding the effects of the programme on health indicators, the results show that the gas programme induced a decrease in both the occurrence of respiratory diseases, flu, and fever as well as in the incidence of gastrointestinal diseases (although this result is less robust). The *intention-to-treat* estimator suggests a decrease of 18 to 45 per cent in the cases of flu or fever cases, and a reduction of 4 to 18 per cent in the cases of respiratory diseases. The IV estimator reports stronger effects, with a decrease of 55 per cent for the flu and fever cases and 43 per cent for respiratory diseases. As for the cases of gastrointestinal diseases, although the highest *intention-to-treat* coefficient was found (the estimates indicate that there was a reduction of between 37 to 100 per cent), the effect seems less robust across specifications since it disappears in the IV treatment estimation.

It is important to bear in mind that the effects of the programme on disease may be a consequence not only of the direct effect of the gas installation – such as better heating, better cooking facilities, and an improvement in air quality – but also of the indirect results that were obtained due to the (measured) improvement in the conditions and infrastructure of the dwelling.

Finally, Table 10.3 shows that the gas programme produced a positive effect on the level of satisfaction as advised by residents with respect to their dwellings. On a scale of 1 to 10, those households in the neighbourhood that benefited from the programme gave a score that was, on average, 0.26 to 0.45 per cent higher than those in the control group. This implies that the gas programme, through the changes that it brought in the dwellings, may have improved the perceptions of the families with regard to their level of satisfaction. The result holds even when controlling for the general level of reported satisfaction of each head of household; in other words, an individual's overall tendency towards optimism or pessimism was considered when evaluating his or her perception with respect to his or her dwelling.

5 Conclusions

As in most developing economies, informal neighbourhoods in the MRBA are affected by a lack of access to public services. The imbalances in the supply of such services cannot be solved by simply extending traditional mechanisms. Informality and low-quality infrastructure in the dwellings are some of the factors that hinder access to services. Access to credit must be provided and legal, logistic, and technical problems must be solved. In line with the concept of coproduction, the programme *Redes Solidarias* tackled these issues by coordinating institutions, generating trust among neighbours, and paving the way for families to become customers of the gas company (Goytia, 2009).

This chapter provides evidence about the importance of infrastructure inputs for achieving some development goals. The evaluation of the programme's impact to date reports effects on several dimensions of the households. Improvements in infrastructure have been found. Strong positive effects are found on the existence of walls with cement plasterwork and also on the installation of hot water in the bathrooms. In the case of ceramic floors, however, results suggest that the effects are less significant.

Some of these improvements in infrastructure may have been related to the process of formalization induced by the gas programme, in particular, the regulations on gas connections. Other improvements – such as the installation of water inside the bathroom – may have been a consequence of the new possibilities that the gas connection offered. The gas programme substituted the purchase of gas in tanks with a lower-cost network gas, generating new resources that allowed the financing – in some cases with micro-credit – of internal water installations and possibly several other infrastructure improvements.

The programme has also been found to generate strong reductions in the frequency of cases of flu, fever, and respiratory diseases. A less significant effect was found for gastrointestinal diseases. Reductions of at least 30 per cent in the probability of falling ill with flu or fever were found, whereas a reduction of at least 14 per cent took place in the case of respiratory diseases. The gas connection allowed families to enjoy several improvements in their standard of living: heating and better regulation of room temperature, hot water in the kitchen and bathroom, improved personal and food hygiene, and faster and better quality food preparation. All of these improvements are theoretically related to a decrease in the risk factors for contracting diseases, and may explain the results.

Finally, these improvements might also be related to effects resulting from the increased level of satisfaction of individuals with respect to their dwelling.

Our results have a number of important policy implications. First, the access to infrastructure services appears to be a relevant component in the formalization of the dwelling, and our results show that several improvements are induced by the connection to the network. These compare favourably to the improvements in wall quality that are reported in empirical studies that estimate the effects of land titling programs (Galiani and Schargrodsky 2010), suggesting that the provision of services can constitute a valuable incentive for the formalization of the dwelling, as the poor invest in improving their dwelling when services are provided.

Second, we provide new evidence that housing and infrastructure are strongly complementary to health. Further studies providing more detailed analysis of the importance of combining direct health interventions with infrastructure provision policies in order to achieve health outcomes (such as the MDGs) are desired.

All of these issues point to some omissions in the academic literature and in policy recommendations which do not consider the potential impact upon wellbeing brought by the physical upgrading of infrastructure and the dwelling., It would be interesting, therefore, to complement this study with an assessment of the long-term quality of life effects, whilst including other related effects such as labour and income-generating activities which might be enhanced by having an improved source of energy in the dwelling.

Notes

We want to give special thanks to participants at the UNU-WIDER conference in Buenos Aires (May 2009) for their comments.

1. The additional cost of installation that might be necessary for the expansion of the network, if crossing through an inter-municipal road, was considered. In particular, the temporary closing of roads and the effect that this would have on traffic in the region was evaluated. The decision was made to start the first

stage of the gas network expansion programme in the area that was closer to the trunk network. The second stage of the programme, currently underway, has expanded the network to other neighbourhoods (Goytia 2009).

2. As is usual in this kind of survey, it was quite difficult to obtain answers from households in the control group that did not have any interest in joining the programme in the future. Although this fact implies a certain self-selection bias in the programme's estimated results, this bias would tend to underestimate the real effect of the programme on those treated, and therefore does not represent a serious problem for the purpose of measuring whether there was an impact on those treated.
3. According to the National Statistics Institute (INDEC), UBN is a quality of life indicator. Households are considered to have UBN when reporting more than three people per room, an inappropriate type of dwelling, lack of bathroom with a water tank, children of school age (6 to 13 years of age) who do not go to school, or an adult who has not completed secondary education.
4. Nevertheless, there are no significant differences in the per capita income between the households in the treatment group and the control group during 2006, as it will be shown.
5. Nonetheless, notice that the omission of this variable would tend to underestimate the impact of the programme.
6. It is important to clarify that the classification of the census for such a variable does not distinguish the kind of network to which each and every house is connected. The variable measures the way in which the dwelling receives the water without making any distinction between the quality and the type of network. The households in these neighbourhoods receive water either from pipes coming from community networks without any intervention from a purifying plant, from a connection to a public tap made by the neighbours, or from their land.
7. These results are not included here, but are available upon request.
8. See Goytia (2009) for the complete regressions output.
9. According to the *intention-to-treat* effect.
10. See Section 3 Methodological above.

References

Amis, P. (2001). 'Rethinking UK aid in urban india: reflections on an impact assessment study of slum improvement projects', *Environment and Urbanization*, 13(1): 101–13.

Besley, T. (1995). 'Property rights and investments incentives: theory and evidence from Ghana', *Journal of Political Economy*, 103: 903–37.

Brasselle, A.-S., F. Gaspart, and J.-P. Platteau (2002). 'Land tenure security and investment incentives: puzzling evidence from Burkina Faso', *Journal of Development Economics*, 67(2): 373–418.

Briceño-Garmendia, C., A. Estache, and N. Shafik (2004). 'Infrastructure services in developing countries: access, quality, costs and policy reform'. *Working Paper* 3468. Washington, DC: World Bank.

Budds, J., and G. McGranahan (2003). 'Are the debates on water privatization missing the point? experiences from Africa, Asia and Latin America'. *Environment and Urbanization*, 15(2): 87–113.

Cappelletty, D. (1998). 'Microbiology of bacterial respiratory infections', *Pediatric Infectious Disease Journal*, 17: 55–61.

Cattaneo, D., S. Galiani, P. Gertler, and R. Martinez (2007). 'Housing, health and happiness'. *World Bank Policy Research Working Paper* 4214. Washington DC: World Bank.

Cook P., and C. Kirkpatrick (1988). *Privatisation in Less Developed Countries*. Hemel Hempstead: Harvester Wheatsheaf.

Dasgupta, S., M. Huq, M. Khaliquzzaman, K. Pandey, and D. Wheeler (2004). 'Who suffers from indoor air pollution? evidence from Bangladesh'. *World Bank Policy Research Paper* 3428. Washington DC: World Bank.

D'Souza, R. (1997). 'Housing and environmental factors and their effects on the health of children in the slums of Karachi, Pakistan'. *Journal of Biosocial Science*, 29: 271–81.

Duflo, E., M. Greenstone, and R. Hanna (2008). *Indoor Air Pollution, Health and Economic Wellbeing*. Abdul Latif Jameel Poverty Action Lab, Cambridge MA: MIT.

Engvall, K., C. Norrby, and D. Norback (2003). 'Ocular, nasal, dermal and respiratory symptoms in relation to heating, ventilation, energy conservation, and reconstruction of older multifamily houses', *Indoor Air*, 13: 206–11.

EPA (Environmental Protection Agency) (2006). 'Health and Environmental Effects of Particulate Matter', US Environmental Protection Agency, available from: http://www.epa.gov/air/particles/actions.html.

Estache, A., and M. Fay (2007) 'Current debates on infrastructure policy'. *Policy Research Working Paper* 4410. Washington DC: The World Bank.

Estache, A., V. Foster, and Q. Wodon (2002). 'Accounting for poverty in infrastructure reform: learning from Latin America's experience'. *Studies in Development Series*, Washington DC: World Bank.

Fay, M., and M. Morrison (2007). *Infrastructure in Latin America and the Caribbean: Recent Developments and Key Challenges*. Washington, DC: World Bank.

Field, E. (2005). 'Property rights and investment in urban slums'. *Journal of the European Economic Association Papers and Proceedings*, 3(2–3): 279–90.

Galiani, S. and E. Schargrodsky (2010). 'Property rights for the poor: effects of land titling'. *Journal of Public Economics*, 94(9–10): 700–29.

Galiani, S, P. Gertler, and E. Schargrodsky (2005). 'Water for life: the impact of the privatization of water services on child mortality'. *Journal of Political Economy*, 113(1): 83–120.

Gilbert A. (2007). 'Water for all: how to combine public management with commercial practice for the benefit of the poor?' *Urban Studies*, 44(8): 1559–79.

Goytia, C. (2009). 'Issues about formalization in informal settlements of Buenos Aires : legality, services and investment'. Unpublished mimeo.

Goytia C., and G. Lanfranchi (2009). 'Informal neighborhoods in Buenos Aires metropolitan region: understanding the effects of land regulation on the welfare of the poor'. In S.V. Lall, M. Freire, B. Yuen, R. Rajack, and J.-J. Helluin (eds), *Urban Land Markets Improving Land Management for Successful Urbanization*. Springer : XXXVII.

Goytia C., R. Pasquini, and P. Sanguinetti (2009). 'Public-Private Co-operation for Gas Provision in Poor Neighbourhoods of Buenos Aires: Institutional Framework and Impacts', mimeo.

Hirschman, A. (1984). *Getting Ahead Collectively: Grassroots Experiences in Latin America*. New York: Pergamon Press.

INDEC (Instituto Nacional de Estadísticas y Censos [National Institute of Statistics and Census of Argentina]) (2001). *National Population Household and Housing Census, year 2001.*

Kessides, I.N. (2005). 'Infrastructure privatization and regulation: promises and perils'. *World Bank Research Observer*, 20(1): 81–108. Oxford University Press.

Ostrom, E. (1996). 'Crossing the great divide: coproduction, synergy, and development'. *World Development*, 24(6): 1073–87.

Shaw, M. (2004). 'Housing and public health'. *Annual Reviews of Public Health*, 25: 8.1–8.22.

Spiller, P.T., and W.D. Savedoff (1999). 'Government opportunism and the provision of water'. In W.D. Savedof, and P.T. Spiller (eds), *Spilled water: Institutional Commitment in the Provision of Water Services*. Washington, D C: Inter-American Development Bank.

Strassman, W.P. (1984). 'The timing of urban infrastructure and housing improvements by owner occupants', *World Development*, 12(7): 743–53.

Triche, E., K. Belanger, W. Beckett, M. Bracken, T. Holford, J. Gent, T. Jankum, J. McSharry, and B. Leaderer (2002). 'Infant respiratory symptoms associated with indoor heating sources', *American Journal of Respiratory and Critical Care Medicine*, 166: 1105–11.

Willoughby C. (2004). 'How Important Is Infrastructure for Achieving Pro-Poor Growth?' DAC Network on Poverty Reduction Global Picture for Infrastructure and Pro-Poor Growth Paris, 29–30 March 2004. OECD/DFID.

World Bank (1994). 'Infrastructure: Achievements, Challenges, and Opportunities'. In *World Development Report 1994: Infrastructure for Development*. Washington, DC: The World Bank: 13–22.

World Bank (2004). *World Development Report 2004: Making Services Work for Poor People*. Washington, DC: World Bank.

WHO (World Health Organization) (2002). 'Addressing the Links between Indoor Air Pollution, Household Energy and Human Health,' Washington, DC: WHO-USAID.

11
A New Way of Monitoring the Quality of Urban Life in Latin America

Eduardo Lora and Andrew Powell

1 Introduction

Quality of life rankings across major cities frequently attract a great deal of global press. The often-quoted Mercer (2010) ranking currently ranks Vienna as the city with the highest quality of life of the 221 cities covered, with Zurich and Geneva not far behind. The declared intention of the Mercer ranking is to 'help governments and major companies place employees on international assignments'. However, the factors that are important for international executives are quite different to those that are of importance to residents. In Europe the Urban Audit system of Eurostats monitors the quality of life in 357 cities with more than 300 indicators more aligned to residents' likes and dislikes. This system has the explicit (and ambitious) intention to shed light on 'most aspects of quality of life, e.g., demography, housing, health, crime, labour market, income disparity, local administration, educational qualifications, environment, climate, travel patterns, information society and cultural infrastructure' (Feldman 2008).

Efforts to monitor quality of life in other world regions tend to have less geographic coverage, but are equally ambitious. The Quality of Life Report of New Zealand's Cities, which covers a dozen cities, encompasses 186 individual measures across 11 domain areas (Quality of Life Project 2007). In the developing world, initiatives in several cities of Colombia and Brazil stand out. Though less structured than their counterparts in Europe and New Zealand, some of their monitoring systems have greater flexibility for exploring issues of immediate interest to citizens. In Bogotá, Colombia, the *Cómo Vamos* system, for instance, is a veritable barometer of public opinion on the principal aspects of the city's conditions (Bogotá Cómo Vamos 2009).

These systems for monitoring residents' quality of life share two interesting yet problematic traits. In contrast to the indices for executives or international businesses, which are based exclusively on objective data, systems for monitoring the quality of life of the population at large combine objective information with opinion, albeit in a variety of manners and with varying weights. While the Quality of Life Report of New Zealand's Cities attempts to strike a balance between objective and subjective indicators, *Bogotá Cómo Vamos* has gradually moved from its origin as an opinion survey in the late 1990s to a mix of subjective and objective indicators. A remarkable feature of both, however, is the lack of interconnection between the objective and subjective indicators. In the New Zealand system, for instance, the most comprehensive measures of subjective wellbeing are reported as part of the health indicators, with no attempt to understand their relationship with the objective indicators in that domain or others. The same concerns apply to other systems that mix objective and subjective indicators (Santons and Martins 2007). It is hard to argue that the quality of urban life can be satisfactorily monitored with the exclusive use of either objective or subjective indicators. Many important aspects of people's lives do not lend themselves to objective measurement, such as the beauty (or lack thereof) of the urban environment, feelings of insecurity, or the quality of relations between neighbours. However subjective measures may also be misleading, due to lack of public information, cultural biases, habituation, or aspiration factors.

Partially for these reasons, international monitoring systems (including Eurostats' Urban Audit) avoid subjective variables as much as possible since they limit international comparability. This limitation, though, amounts to throwing out the baby with the bathwater. An alternative solution is to understand the relationship between objective and subjective indicators and exploit it in a complementary manner so as to enrich the interpretation of both.

A second problematic feature is the inclusion of a large number of topics. Since the very essence of urban life is the meeting of diverse individuals who undertake a variety of activities, and possibly have greatly differing interests and tastes, it may seem necessary for a monitoring system to cover many dimensions of a city's services and amenities and the way in which residents utilize and value them. While the European Urban Audit has more than 300 indicators which address the interests of many different users, that very breadth may hinder rather than facilitate the policy-making process because it does not provide any ranking of needs or priorities. Moreover, the development of a universal set of indicators that would facilitate national or even world-wide comparisons among cities is a futile undertaking: huge differences exist in geographical, economic, and socio-cultural contexts, and many aspects of quality of life are qualitative in nature. For instance, while social ills such as inequality, exclusion, or violence may be considered detrimental to quality of life, it is in no way obvious how they should be measured and weighted in the construction of a quality of life index, taking into account that the impact of these problems on wellbeing may differ widely across cultures.[1] One possible solution is to use participatory approaches to elicit residents' degree of concern about different domains or their relative importance (Fahy 2009). An alternative, which is explored in this chapter, is to employ objective and subjective information jointly, using statistical methods to deduce which dimensions and aspects of urban conditions are important, and to what degree, according to two complementary criteria.

In this chapter, we propose a methodology to attempt to resolve the problems resulting from the use of a combination of both objective and subjective information, and we suggest techniques to identify and rank issues of potential importance for urban dwellers. In order to combine objective and subjective information in a coherent manner and focus on the most relevant dimensions of the quality of life in a city or neighbourhood, we attempt to exploit the complementary nature of two approaches: the 'hedonic approach', which employs market prices for housing, and the 'life satisfaction approach', which makes use of information on individuals' subjective wellbeing.

Housing market prices (or rentals) reflect the market's recognition of the characteristics of both the dwelling itself and the neighbourhood where it is located. House prices offer a good summary gauge of the quality of urban life enjoyed by residents, assuming prices reflect all of the characteristics of cities which impact upon people's wellbeing. This so-called 'hedonic approach' has a long tradition in urban economic literature as a method of placing monetary value on the welfare impact of city amenities and public 'goods', as will be discussed below. Implicit values estimated with this approach can then be used to construct price-weighted quality of life (QoL) indices.

An alternative and complementary method is to ask people how satisfied (or happy) they are with their life, their city, or their neighbourhood.[2] A more recent literature surveyed below (in Section 3) has emphasized this utilization of subjective satisfaction or happiness indicators for evaluating wellbeing. As income is included as an explanatory variable in the standard life satisfaction regression, the marginal valuations of other significant variables included in the analysis may be computed. Under certain circumstances this allows for the calculation of an implicit price for various QoL attributes, which again may yield a scheme to weight variables to generate an aggregate QoL index.

As two methodologies can be used to derive a QoL index, it is imperative to understand the relationship between them. It is argued below that they are complementary. Indeed, under some circumstances the most appropriate valuation may be the sum of the prices from each (van Praag and Baarsma 2005). However, comparing the two approaches may also yield interesting information regarding the functioning of housing and land markets.

There is a small but growing literature on estimating other types of QoL indices for Latin American cities. For example, Amorin and Blanco (2003) employed census data for Rio de Janeiro in order to construct a human development index (HDI) for 126 neighbourhoods.[3] Also for Rio de Janeiro, Cavallieri and Lopes (2008) present the estimation of a social development index (SDI), an equally-weighted average of 11 socioeconomic variables normalized between 0 and 1, covering 8045 subcity areas defined by census radiuses.[4] For the case of Colombia, using the data provided by the National Survey on Quality of Life, Acosta, Guerra, and Rivera (2005) construct a city-level indicator based on the methodology proposed by Cortés, Gamboa, and González (1999) which includes sanitary and water services, garbage collection, schooling, overcrowding, and certain housing construction characteristics (the quality of floors and walls). A potential drawback of these analyses, however, is that both the selection of the QoL indicators and the weights employed to construct an index tend to be arbitrary.[5] In the analyses in this chapter, on the other hand, the hedonic and the life satisfaction methodologies each allow the data to determine which indicators should be included and what the weights should be in any QoL index.

The proposed two-pronged methodology has been applied in pilot studies conducted in several Latin American cities: Buenos Aires in Argentina, Bogotá and Medellín in Colombia, San José in Costa Rica, Lima in Peru, and Montevideo in Uruguay.[6] Although these cities cannot be considered as a representative sample of all Latin American urban population centres, they are certainly diverse in terms of their history and socioeconomic characteristics. One key aspect that will differentiate this analysis, in relation to recent academic and policy work, is the level of disaggregation. Here, the objective is to consider a within-city analysis, thus many of the QoL indicators that are analysed are computed at the neighbourhood level. In some cases these sub-city areas represent districts or localities within large urban agglomerations; in other cases they refer to census tracts. This level of disaggregation allows us to gauge the extent to which QoL indicators vary across the city space and so consider whether differences in this indicator across households display some spatial pattern.

The rest of this chapter is organized as follows. In the Section 2 the hedonic price approach is discussed and the results of its application to the selected cities are summarized. In the Section 3, the results from employing the life satisfaction approach are summarized. The Section 4 discusses the relationship between the two approaches. The chapter concludes with a brief discussion of the potential uses of the two-pronged methodology for policy analyses.

2 The hedonic price approach

A traditional method of estimating monetary values for local public 'goods' and neighbourhood amenities is hedonic pricing.[7] Families' location decisions implicitly reflect preferences regarding a set of characteristics pertaining to the house purchased or rented and the neighbourhood where the house is located, as well as the amenities offered in that location. In turn, these preferences will affect property prices in the market for land. A better quality house in a location that offers a wider set of amenities and fewer 'bads' will command a higher price. Given sufficient variation in the house and location combinations present in the market, and assuming that the market functions smoothly, house prices will fully reflect the value of the full set of relevant housing and neighbourhood features and amenities. As examples of this approach, Roback (1982) and Blomquist et al. (1988) use hedonic price methods to estimate the implicit values of local amenities. These valuations can be derived from microeconomic fundamentals considering households' and firms' location decisions as a function of the characteristics of neighbourhoods and houses. Intuitively, implicit prices for various QoL attributes are obtained from a 'spatial equilibrium' where a worker-resident receives an equilibrium wage and pays an equilibrium price for housing services. At this equilibrium, the worker-resident is just as happy living in that location as moving to a different one. For the equilibrium to be sustainable, differences in urban amenities between alternative locations must be compensated by differences in housing prices and wages, for example.[8]

The urban economics literature has usually assumed that city amenities affecting the QoL are reflected not only in land or housing prices, but also in wages. The key assumption is that city borders also place limits on labour markets in the sense that the choice of residence affects access to job opportunities. In contrast, the analysis presented in this chapter focuses on within-city variations in QoL. As it is reasonable to assume that job opportunities do not differ greatly among workers within neighbourhoods, valuations of amenities will be captured for house prices and not for wage differentials. Within-city location is not expected to limit labour opportunities if worker mobility is relatively high. In order to empirically implement this methodology, complementary data on real estate prices are needed. Ideally, for each sub-city area j, information on house prices and characteristics needs to be collected for a representative sample of housing units. Thus the hedonic regression to be estimated would have the following form from Gyourko et al. (1999):

$$\text{Ln}\, p_{ij} = \text{constant} + \gamma_1 H_i + \gamma_2 Z_j + v_{ij},\; v_{ij} = \delta_j + \eta_i \qquad (1)$$

where p_{ij} is the rental price of house i located in neighbourhood j, H_i is a vector of individual house features (number of rooms, quality of construction, square metres, and so forth), Z_j is a vector of neighbourhood j amenities (for example, crime rate, green space), and v_{ij} is the composite error term which is a combination of a neighbourhood-specific error component, δ_j, and a house-specific error component, η_i. The city-specific error component is common to all houses in the neighbourhood and represents systematic uncontrolled differences in amenity characteristics across sub-city areas, but it may also capture systematic uncontrolled differences in *house quality* across neighbourhoods. Either of these two factors would imply that the composite error term across houses within the same sub-city area will be correlated, violating the ordinary least squares (OLS) independence assumption.[9]

The above brief discussion of the hedonic methodology already suggests the rather restrictive assumptions made by this theory. The presumption that the real estate market is in equilibrium implies that households have a great deal of information on buying-selling opportunities in the real estate market, that prices of houses and land adjust rapidly, that transaction and moving costs are low, and that there are no other market restrictions (such as prices controls). Only if these assumptions are met would we expect the impact of public 'goods' or 'bads' to be fully reflected in housing rents and prices.

Beyond the theoretical concerns regarding whether the application of hedonic pricing is justified or not, from the empirical point of view there is the abovementioned problem of unobserved house and neighbourhood characteristics and the consequent bias produced by omitted variables. In the literature this problem is manifested in results that vary across different regression specifications or, occasionally, in variables that even appear to have the wrong sign. The practical relevance of this problem is discussed in the context of the estimation results presented below.

Table 11.1 shows a summary overview of the results of the hedonic regressions. There is considerable variation across the examined urban areas in terms of features that affect house prices. For example, in the San José metropolitan area (Costa Rica), the slope of the land in a neighbourhood and vulnerability to volcanic eruptions negatively affect property values (see Table 11.2). In Montevideo, proximity to the coastal promenade (La Rambla) is an important feature of a neighbourhood, and contributes to the values of the houses. In some cities, proximity to a main avenue or thoroughfare may be considered an asset, whereas in another context it may indicate congestion or pollution. Thus, while in Buenos Aires or in Medellín proximity to a subway station contributes to higher house prices, in Bogotá the distance to the 'Transmilenio' transport system does not affect house prices. In those cities where basic domiciliary services coverage is still deficient in some areas, its influence on house prices can be gauged. The results indicate that access to running water, access to sewage, and access to piped gas are all associated with higher house prices.

Other neighbourhood variables which proved to be important in several of the cities under consideration include proximity to schools, proximity to a park or a green space, and security. Interestingly, in some cities it is noted that variables which relate to segregation by socioeconomic characteristics also have effects on property prices. In the case of Bogotá and Medellín, it has been observed that the proportion of people belonging to the highest socioeconomic stratum and the average level of education by census tract have a significant positive impact on property values (even after controlling for housing and other neighbourhood characteristics). In fact, these two variables explain around 20 per cent of the variance of house prices in Bogotá, and 30 per cent in Medellín.

These quantitative estimates should be considered with caution, as identification problems may produce biases in the results. Segregation is an endogenous response of location decisions to market prices so that

Table 11.1 Significant house and neighbourhood characteristics revealed in house prices, selected cities

Argentina (Buenos Aires)	Colombia (Bogotá)	Colombia (Medellín)	Costa Rica (San José)	Uruguay (Montevideo)
Housing characteristics				
	Number of rooms	Number of rooms	Number of rooms	Number of rooms
Garage	Garden	Number of bathrooms	Number of bathrooms	Number of bathrooms
Quality of construction	Garage	Fixed phone line	Condition of walls	Condition of walls
	Condition of floors	Internet or satellite TV	Condition of floor	Condition of floor
	Size of house	Garage	Condition roof	Condition of roof
Number of bathrooms	Size of plot	Condition of floors	Exclusive bathroom	Exclusive kitchen
		Condition of walls		
Neighbourhood characteristics				
Drug dealing	Homicide rate	Environmental risks	Safety	Access to running water
Public transportation stops	No bus/train terminal	Distance to subway	Slope	Access to sewerage
	Distance to restaurant	Distance to bus terminal	Eruption vulnerability	Access to gas
Distance to subway	Running water	Distance to main/ connector street	Distance to fire departments	Condition of street
	Average education	Running water	Neighbourhood road	Condition of sidewalk
Distance to green space	Education inequality	Pipe gas	Length of primary road	Street lights
	Schools per capita	Average education	Length of secondary road	Access to La Rambla (Ocean Promenade)
	Distance to universities	Distance to university	Distance to parks	
	Lower unemployment	Distance to places of cultural value		

Source: Authors' compilation based on the IDB (2007).

causality could go from prices to the chosen indicator of segregation. At the same time, these neighbourhood-level variables may be capturing other unobservable characteristics of houses and neighbourhoods. Still, at least qualitatively, these results suggest that in fact spatial segregation could result in a negative externality for poor/low educated families living in those city areas. The issue is discussed below when addressing policy implications.

House prices also strongly depend on the characteristics of the particular home in question. Here there is more homogeneity regarding the variables found to be significant. In particular, the number of rooms (total rooms or bedrooms), the number of bathrooms, and the condition of walls, roof, and floors are typically found to be significant. In Buenos Aires, the age of the house is found to be important (with a negative coefficient), and in some cities the presence of a garage and an exclusive kitchen appear to be important.

In the case of Bogotá, around 30 per cent of the variance in housing prices is explained by identified neighbourhood amenities, while 51 per cent of price variation is explained by housing attributes. For Medellín the numbers are 37 per cent and 25 per cent, respectively. In the Metropolitan Area of San José, neighbourhood amenities explain 39 per cent of the variation in rents. Neighbourhood features, while not everything, are definitely significant.

Using the coefficients from the regressions, an implicit price can be estimated (expressed in monthly terms) for different housing and neighbourhood characteristics. These prices indicate that, for example, each degree of slope of land implies a lower housing cost of about 60 cents (US$0.6) per month, whereas an extra unit of safety (measured as reported crimes per week in the neighbourhood) would imply a higher cost for housing of over US$20 per month.[10]

Using these implicit prices, an index of the overall value of neighbourhood characteristics can be generated and, combining this with the average value of housing characteristics, an overall neighbourhood QoL index expressed in monetary terms can be calculated. Employing this technique, it is possible to obtain the average QoL index measured in terms of monthly rental value of houses by district (including both housing and neighbourhood characteristics across 51 districts), which in San José ranges from US$143 to US$370 per month. Table 11.3 lists the top 10 and bottom 10 neighbourhoods in San José according to this measure. The contribution to the rental value of the neighbourhood amenities and other characteristics ranges from –US$67 to US$27; the contribution can take negative values as some neighbourhood

Table 11.2 Hedonic estimation of implicit prices for housing and neighbourhood characteristics, metropolitan area of San José de Costa Rica

Amenities/Disamenities	**Estimated coefficient**	**Implicit price (2000 US$)**
Housing characteristics		
Number of bedrooms	0.55***	30.84
Number of rooms (not bedrooms)	0.33***	18.80
Floor in good condition	0.24***	13.63
Walls in good condition	0.44***	24.82
Walls of cinder blocks	0.82***	45.72
Roof in good condition	0.32***	18.23
Ceiling in good condition	0.43***	24.46
Water source: communal organization	–0.36***	–20.24
Water source: rain	–0.82**	–46.07
Water source: well	0.13	7.44
Water source: river	–0.89***	–49.63
Sewer (septic tank)	–0.10***	–6.03
Sewer (latrine)	–0.21*	–11.72
Sewer (other)	–0.33***	–18.60
No sewer	0.09	5.05
Exclusive bathroom for the household	0.48***	27.07
Electricity not supplied by Instituto Costarricense de Electricidad	–0.24***	–13.66
No electricity supplied	–0.70**	–39.15
Total contribution of housing characteristics (%)	*60.84*	
Neighbourhood characteristics		
Safety index	0.46***	25.82
Degree of slope	–0.01***	–0.57
Precipitation (mm^3)	–0.12**	–6.99

Risk of eruption	–0.13**	–7.52
Distance to national parks (km)	–1.25***	–70.09
Distance to clinics (km)	0.01	0.57
Distance to secondary schools (km)	0.02	1.18
Distance to primary schools (km)	0.00	0.19
Distance to rivers (km)	0.06***	3.42
Distance to fire departments (km)	0.05**	3.14
Closeness to Sabana Park	–0.54***	–30.58
Distance to Peace Park	1.35***	75.56
Length of primary roads (km)	–0.46***	–25.89
Length of secondary roads (km)	0.23***	13.31
Length of urban-neighbourhood roads (km)	0.57***	31.77
Neighbourhood classified as poor	–0.35***	–19.91
Total contribution of neighbourhood characteristics (%)	*39.15*	

Notes: Km = kilometres; mm^3 = cubic millimetres. The price of amenities is measured at mean prices in 2000 US$ (308 colones = 1$).
*Coefficient is statistically significant at the ten per cent level; ** at the five per cent level; *** at the one per cent level; no asterisk means the coefficient is not different from zero with statistical significance.

Source: Hall et al. (2008).

Table 11.3 Ranking of districts by housing and neighbourhood characteristics, using hedonic prices to construct a QoL index, Metropolitan San José, Costa Rica

		Neighbourhood plus housing characteristics		Neighbourhood characteristics		Housing characteristics	
	Neighbourhoods	**Ranking**	**Value (US$)**	**Ranking**	**Value (US$)**	**Ranking**	**Value (US$)**
Top 10	Sánchez	1	370	1	27	1	343
	San Rafael	2	285	2	9	8	275
	Mata Redonda	3	275	10	–23	2	299
	Carmen	4	264	11	–24	3	287
	San Vicente	5	258	8	–20	6	277
	Anselmo Llorente	6	254	13	–28	4	281
	San Isidro	7	245	3	–5	23	250
	San Pedro	8	238	20	–32	10	271
	San Juán	9	237	16	–30	11	267
	Sabanilla	10	237	35	–39	7	276
Bottom 10	Alajuelita	42	172	48	–59	34	230
	Hospital	43	169	40	–42	42	211
	San Jocesito	44	166	46	–54	38	220
	San Felipe	45	165	36	–40	46	205
	Cinco Esquinas	46	164	28	–37	48	200
	Patarrá	47	154	15	–29	51	183
	San Juánde Dios	48	148	50	–62	45	210
	Tirrases	49	144	51	–67	43	211
	Concepción	50	143	49	–61	47	204
	Aserri	51	143	47	–57	49	199

Note: Rounding errors may mean sums are not exact.

Source: Hall et al. (2008).

characteristics, such as the probability of a volcanic eruption, are 'bads' rather than 'goods'. The contribution of housing characteristics ranges from US$183 to US$343, reflecting the differing quality of housing construction across districts in San José.

As expected, wealthier districts such as Sánchez, San Rafael, and San Isidro have relatively high rental values attributable to neighbourhood variables, while poorer areas such as Patarrá, San Juán de Dios, and Tirrases have lower values. Although this is not surprising, it illustrates how neighbourhood characteristics may exacerbate income differentials in terms of the distribution of quality of life. These valuations also provide a guide to where scarce resources might be concentrated, in order to best improve that distribution. However, there are some unexpected results. For example, Mata Redonda ranks very high in housing characteristics (3rd) but rather poorly in neighbourhood amenities (10th), while Patarrá ranks poorly in housing characteristics (47th) but relatively high in neighbourhood amenities (15th). This illustrates that there is indeed considerable space for action. Public policy has contributed to these results and may be used further to enhance the welfare of those living in districts where neighbourhood valuations are currently at the lower end.

A similar exercise of calculating monetary values for neighbourhood amenities using the hedonic method is presented here for Buenos Aires. Table 11.4 ranks the top 10 and the bottom 10 neighbourhoods. Neighbourhood characteristics include the distance to different urban infrastructures such as avenues, schools, parks, freeways, train stations, and subways. The first column of the table represents the estimated value (in 2006 US dollars) of the neighbourhood characteristics for the average house in the indicated city area. The second column indicates the percentage difference in price given by the considered amenities (0.05 means that property values rise by 5 per cent). As seen for some neighbourhoods, even the rather small number of amenities considered imply a significant increase in property values (18 per cent for Chacarita, 17 per cent for Colegiales). At the other extreme, for some other areas the lack of these amenities implies a significant reduction in property prices (e.g. –16 per cent for Vila Real and –12.5 per cent for Villa Riachuelo). Overall, wealthier neighbourhoods (as judged by average price of property per square metre) such as Recoleta and Palermo are included in the top 10, while poorer ones, such as Villa Lugano and Mataderos, in the south of the city, are in the bottom 10. However, there are some relatively expensive neighbourhoods at the bottom of the table (Villa Devoto), and neighbourhoods in the middle of the income distribution

Table 11.4 Using hedonic prices to construct a QoL index, by neighbourhood, City of Buenos Aires

	Neighbourhood	Average index implicit price difference(value, 2006 US$)	Average amenities index (–1 to 1, scale)	Ranking by amenities index (of 47 neighbourhoods)	Average price per square metre (US$)	Ranking by price per square metre (of 47 neighbourhoods)
Top 10	Chacarita	218.7	0.186	1	1,021	14
	Colegiales	214.0	0.166	2	1,174	7
	Puerto Madero	209.2	0.064	18	2,810	1
	San Nicolás	204.2	0.159	3	1,159	8
	Palermo	202.9	0.129	7	1,507	3
	Belgrano	184.7	0.136	5	1,269	5
	Villa Ortuzar	178.0	0.148	4	1,118	9
	Recoleta	158.2	0.105	10	1,453	4
	Retiro	154.3	0.091	14	1,721	2
	Villa Crespo	138.8	0.128	8	1,016	16
Bottom 10	Monte Castro	–42.8	–0.051	36	862	30
	Villa Devoto	–44.5	–0.056	38	960	22
	Villa Soldati	–44.9	–0.070	40	680	45
	Villa Lugano	–46.4	–0.081	43	605	47
	Mataderos	–60.4	–0.082	44	754	42
	Villa Luro	–63.1	–0.079	42	836	36
	Liniers	–63.6	–0.076	41	852	34
	Versalles	–89.0	–0.108	45	873	28
	Villa Riachuelo	–90.0	–0.124	46	760	41
	Villa Real	–126.6	–0.164	47	850	35

Source: Cruces et al. (2008).

(such as Chacarita and Villa Crespo) are among the top 10. With respect to the 2006 average price of real estate in the city of about US$1041 per square metre, the implicit price differences given by this index range from US$219 to –US$126, with an average of US$72.5, or just under seven per cent of the average property value.

The correlation between the price per square metre and the index is positive, but it is far from 1, reflecting a significant but imperfect relationship between the index and property prices (the price/index correlation is 0.43, and the price/rank correlation is 0.71). This imperfect correlation again suggests that there are additional factors that determine real estate prices, other than basic housing features and neighbourhood characteristics.

3 The life satisfaction approach

Life satisfaction (LS) is a relatively new approach to placing a value on public 'goods' (Frey et al. 2004; van Praag and Baarsma 2005). The approach is an important methodological by-product of the new 'happiness science', a term first coined by Clark and Oswald (1994), with predecessors in van Praag (1971) and Easterlin (1974).[11] Happiness economics is diametrically opposed to mainstream neoclassical economics in that it does not assume that individuals make the right decisions based on observed prices to be able to maximize utility, which is assumed unobservable. Happiness economics posits that subjective wellbeing, as reported by individuals in surveys, can serve as an empirically adequate and valid approximation for individual utility. Subjective wellbeing information provides an obvious and straightforward strategy for directly evaluating public 'goods' in utility terms. By measuring the marginal utility of a public 'good' as well as the marginal utility of income, the trade-off between income and public 'goods' (the implicit price) can be calculated.[12]

Examples of this approach include Frey et al. (2004), Winkelman and Winkelman (1998), Di Tella and MacCulloch (1998), and Gardner and Oswald (2001).[13] A recent Inter-American Development Bank book (IDB 2008) which considers many aspects of this approach is devoted to the analysis of life satisfaction in general in Latin America and the Caribbean.

Life satisfaction has certain advantages with respect to hedonic methods. First, as this method is not based on observed behaviour, the underlying assumptions are less restrictive and non-use values can be measured, to some extent. Furthermore, individuals are not asked to value the public 'good' directly, but to evaluate their general subjective satisfaction. Arguably, this is a less cognitively demanding task and also one that does not allow for strategic behaviour – two issues that have been critical problems affecting contingent valuation methods.

LS methods have been successfully applied to value different public 'goods' and policies. For example, the approach has been successfully applied to value environmental externalities: van Praag and Baarsma (2005) analysed the noise nuisance in the area of the Amsterdam Airport. For the case of housing and neighbourhood amenities, Cattaneo et al. (2007) provided evidence that certain basic housing characteristics generate significant improvements in health and self-reported levels of QoL satisfaction even though they are poorly correlated with family income.

In the basic empirical analysis of the LS approach, a micro-econometric happiness function is estimated in which an individual's utility is approximated by self-reported subjective wellbeing. Explanatory variables are his/her income and a vector of socioeconomic variables. In addition, exposure to different neighbourhood and city amenities (or disamenities) could also be included. The typical regression has the following form,

$$LS_{ij} = a + b\,y_{ij} + c\,age_{ij} + d\,age_{ij}^2 + e\,fs_{ij} + g\,H_{ij} + h\,Z_j + v_{ij} \qquad (2)$$

where *y*, *age* and *fs* represent income, age, and family size of individual *i* living in neighbourhood *j*. *H* and *Z* are two vectors of housing and neighbourhood characteristics, respectively. The error term $v_{ij}=n_i+z_j$ is a composite error term which is a combination of a neighbourhood-specific error component (*zj*) and a house-specific error component (n_i). Equation (2) is the typical LS regression with the addition of housing and neighbourhood features. In this regard it is important to mention that empirical applications of this approach have consistently found that income has a positive effect on LS and that age has a negative but decreasing impact (*b* negative and *d* positive).

The estimation of Equation (2) is subject to potential omitted variables bias. In cross-section applications of these regressions, which will be summarized in a later section, estimation can be seriously biased if unobserved factors covariate with life satisfaction and the measured public 'good'. A key issue is then to control for potentially co-linear variables, though the lack of the relevant indicators generally limits this procedure. Alternatively, instruments for the public 'good' variables could be used.

Table 11.5 presents an overview of the results. A set of housing and neighbourhood characteristics are found to be important for each city, with reasonable homogeneity across different urban areas. The table indicates statistically significant coefficients in a regression of life satisfaction on a set of standard variables (income, age, sex, marital status, and so forth) and then a set of house and neighbourhood characteristics.[14]

At least one indicator of the quality of house construction appears as significant in all cases.[15] The particular proxy varies between the quality of floors and the quality of walls, but at least one appears in each case. In the case of the two Colombian cities (Bogotá and Medellín), the number of rooms also appears as significant, although this is not the case in the other cities.

With respect to neighbourhood characteristics, security appears as perhaps *the* most important and consistent issue in Latin American cities, which is consistent with the cross-country findings on city satisfaction reported by Lora et al. (2010: chapter 1). For example, in the case of San José, the presence of gangs negatively affects life satisfaction. In the case of Bogotá, Lima, and Montevideo safety is seen as an important neighbourhood attribute. Access to basic services such as electricity, water and sewage, garbage collection, and telephone services also appear as important neighbourhood characteristics. For Bogotá, inefficiencies in the provision of certain infrastructure services such as energy, garbage collection, and telephone services have a negative and significant impact upon subjective wellbeing.

Note that some neighbourhood characteristics are objective, in the sense that they can be verified by an external observer, such as the presence of garbage in the streets, or the availability of payphones (in general the information on the objective variables was reported by interviewers in this project). However, several subjective neighbourhood characteristics were also included, which were based on residents' own opinions. Among those subjective variables, good neighbours are found to be particularly valuable in Argentina and in Peru, as is the perceived condition of the streets in Peru.

Several neighbourhood characteristics that might be considered important *a priori* do not seem to influence individuals' satisfaction. Perhaps surprisingly, traffic (or congestion) was only significant in the case of Buenos Aires. This is also consistent with the cross-country results reported in Lora et al. (ibid.), where traffic problems did not affect city satisfaction. However, one view is that this is a disamenity that people become used to and over time even become unaware of, and hence do not consider it to be important when asked.

Table 11.5 Overall life satisfaction regressions for the six case cities: summary of results and significant factors

Argentina (Buenos Aires)	**Colombia (Bogotá)**	**Colombia (Medellín)**	**Costa Rica (San José)**	**Peru (Lima)**	**Uruguay (Montevideo)**
Housing characteristics					
Not included (because a two-stage technique was used)	Number of rooms	Number of rooms	Quality of floors	Condition of walls	Quality of walls
	Quality of floors	Satellite TV services			
		Quality of floors			
Neighbourhood characteristics					
Security during the day	Safety in the neighbourhood	Presence of prisons	Safety (presence of gangs)	Safety (robbery)	Safety (vandalism in neighbourhood)
Sidewalk condition when raining	Robbery				
Noise during the day	Drug dealing			Condition of street	Running water
Cultural and sports activities	Recreation/sports centres	Distance to places of cultural value		Trust in neighbours	Street lights
Amount and quality of green areas	Quality of energy services				
	Quality of garbage collection	Distance to main/ connector street			
Traffic	Quality of telephone services				
Evaluation of neighbours					
	Average education in the neighbourhood				
Other controls					
Income	Income	Income	Income	Income	Income
Age	Age	Age	Age	Age	Age
Marital status	Marital status	Marital status	Marital status	Marital status	Marital status
Household size	Family size	Family size	Family size	Family size	Family size
Education	Health variables				

Source: Authors' compilation based on the IDB (2007).

As well as judging which housing and neighbourhood characteristics are particularly important, the life satisfaction approach can also be used to place a value on living in a neighbourhood, or to place a value upon a particular house or neighbourhood characteristic.[16] As income influences life satisfaction along with certain characteristics (say, the condition of streets), the trade-off between greater income and better streets can be used to estimate the value of street improvements. At no point do interviewed people actually express how much they are willing to pay for these characteristics. The life satisfaction approach, then, is particularly useful as it can be used to value amenities that do not yet exist or where there is no market price available.

In order to illustrate how the life satisfaction approach can be used to price or value neighbourhood amenities, Table 11.6 shows the values for those neighbourhood characteristics that turned out to be significant for three neighbourhoods in Buenos Aires.[17] The table not only presents the valuation of individual neighbourhood characteristics and amenities, but also how they are combined into a QoL index. Thus the approach can be used to place a value on a neighbourhood as such, as well as the specific characteristics of those places. For instance, good condition of paved streets has an estimated value of a monthly payment of US$3. In the same way, living near green areas and parks commands a monthly income of around US$2.5. The significant value for the neighbourhood dummies suggest that differences in value go beyond the differences in the set of characteristics considered. In other words, this value is in addition to the measured differences in neighbourhood characteristics as reflected in the regression results. Overall the combination of all these characteristics (those that are observable and those captured by the dummies) imply that people living in Caballito and Palermo enjoy a quality of life that is equivalent to a monthly payment of aroundUS$450 per month, as compared to that of people living in a neighbourhood with the average supply of local public services and amenities.

The life satisfaction approach, then, provides one possible route for ascertaining which amenities are actually considered to be valuable, and also for placing values on those characteristics and monitoring these valuations over time to see if they change depending on socioeconomic developments and changes in the characteristics of cities.

4 The relation between both approaches

As discussed above, the hedonic and life satisfaction approaches can be viewed as complementary. To understand their relationship, consider

Table 11.6 Values of neighbourhood characteristics in selected Buenos Aires neighbourhoods

Monthly income compensation		
Neighbourhood characteristics	**%**	**US$**
Neighbourhood dummies		
Avellaneda	0	0
Caballito	-1.47	-11.66
Palermo	-1.28	-10.15
Neighbourhood characteristics		
Annoying noise during the day	0.38	3.01
Good sidewalk conditions when raining	-0.38	-2.99
Good conditions of pavement/streets	-0.40	-3.13
Cultural and sports activities	-0.22	-1.75
Amount and quality of green areas	-0.32	-2.51
Low traffic in neighbourhood	-0.23	-1.86
Security during the day	-0.45	-3.59
Evaluation of neighbours	-0.64	-5.10
Payphones	-0.35	-2.78
Change from average to own neighbourhood (income variations)		
Neighbourhood	**Neighbourhood QoL Index (US$)**	**Average monthly income (US$)**
Avellaneda	-319	763
Caballito	463	807
Palermo	455	866
San Cristóbal	-558	704

Source: Cruces et al. (2008).

an extreme case where markets function perfectly and where there is ample variation in the housing stock so that there are houses with differing characteristics and that display a wide variation of neighbourhood amenities and disamenities ('bads'). Under these circumstances house prices may reflect all the valuations of the relevant neighbourhood and housing characteristics, and hence suitably specified regressions with house prices as the dependent variable may reveal those valuations.

In the extreme case where markets function perfectly, those same characteristics may not be at all significant in the life satisfaction regressions. The reason for this is that income is already included as one explanatory variable, and as the various characteristics are priced correctly, individuals may already buy them through their market-based housing decisions. This then implies that there is no extra effect to be found by regressing life satisfaction on individual house or neighbourhood characteristics. In essence, the importance of a neighbourhood amenity is already priced and paid for through the value of the house. The interpretation is, then, that not that all of these factors are unimportant, but rather that markets work well and are in equilibrium.

This implies that using the results of the hedonic regressions to calculate prices and using those prices as the weights to develop a QoL index is appropriate. In this case the life satisfaction approach would not be expected to reveal very much. As income is included in the regression and markets are in equilibrium, no additional welfare is obtained from the relevant 'good' (or reduction in welfare from a 'bad'). These factors are therefore already reflected in prices and affect welfare through the income variable.

A more realistic case, however, is that housing markets are not perfect. Information problems and transaction costs may be significant, suggesting that disequilibria may persist in housing markets for a considerable period of time.[18] In this case, it is possible that both the life satisfaction and the hedonic regression approach will find significant effects for a particular characteristic. Moreover some characteristics change quite quickly over time: for example, bus routes change, patterns of crime may shift, and some neighbourhoods become 'gentrified'. Other characteristics, though, are much more permanent. A river or coastal area, for instance, is a fixture, the slope of the land cannot be changed easily, and parks rarely move (although they may be improved). These more structural features (again assuming there is enough variation in the housing stock) may be priced in the cross-section of house prices at a given time, whereas characteristics that shift over time may not be priced appropriately in the snapshot of house prices typically available. This implies that hedonic regressions may reveal some valuations but not others, depending on the nature of the characteristic in question. And where hedonic regressions do reveal values, they may only reveal those valuations imperfectly as the market may be slowly moving towards equilibrium.

Moreover, there may be insufficient variation in a particular characteristic across the housing stock for that characteristic to be priced. For example, if all houses have exactly the same type of roof, then the quality of roofing will not be reflected in house prices. Likewise, if the crime level is constant across neighbourhoods this disamenity will not be priced. In these cases, prices will not reflect the full marginal effect of these characteristics on welfare. Subsequently, hedonic regressions may not find the characteristic significant, whereas these factors may well be picked up by the life satisfaction approach.

These issues are discussed further in van Praag and Baarsma (2005), where it is suggested that the hedonic and the life satisfaction approaches are complements. Indeed, it is shown that, if certain conditions are met, the correct valuation is actually the sum of the coefficients from the two approaches. However, this is only feasible if the same sample and the same variable are included in both analyses, and in general this is not the case. Moreover, it is also of interest to compare the two approaches and to understand what the combination of results implies for how housing markets operate in the region.

Any neighbourhood characteristic (ranging from the quality of sidewalks, safety conditions, or proximity to public transportation routes) can be classified as one of four options, according to their effect or lack of effect on housing costs, and their effect or lack of effect on subjective wellbeing or life satisfaction *beyond what is paid for it.*

As mentioned, the simplest case is that of characteristics affecting housing costs, which do not have an additional effect on life satisfaction. A typical example is access to types of transportation. The housing units that are closest to a subway station or public transportation routes often are worth more than those that are located at a greater distance. That people pay more for the former units implies that proximity to transportation has an impact upon people's quality of life. But it does not *additionally* influence life satisfaction, which suggests its value is its price.

If a city spends more on the delivery of goods and services which influence housing costs, it makes an implicit transfer of wealth to owners of certain homes and not to others. This has two important implications. One is the type of goods or services that can, or perhaps should, be financed through real estate taxes. The other is that, unless goods and services are delivered equally across the board, the poorest residents of beneficiary neighbourhoods will become displaced by those more fortunate people who are willing to pay higher prices for their housing. Thus, these types of 'goods' can be a major cause of urban economic segregation, a problem that in itself is quite severe in many cities of Latin America.

For the reasons mentioned, not all 'goods' and services that people care about are reflected in housing prices. Some contribute to life satisfaction without having any impact upon the housing market. Typical examples are recreational centres and places of cultural interest. Those who have easy access to these places may enjoy a more relaxing lifestyle and lead more satisfactory lives, perhaps because sports and culture contribute to health, intellectual enrichment, and socialization. Since they do not contribute to inflating the prices of nearby housing it is not feasible or desirable to finance them with property taxes, but at the same time it should be noted that they do not exacerbate urban social segregation. On the contrary, the areas around these facilities may attract people from diverse socioeconomic backgrounds who appreciate health and culture, thus contributing to the diversity and vitality of the beneficiary zones. Since people appreciate investments of this type but do not pay for them, it is hardly surprising that they are an effective instrument for politicians seeking to increase their popularity and garner votes.

Some neighbourhood characteristics are reflected partially in housing costs and partially in life satisfaction. Safety is a common case in point, as already seen. The implication of improving safety or security conditions is that, although some residents may be pushed out, the effect is quite limited, given that the benefit in subjective perceptions will be far greater than the costs for the increase in security.

Finally, it is important to bear in mind that there are 'goods' and services which, even though they may be potentially important factors for quality of life, are not reflected in the costs of housing or in life satisfaction, as reported by individual survey respondents. This can occur for purely statistical reasons (for example, because the data on housing costs and life satisfaction are not sufficiently precise to take account of their impact, or because the problem is common to every city or group of neighbourhoods under consideration, such that the effect tends to be the same for the vast majority of homes and persons, as, for example, with the issue of air quality).[19] But this may also occur with problems which people are largely unaware of, or to which they are excessively accustomed. A potential example is poor citizen culture where there is a pervasive absence of respect for norms and standards (zones where parking is permitted, respect for pedestrians, facilities for persons with disabilities, cleanliness of public areas, and so forth). Another example is that of moderate traffic problems. It is important to know which of these are characteristic of particular neighbourhoods or cities, because their solution will not be easily financed, nor will it reflect recognition for local government efforts, unless a campaign is first carried out to raise awareness of the problem and its implications.

5 The monitoring system and public decisions

The monitoring system described here facilitates public decision-making in many ways. It allows public officials to know what city attributes individuals value the most and which problems require most urgent amendment. Ultimately it provides a methodology for officials to place a monetary value on city characteristics. Combined with cost information, this facilitates planning and investment decisions. These characteristics may range from physical amenities to issues such as pollution or crime. The methodology can be used to develop a weighting system which can then be employed to calculate overall quality of life indices for different neighbourhoods or other city areas. These indices then allow for a comparison of neighbourhoods or population groups, and may reveal where interventions to improve wellbeing are most urgently required.

Regular surveys can reveal how certain interventions affect life satisfaction over time and gauge how city officials are responding to those demands revealed by published survey results. Moreover, monitoring systems across neighbourhoods can generate a type of 'yardstick competition' among officials to increase wellbeing within their neighbourhood or municipality. A further interesting aspect of the monitoring methodology proposed here is that it can be used to promote dialogue between public officials and the city public, and enhance participation in decision-making. In many cases, the process of decision-making and ensuring adequate consultation is as important as the final decision itself. A well-functioning monitoring system can be used to request opinions on particular issues faced by communities and to enhance participation in critical decisions.

The methodology proposed here may also allow officials to assess how investments for improvements to city wellbeing may be appropriately financed. Investments to improve characteristics that are fully valued through house prices (and are not found to be significant in life satisfaction regressions) may be recouped through property taxes from those houses which will experience an increase in value as a result. Other improvements to city wellbeing that are not revealed through enhanced house prices would have to be financed through more general taxation.

For local authorities and for citizens, one attractive feature of the proposed system of monitoring is that it can be employed on a regular basis to gauge the progress of the city and its neighbourhoods. Over time, this monitoring system makes clear whether enhancements in specific aspects of the city are important to people. It also helps to reveal which efforts by builders, on the one hand, and by local authorities, on the other, are concentrated more in some neighbourhoods, or among certain socioeconomic groups, than in others. If subjective information is collected regarding people's satisfaction with specific aspects of their cities, it will be possible to assess people's perceptions of the severity of problems in accordance with objective indicators, and whether the gaps between perceptions and reality differ in different zones of the city, especially between high-income and low-income areas. Since valuations are based on regressions by city, this method does not permit comparison of the quality of life of different cities nor, consequently, can it provide city rankings.

A book recently published by the World Bank and the IDB[20] (in which the application of this methodology is presented in greater detail) discusses additional aspects regarding how this type of inquiry should be carried out, and how a system to monitor the quality of urban life – one that is easy to operate at a reasonable cost on the basis of solid conceptual foundations – can be carried out in practice. This is the ideal of many scholars and observers of urban issues, and its application in reality may not be too far off in the future. A good monitoring system should enable local governments, analysts of urban problems, and local communities to engage in informed debate over the problems of cities and their possible solutions.

Notes

The authors gratefully acknowledge comments made by Vicente Fretes, Rita Funaro, Carlos Alberto Medina, an anonymous reviewer, and the organizers and participants of the UNU-WIDER Project Workshop 'Beyond the Tipping Point: Latin American Development in an Urban World', held in Buenos Aires, Argentina, 22–24 May 2009.

1. For instance, Alesina et al. (2001) have argued that Americans are more tolerant of inequality than Europeans because the expectations of social mobility are higher among the former. Among Latin American countries, public concern about violence is highest in some of the countries with the lowest homicide rates, such as Uruguay, and lowest in countries where street crime is more rampant and homicide rates higher, such as some of the Central American countries (IDB 2008: 226–8).
2. This question can also be applied to a specific dimension of life satisfaction, such as how satisfied an individual is with their house.
3. The human development index (HDI) is a welfare measure that combines three indicators: (i) longevity as measured by life expectancy at birth; (ii) educational attainment, measured as a weighted average of (a) adult literacy rate with a two-third weight, and (b) combined primary and secondary

gross enrolment rates with a one-third weight; and (iii) standard of living as measured by income per capita.

4. The 11 indicators are: access to a water network within the house; access to sewage services; proper waste disposal collection; average size of household; number of bathrooms per house; percentage of illiteracy among household members older than 15 years; percentage of heads of household with less than 4 years of school; percentage of heads of household with 15 or more years of schooling; average income of heads of household (in terms of minimum wages); percentage of heads of household with income up to two minimum wages; percentage of heads of household with income of ten or more minimum wages.
5. An exception is Acosta et al. (2005). While the authors select the indicators arbitrarily, they determine the weights across nine regions of Colombia using a principal component analysis.
6. The project also included La Paz and Santa Cruz in Bolivia, but due to substantial methodological differences the results are not considered here.
7. Pioneering work using hedonic methods to evaluate, for example, the impact of air pollution can be found in Ridker (1967) and Ridker and Henning (1967). Chay and Greenstone (2005) provide a more updated treatment of the same issue, taking into account identification problems. Another area where hedonic methods have been widely used is to estimate the value of school quality. Early work for the United States is presented in Kain and Quigley (1975) and Li and Brown (1980). See Black (1999), Clapp and Ross (2002), and Bayer et al. (2003) for more recent estimations.
8. For a description of the microeconomic fundamentals behind hedonic pricing of quality of life indicators, see Gyourko et al. (1999).
9. In particular it will imply a downwards bias to OLS-based standard errors (Moulton 1986). Thus the potential problem of the presence of group effects needs to be addressed by correcting the standard error by clustering or running a random effect E estimation (assuming city fixed effects are not correlated with any of the Z variables). Of course this problem will be minimized the better the data on individual housing characteristics and also the more data we have for neighbourhood-level QoL attributes.
10. Housing costs refers to 'equivalent rents', which is either the rent itself or a calculation of the opportunity cost of inhabiting the self-owned house (as estimated, albeit somewhat subjectively, by the owner). Any differences between renters and owners in relation to their preferences are ignored in this analysis.
11. Useful surveys include Layard (2005), Frey (2008), van Praag and Ferrer-i-Carbonell (2008), and Graham (2010).
12. As indicated in Frey et al. (2004), measures of self- reported subject wellbeing passed a series of validation exercises in the sense that they reflect objective circumstances affecting individuals' wellbeing. Another critical assumption made by this approach, which makes it possible to identify the impact on welfare of public goods, is that utility is cardinal and interpersonally comparable. This assumption, though problematic on theoretical grounds, proved to be less problematic empirically. For example, Frey and Stutzer (2002) report very similar quantitative results in micro econometric estimations of happiness function using ordinal and cardinal measures of satisfaction.

13. For application to other economic issues like the costs of unemployment, the inflation-unemployment trade-off, macro volatility, and inequality see, respectively, Clark and Oswald (1994), Di Tella et al. (2001), Wolfers (2002), and Alesina et al. (2001).
14. Here, the distinction is somewhat artificial between what is considered a house characteristic and what is considered a neighbourhood characteristic, as the data are at the level of each household. In practice the distinction may be drawn, given the relative variation across individual houses in a sub-neighbourhood. For example in a (small) sub-neighbourhood most houses will have or will not have access to water, hence this is considered as a neighbourhood characteristic here.
15. The Argentina study adopted a slightly different methodology where housing satisfaction was included in the regression and so individual housing characteristics were not included. However, a second stage regression was performed to explain housing satisfaction and here too the quality of house construction was found to be a significant variable.
16. Lora et al. (2010: chapter 3) provide a description of the theory and applications of these techniques in practice. See also Frey et al. (2004) and van Praag and Ferrer-i-Carbonell (2008).
17. These valuations stem from a two-stage technique (developed by van Praag et al. 2003) where, in the first step, overall life satisfaction is regressed on income and a set of domains (including satisfaction with the neighbourhood), and then, in the second step, neighbourhood satisfaction is regressed on a set of more objective neighbourhood characteristics. The coefficient on income in the first regression and the coefficients on neighbourhood satisfaction and the coefficients in the second step are then combined to find the trade-off between income and, say, improved security during the day. This trade-off suggests how much someone would be willing to pay to obtain a little more security and hence can be interpreted as the price of additional security.
18. For example, because of imperfect information with respect to certain features like crime, which cannot be associated easily with a specific location due to its transitory nature.
19. Another possible statistical reason is that a neighbourhood characteristic, such as safety, is so closely correlated to a separate trait, such as the condition of public zones, that it is not statistically possible to disaggregate the two effects.
20. Lora et al. (2010).

References

Acosta, O., J.A. Guerra, and D. Rivera (2005). 'Acceso de los Hogares a los Principales Servicios Públicos y Sociales y Percepciones de Calidad sobre estos Servicios'. Serie Documentos de Trabajo 76. Bogotá, Colombia: Colegio Mayor de Nuestra Señora del Rosario.

Alesina, A., R. Di Tella, and R. MacCulloch (2001). 'Inequality and happiness: are Europeans and Americans different?'. *NBER Working Papers*, 8198.

Amorin, É., and M. Blanco (2003). 'O Indice do Desenvolvimento Humano (IDH) na Cidade do Rio de Janeiro'. Rio de Janeiro: Coleçao Estudos Da Cidade. Prefeitura Da Cidade do Rio de Janeiro.

Bayer, P., R. McMillan, and F. Ferreira (2003). 'A unified framework for measuring preferences for schools and neighbourhoods'. *Economic Growth Center Discussion Papers*, 872. New Haven: Yale University.

Black, S.E. (1999). 'Do better schools matter? parental valuation of elementary education'. *Quarterly Journal of Economics*, 114(2), 577–99.

Blomquist, G., M. Berger, and J. Hoehn (1988). 'New estimates of quality of life in urban areas'. *American Economic Review*, 78(1): 89–107.

Bogotá Cómo Vamos (2009). *Bogotá Cómo Vamos*. Available at: www.bogotacomovamos.org/scripts/home.php.

Cattaneo, M., S. Galiani, P. Gertler, S. Martínez, and R. Titiunik (2007). 'Housing, health, and happiness'. *WB Policy Research Working Papers*, 4214. Washington, DC: World Bank.

Cavallieri, F., and G. Lopes (2008). *Índice de Desenvolvimento Social*. Washington, DC: Inter-American Development Bank.

Chay, K.Y., and M. Greenstone (2005). 'Does air quality matter? evidence from the housing market'. *Journal of Political Economy*, 113(2): 376–424.

Clapp, J., and S. Ross (2002). 'Schools and housing markets: an examination of school segregation and performance in connecticut'. *Economic Working Papers*, 200208.

Clark, A.E. and A.J. Oswald (1994). 'Unhappiness and unemployment'. *Economic Journal*, 104: 648–59.

Cortés, D., L.F. Gamboa, and J.I. González (1999). 'ICV: Hacia una Medida Estándar de Vida'. *Coyuntura Social*, 159–80.

Cruces, G., A. Ham, and M. Tetaz (2008). 'Quality of Life in Buenos Aires Neighbourhoods: Hedonic Price Regressions and the Life Satisfaction Approach'. Washington, DC: Latin American and Caribbean Research Network, Inter-American Development Bank and Center for the Study of Distribution, Labor and Social Affairs (CEDLAS). Unpublished document.

Di Tella, R., and R. MacCulloch (1998). 'Partisan Social Happiness'. Cambridge, MA. Mimeo.

Di Tella, R., R.J. MacCulloch, and A.J. Oswald (2001). 'Preferences over inflation and unemployment: evidence from surveys of happiness'. *The American Economic Review*, 91(1): 335–41.

Easterlin, R.A. (1974). 'Does economic growth improve the human lot? Some empirical evidence'. In P.A. Daid and M.V. Reder (eds), *Nations and Households in Economic Growth: Essays in Honor of Moses Abramowitz*. New York: Academic Press.

Fahy, F. (2009). Environmental Protection Agency Publications and Reports. Washington, DC: Environmental Protection Agency. Available at: www.epa.ie/downloads/pubs/research/econ/galway21_fahy_guide.pdf.

Feldman, B. (2008). 'The Urban Audit – Measuring the Quality of Life in European Cities'. Eurostat, Statistics in Focus. Available at: www.epp.eurostat.ec.europa.eu/ cache/ITY_OFFPUB/KS-SF-08–082/EN/KS-SF-08–082-EN.PDF.

Frey, B. (2008). *Happiness: A Revolution in Economics*. Cambridge, MA and London: The MIT Press.

Frey, B., S. Luechinger, and A. Stutzer (2004). 'Valuing public goods: the life satisfaction approach'. *CESifo Working Papers*, 1158. Munich: CESifo.

Frey, B., and A. Stutzer (2002). *Happiness and Economics: How the Economy and Institutions Affect Human Wellbeing*. Princeton: Princeton University Press.

Gardner, J., and A.J. Oswald (2001). 'Does money buy happiness? a longitudinal study using data on wind falls'. Coventry: University of Warwick. Unpublished manuscript.

Graham, C. (2010). *Happiness around the World. The Paradox of Happy Peasants and Miserable Millionaires*. Oxford: Oxford University Press.

Gyourko, J., P. Linneman, and S. Wachter (1999). 'Analysing the relationships among race, wealth and home ownership in America'. *Journal of Housing Economics*, 8(2): 63–89.

Hall, L.J., R. Madrigal, and J. Robalino (2008). 'Quality of Life in Urban Neighbourhoods in Costa Rica'. Washington, DC: Latin American and Caribbean Research Network, Inter-American Development Bank and Centro Agronómico Tropical de Investigación y Enseñanza (CATIE). Unpublished document.

IDB (Inter-American Development Bank) (2007). 'Latin American Research Network Project on Quality of Life in Urban Neighbourhoods in Latin America and the Caribbean'. Available at: www.iadb.org/res/projects_detail.cfm?id=91.

IDB (Inter-American Development Bank) (2008). *Beyond Facts: Understanding Quality of Life. Development in the Americas*. Washington, DC: IDB and David Rockefeller Center for Latin American Studies.

Kain, J.F., and J.M. Quigley (1975). *Housing Markets and Racial Discrimination: A Microeconomic Analysis*. Cambridge, MA: National Bureau of Economic Research.

Layard, R. (2005), *Happiness: Lessons from a New Science*. Penguin.

Li, M., and J. Brown (1980). 'Micro-neighbourhood externalities and hedonic prices'. *Land Economics*, 56(2): 125–41.

Lora, E., A. Powell, P. Sanguinetti, and B. van Praag (2010). *The Quality of Life in Latin American Cities: Markets and Perception*. Washington, DC: Inter-American Development Bank and World Bank.

Mercer (2010). Quality of Living Worldwide City Ranking – 2010 Mercer Ranking. Available at: www.mercer.com/qualityoflivingpr.

Moulton, B. (1986). 'Random groups effect and the precision of regression estimates'. *Journal of Econometrics*, 32(3): 385–97.

Quality of Life Project (2007). 'Quality of Life '07'. Available at: www.bigcities.govt.nz/pdfs/2007/Quality_of_Life_2007.pdf.

Ridker, R. (1967). *Economic Costs of Air Pollution, Studies in Measurement*. New York: Frederick A. Praeger.

Ridker, R., and J. Henning (1967). 'the determinants of residential property values with special reference to air pollution'. *Review of Economics and Statistics*, 49(2): 246–57.

Roback, J. (1982). 'Wages, rents, and the quality of life'. *The Journal of Political Economy*, 90(6): 1257–78.

Santons, L.D., and I. Martins (2007). 'Monitoring the urban quality of life: the Porto experience'. *Social Indicator Research*, 80: 411–25.

van Praag, B.M.S. (1971). 'The welfare function of income in Belgium: an empirical investigation'. *European Economic Review*, 2(3): 337–69.

van Praag, B.M.S, and B. Baarsma (2005). 'Using happiness surveys to value intangibles: the case of airport noise'. *Economic Journal*, 115(500): 224–46.
van Praag, B.M.S., and A. Ferrer-i-Carbonell (2008). *Happiness Quantified. A Satisfaction Calculus Approach*. Oxford: Oxford University Press.
van Praag, B.M.S., P. Frijters, and A. Ferrer-i-Carbonell (2003). 'The anatomy of subjective well-being'. *Journal of Economic Behavior & Organization*, 51(1): 29–49.
Winkelman, L., and R. Winkelman (1998). 'Why are the unemployed so unhappy'. *Economica*, 65(257): 1–15.
Wolfers, J. (2002). 'Is business cycle volatility costly? evidence from surveys of subjective well being'. *Stanford Graduate School of Business Research Papers*, 1751, Stanford University.

Part IV

Conclusion

12

Towards a New Research Agenda for 21st Century Latin American Urban Development

Dennis Rodgers, Ravi Kanbur, and Jo Beall

The starting premise of this volume was the contention that there exists a real need for Latin American urban development research to engage with cities in a more systemic manner than is currently the case. The dominant discourse about urban contexts in the region sees cities principally as fragmented social spaces, and this has arguably led to something of an intellectual 'impasse'. In particular, it promotes fundamentally dystopian visions of both the nature and potential developmental role of cities in Latin America. However, as all of the contributions to this volume highlight in a range of different ways, even in the most fractured of cities disparate locales, networks, and processes are inevitably relationally connected to each other, and understanding this is critical in order to properly get to grips with contemporary Latin American urban dynamics. Rodgers' contribution, for example, highlights how socio-spatial segregation in São Paulo and Buenos Aires can be fundamentally linked to its seemingly anti-thesis, participatory democracy, while Navarro's chapter explores the integration between the illegal drugs market and the legal urban real estate market in Bolivian cities.

The case for focusing on cities as wholes rather than parts is explicitly made by Jirón in her contribution, which highlights the need to pay attention to the mobility practices of urban inhabitants in order to properly understand their socioeconomic condition. As such, she innovatively offers movement within cities as a fundamental vector for measuring urban quality of life. In a related manner, the contributions by Goytia et al. and Lora and Powell similarly propose more holistic approaches to the measurement of the good life in urban contexts, treating the city as common property rather than simply as epiphenomenal context. At the same time, as economists, they approach measuring the advantages and disadvantages of urban life in terms of benefits and costs. Put simply, agglomeration has economic benefits – economies of scale and scope, for example – and it has costs – congestion, information overload, and so forth. Seen from a policy perspective, an economist's approach, therefore, would effectively be to encourage agglomeration until the marginal costs equal the marginal benefits. In practice, however, managing the balance between the costs and benefits of agglomeration requires purposive action to ensure that the spillover benefits and spillover costs of individual action are appropriately priced. As the contribution by Aliaga-Linares on street market regulation in Santiago de Chile illustrates very well, such action inevitably has distributional consequences, generating both winners and losers, and whether the policies needed to balance costs and benefits will actually emerge depends on how these gains and losses are perceived, and how individuals and communities organize themselves to support or resist the policies. Economic assessment can thus be only one part of an overall study of urban policy.

Davis' contribution on urban violence in Mexico City describes how urban politics are fundamental to dealing with such trade-offs. She draws particular attention to the way that urban political discourse often contains both utopian and dystopian elements, but also highlights how the line between the two is often a very fine one. On the one hand this depends on whose perspective one adopts, as the contribution by Gutiérrez et al. illustrates well, emphasizing how much of contemporary urban politics in Latin American cities revolves around juxtaposing utopian and dystopian elements within the context of a new politics of 'signalling' that is very different from more traditional patron-client or programmatic forms of politicking. Sometimes, however, utopia and dystopia can become blurred. Earle's contribution on illegal occupations by informal housing movements in São Paulo, who justify their actions in terms of legal rights enshrined in the Brazilian constitution, is a case in point in this respect.

The politics of city life are explored at a more prosaic level by Risør in her contribution, which describes how indigenous and class-based traditions of political organization in Bolivia have been re-articulated into a residence-based notion of urban citizenship. She provides a detailed description of the processes of local territorialization through which poor urban dwellers have sought to attain their social, economic, and civil rights, and argues that rather than focusing on traditional forms of (identity) politics, it is now more important to take into account such local urban practices in order to understand contemporary forms of citizenship in Bolivia. This is a point worth dwelling on in a broader Latin American context where the notion of 'citizen security' has become a ubiquitous lens through which to view development in the region (see, for example, Rico and Chinchilla 2002). Although the expression is used to refer to a whole range of social, economic, legal, and political concerns, the etymological root of the word 'citizen' is of course 'city', and in many ways it can be argued that it is perhaps time to return to a more original conception of the word in order to get to grips with contemporary Latin America's development predicament. Cities are not only demographically and economically important in the region, but as almost all of the contributions to this volume highlight, they are also hotbeds of new forms of political action, and the sources of important new policy innovations.

Seen from this broad perspective, what might a new research agenda for 21st century Latin American urban development include? In our introduction to this volume we highlighted how past concerns tended to follow broader development concerns that were often not intrinsically linked to urban dynamics, such as international migration or import substitution, for example. Perhaps the first item for a new Latin American urban development research agenda is to place the city in and of itself at the centre of debates. Although, as the celebrated Nicaraguan poet Pablo Antonio Cuadra put it in a famous essay entitled 'An illness called Managua', cities fundamentally reflect society – 'its grace and its bitterness, its vice and its beauty, its history and its community'[1] – they are also particular entities that both mediate and drive development in ways that have arguably been underexplored in the Latin American context. Of particular importance in this regard, it is clearly critical to also broaden the lens through which we view cities in the region, and that we move away from overly negative visions and towards more holistic approaches that consider both the utopian as well as the dystopian potentialities of urban contexts.

In a related manner, it is also arguably important that Latin American urban research moves towards more syncretic methodological repertoires. As Leeds (1994) famously observed in a still relevant essay reviewing the state of Latin American urban studies, although there are long-standing disciplinary traditions of exploring urban life in the region from a variety of perspectives, most of these tend to focus on a specific location, group, or process within the city – a local neighbourhood, a social network, an economic sector – and rarely connect these to the broader urban context, except at a vague, discursive level. Adopting a more multidisciplinary approach to the study of urban dynamics – both in terms of research methods and thematic focus, but also engagement with a broader, cross-disciplinary secondary literature – would be an obvious means of overcoming this limitation, and would also foster the possibility of making associations that at first glance are by no means obvious, but are potentially highly relevant when thinking about development outcomes. Certainly, as Harriss (2001) has remarked, it is the 'cross-disciplinary' connecting of economic, social, cultural, and political processes that is at the very foundation of development studies, urban or otherwise.

Beyond such general considerations, the contributions to this volume suggest a range of more specific issues that might be part of a new Latin American urban development research agenda. The first is that cities need to be explored in greater detail as systems of order and regulation, be it with regard to the distribution of the economic benefits and costs of agglomeration, the shaping of the nature of political action (both urban and otherwise), or the general conditioning of particular social and cultural practices. In many ways, one could characterize this as a call to revive an urban political economy approach to the study of cities, which, as highlighted in the introduction to this volume, is something that has rather fallen out of favour within the context of Latin American urban development studies during the past quarter-century. At the same time, it is also a way of retaining a sense of the unity of the city, and the way that conceptually distinct elements of urban life are, in practice, deeply interrelated.

A second issue raised by the contributions to this volume concerns the need to rethink conventional understandings of what it means to live in cities. In particular, although there has been something of a 'mobility turn' within the social sciences in recent years – see Sheller and Urry (2006) – mainstream approaches to Latin American urban development have tended to view circulation practices within cities as epiphenomenal rather than inherent to being urban (indeed, it can be argued that the notion of city life is generally approached from decidedly static perspectives such as location, occupation, or identity). Yet, as was famously observed almost a century ago by Chicago School sociologists as they attempted to systematically get to grips with the city as a ontological phenomenon (see Wirth 1938), constant and regular movement is one of the primary characteristics of urban contexts, one that fundamentally sets them apart from rural areas (it is also one of the vectors through which different spheres of urban life are connected, and as such it blurs the boundaries between them, making them difficult to consider in isolation, which further emphasizes the need to consider cities in a systemic manner).

The underlying nature of urban life inevitably shapes the politics of the city, yet there is little in-depth research on the way that particular urban morphologies – whether social or material – can shape political action in cities. By focusing on specifically urban processes, many of the contributions to this volume highlight how standard assumptions about political action – that it is, for example, based on identity, on class, on confrontation, on communication – no longer hold true, or are clearly beginning to weaken, and implicitly call for a renewal of thinking about the intersection between geography – whether social or physical – and politics in Latin American cities. Certainly, although urban politics are by no means a new focus of investigation within the context of Latin American urban development research, it has been a while since new concepts and approaches have been put forward, with the 'new social movements' cultural turn at the beginning of the 1990s – see Alvarez and Escobar (1992) and Alvarez et al. (1998) – probably representing the last significant evolution in this respect. At the same time, it should be stressed that this is not simply a question of replacing one type of categorization with another. One issue specifically raised by contributions to this volume, with regard to both economic and political activity, concerns the way that viewing them through the lens of a formal–informal duality is extremely restrictive due to the fact that such processes often contain both formal and informal elements, and can also move very fluidly between the two states of being.

These issues are admittedly very broad ones, and our discussion in this conclusion has by no means been exhaustive. Generally, though, it has not been our intention to provide a checklist of issues for future research; rather, what we have sought to delineate is an alternative ethos through which to approach Latin American urban development research in the 21st century, one which we hope will be a potential starting point, rather than an end point. As we highlighted in our introduction, thinking about Latin American cities has undergone multiple pendulum swings over the past half-century. This is not necessarily problematic, of course, since it allows for urban development research on the region to regularly renew itself. Over the past few years, however, an impasse has arguably been reached, both theoretically and empirically. To this extent, we contend that it is time to swing the pendulum once again. The direction is open to debate, however, and ultimately what this volume aims to do more than anything else is to encourage the wide community of researchers, policymakers, and activists working on Latin American urban development issues to engage in renewed discussions about current urban conditions in the region. In this way, we hope that new issues will be identified both for the present and the future, whether emergent, seen from new perspectives, through the questioning of received wisdoms, or simply by being re-emphasized.

Note

1. Quoted in Ezequiel D'León Masís, 'Entrevista con Alina Sálomon: Reactivar el viejo centro de Managua', *La Prensa*, 13 December 2002, http://www-ni.laprensa.com.ni/archivo/2002/diciembre/14/literaria/comentario/.

References

Alvarez, S., and A. Escobar (eds) (1992). *The Making of Social Movements in Latin America: Identity, Strategy, and Democracy*. Boulder: Westview Press.

Alvarez S., E. Dagnino, and A. Escobar (eds) (1998). *Cultures of Politics/Politics of Cultures: Revisioning Latin American Social Movements*. Boulder: Westview Press.

Harriss, J. (2001). 'The case for cross disciplinary approaches in international development research', *World Development*, 30(3): 487–96.

Leeds, A. (1994). *Cities, Classes, and the Social Order*. Ithaca: Cornell University Press.

Rico, J.M., and L. Chinchilla (2002). *Seguridad Ciudadana en América Latina*. Mexico City: Siglo XXI.

Sheller, M., and J. Urry (2006). 'The new mobilities paradigm', *Environment and Planning*, A38(2): 207–26.

Wirth, L. (1938). 'Urbanism as a way of life', *American Journal of Sociology*, 44(1): 1–24.

Index

Alliance of Housing Movements, 21
Andean culture, 104
apartheid, 124, 133–4
Apaza, Julian, 119n2
Arequipa, Peru, 7, 24n14
Argentina
see also Buenos Aires
infrastructure services in, 205–24
Autoridad del Centro Histórico, 49–50, 55–6, 58n4

black market, 46–7
Bogotá, Colombia, 22, 187–8, 190–5, 197, 200–1, 227–8, 230, 235
Bolivia, 8, 20
see also specific cities
citizenship in, 103–21, 260–1
cocaine trade and, 62–3
construction in, 73–5
drug production in, 69–76
El Alto, 103–21
indigenous persons in, 105–7
land markets in, 73–6
natural resources in, 120n12
politics, 105–7, 113–14, 260–1
Santiago Segundo, 103–4, 109–18
vecinos, 103–21
Brazil
see also specific cities
urban policies, 130–1
Buenos Aires, Argentina, 6, 9, 22–3, 24n7
crime in, 38
gas programme in, 205–24
housing prices, 235
participatory budgeting in, 135–7
quality of life monitoring in, 230
building occupations, 156–60
business-improvement districts (BIDs), 56

Caldeira, T. P. R., 129–34, 138n9
Calderón, Felipe, 54
Cali, Colombia, 22, 187–8, 193, 194, 198–9, 200
Camacho, Manuel, 58n4
Canada, 169
Caracas, Venezuela, 128
Cardoso, Fernando Henrique, 159
cars, 44
Casarão Santos Dumont, 157–8
cities of hope, 4
citizen participation, 42–3, 53
see also social movements
citizen security, 53, 261
citizenship, 14, 20, 123, 129, 260–1
differentiated, 150–1
indigeneity and, 105–7
insurgent, 15, 117, 145, 150–2
transformation of Bolivian, 103–21
city of walls, 4, 17
see also segregation
civil disobedience, 21, 145, 151–2, 158–61
Civilizacíon y Barbarie (Sarmiento), 4
civil society, 47–9, 114, 131
closed communities, 9–10
closed condominiums, 24n6, 130–1
coca, 61–3, 69–70
cocaine, 19, 61–3
cocaine trade
in Bolivia, 69–76
construction activity and, 71, 73–5
economic effect of, 60–1, 63–9
effects of, 71–3
employment in, 63–6
money laundering and, 66–9
production data, 71–3
coleros, 22
collective action, 42–3, 47–8, 53, 105, 112–16, 127, 145, 160–1, 188–9, 195, 200
Colombia, 22
see also specific cities
cocaine trade and, 62–3

Colombia – *continued*
  crime and violence in, 186–7, 189–90
  inequality in, 187
  politics in, 189–96, 200–1
  taxation in, 196–9
  violence reduction in, 186–202
colonial cities, 6
colonialism, 3, 5–6
common good, 125
community policing, 43
Cómo Vamos system, 227–8
Constitution Plaza, 44
construction, 71, 73–5
contingent democratization, 134–6, 137
coproduction, 206–7
corruption, 38, 42, 49–50, 53, 55
crime, 8–9, 16, 37–9, 60, 186
  see also violence
  in Colombia, 186–7, 189–90
  combating, 53–4
  economic consequences of, 46–7
  fear of, 43–5, 51
  Mexico City, 45, 53
  politics and, 47–50
  property values and, 60
crisis of governance, 14–15
culture of poverty, 11–12

decentralization, 7, 113, 120n11
deliberative democracy, 125–8
democracy, 20–1, 53
  deliberative, 125–8
  participatory, 123–39
  representative, 125
democratization, 123–39
deregulation, 7
de Soto, Hernando, 167
differentiated citizenship, 150–1
disembedding, 9–10, 24n7
downtown areas, 44–6, 148–50
drug trade, 16, 19, 38, 60–77
  in Bolivia, 69–76
  economic effect of, 60–1, 63–9
  land markets and, 63–6
  money laundering and, 66–9
  roots of, 61–3
dystopian representations, 4, 11, 17

Ebrard, Marcelo, 49, 54, 58n4
economy
  effect of drug trade on, 60–9
  impact of violence and insecurity on local, 46–7
El Alto, Bolivia, 20, 103–21
El Salvador, 38
employment
  in cocaine industry, 63–6
  money laundering and, 66–7, 77n6
Empresas Públicas de Medellín (EPM), 197–8
environmental sustainability, 44
Eurostats, 227, 228
extraordinary events, 125, 134–6

Fajaro, Sergio, 192–3, 198
farmers markets, 165–83
fear, 41, 43–5, 51
feriantes (street vendors), 21–2
ferias libres, 165–83
fiscal reforms, 196–9
fortified enclaves, 9
Fox, Vincente, 48–9
fractured cities perspective, 5, 18, 96–7, 124
free market, 7
Fundación Pro Vivienda Social (FPSV), 206

gangs, 16, 186, 243
gas programme, 205–24
gastrointestinal diseases, 210
gated communities, 9, 24n6, 43, 83–4, 97n4, 130–1, 165–6
Geneva, Switzerland, 227
gentrification, 178–80
ghettoization, 186
Giuliani, Rudolph, 41
globalization, 24n7
governance
  Colombia, 194–6
  crisis of, 14–15
  democratic, 123–39
  local, 15, 54–7
  Mexico City, 54–7
  urban, 20–1
grid pattern, 6
Guerrero, Rodrigo, 193

gun trade, 38
Guzmán, Mauricio, 199

Habermas, Jürgen, 44
happiness indicators, 229–30
health impacts, of infrastructure improvements, 205, 207–8, 210–11, 216, 221–3
hedonic price approach, 229, 231–41, 245–9
homicides, 186, 189
housing infrastructure, 205–24
housing market prices, 229, 231–2, 235–7, 239–41, 246–9
housing movements, in São Paulo, 145–62, 260
human development index (HDI), 230

Iberian colonialism, 3, 5–6
identity politics, 260–1
illegal city, 146–50
immigrants, 6, 24n5
import substitution industrialization (ISI), 6–7
income inequality, 8–9, 146
income multiplier, 75
indigenous culture, 104
indigenous people, 105–7
industrial clustering, 6–7
industrialization, 3, 6–7
inequality, 8–9, 20, 80–9, 124, 129, 132, 137, 146, 187, 207
informal economy, 13, 46–7, 166, 167
informal neighborhoods, 208–10
Information System of Ferias Libres (SIFL), 177–8
infrastructure improvements, 205–24
insecurity, 9, 19, 37–8
  see also violence-insecurity nexus
institutional reforms, Mexico City, 54–7
Instituto Ciudadano de Estudios Sobre la Insecuridad (ICESI), 53–4
insurgent citizenship, 15, 117, 145, 150–2
international migration, 6, 24n5
irregular urbanization, 21
irregulatory, 150–2

Johannesburg, South Africa, 133–4

Katari, Tupac, 119n2
kidnapping, 46

labour markets, 8, 11
labour opportunities, 7, 8
land markets
  in Bolivia, 73–6
  cocaine trade and, 63–6
  money laundering and, 66–9
Latin American cities
  see also specific cities
  colonial, 6
  conceptions of, 4
  crime in, 38–40, 186
  democratization and, 123–39
  patterns of development, 5–10
  physical layout of, 6
  quality of life monitoring in, 227–53
  research on, 4–5, 10–16, 259–64
  rethinking, 3–25
  violence in, 37–58
Latin American society, 4
law enforcement, 38, 41–2, 54
  see also police
Law of the City, 130–1, 138n9
Lefebvre, Henri, 153
life opportunities, 150
life satisfaction approach, 229–30, 241–9
Lima, Peru, 7, 167–8, 230
local governance, 15, 54–7
López, Manuel, 48–9
low-income housing, 61, 83, 95, 97n2, 132, 145, 147–9
Lula da Silva, Luiz Inacio, 150

Managua, Nicaragua, 9–10
marginality, 11
marginal settlements, 10
Martínez, Julio César, 199
meandering, 153
Medellín, Colombia, 22, 187–8, 192–5, 197–8, 200–1, 230, 235
media
  politics and, 194–5
  violence in the, 41

mega-cities, 7
mega-projects, 24n6
Mercer rankings, 227
Mexico
  see also Mexico City
  politics, 47–50, 54
  urban-urban migration, 8
Mexico City, 19
  crime in, 38, 45
  fear of public spaces in, 43–4
  institutional reforms, 54–7
  police, 49–50, 54–7, 58n3
  politics, 48–50
  public sphere in, 43–6, 51–2
  renewal of, 45–6, 51–2
  results of changes in, 50–4
  social exclusion/inclusion, 52–3
  social infrastructure, 40
  violence in, 43–6, 260
middle-sized cities, 7–8
migration, 6–8, 11, 24n5
mobility, 19–20, 80–98, 262–3
  conceptualizing, 85–6
  practices, 86–95
  urban inequality and, 80–4
Mockus, Antanas, 191–4, 197
modernity, 4
money laundering, 19, 66–9, 75, 77n6
Montevideo, Uruguay, 128, 230
Morales, Evo, 20, 105, 106
More, Thomas, 126
municipal taxes, 196–9

National Forum for Urban Reform (FNRU), 152–4
natural gas services, 205–24
natural resources, 120n12
neighbourhood characteristics, 233–41, 243, 245–9
neighbourhood organizations, in Bolivia, 103–21
neoliberalism, 14–15, 114, 129–32, 167, 169
new urban segregation, *see* segregation
New Zealand, 227, 228
nongovernmental organizations (NGOs), 43

open-air markets, regulation of, 166–83
over-urbanization, 4, 11

Paraguay, 8
participatory budgeting, 125–6, 128, 135–7
participatory democracy, 123–39
Partido Acción Nacional (PAN), 48
Partido de la Revolución (PRD), 48
Partido Revolucionario Institucional (PRI), 48
patronage politics, 55
peasant wars, 186–7
Peñalosa, Enrique, 191–2, 194
Pérez, Luis, 192
peripheral areas, 146–52, 160
Peru
  see also Lima, Peru
  cocaine trade and, 62–3
police, 38, 41–2
  community policing, 43
  corruption, 42, 49–50, 53, 55
  Mexico City, 49–50, 54–7, 58n3
  private, 42
policy innovation, 188–90, 200–1, 261
political economy problem, 127
politics
  Bolivian, 105–7, 113–14, 260–1
  Colombia, 189–96, 200–1
  identity, 260–1
  in the "margins of the state", 114–17
  Mexico, 47–50, 54
  patronage, 55
  of poverty, 13–14
  of signalling, 194–6, 200
  urban, 22, 24n8, 188–90, 263
  violence-insecurity nexus and, 47–50
pollution, 44
population movements, 6–7
Porto Alegre, Brazil, 126, 128
Portuguese colonizers, 6
post-colonial period, 6
poverty, 8, 38
  culture of, 11–12
  politics of, 13–14

power relations, 135
pre-Columbian societies, 3, 5
primacy effect, 6–7
private security, 42, 47, 50–1
privatization, 44
property rights, 161
property values, 60
public goods, 23, 206–7
public spaces, 135
 fear of, 43–4
 renewal of, 51–2
public sphere, 43–6, 51–2, 135–6
public transportation, 44, 86–97
public utilities, 197–8, 205–24

quality of life (QoL) indices, 230
quality of life monitoring, 227–53
 hedonic price approach, 229, 231–41, 245–9
 life satisfaction approach, 241–9
 public decision-making and, 250–1
Quality of Life Report, 227, 228

real estate
 cocaine trade and, 63–6
 money laundering and, 67–9
Redes Solidarias programme, 22–3, 205–24
regulations, on open-air markets, 166–83
representative democracy, 125
Residential Leasing Programme (PAR), 159
residential segregation, 20, 80–4, 97n3, 132, 146–50, 166, 178–81
respiratory diseases, 208, 210
right to the centre, 154–6
right to the city, 153–6
Rio de Janeiro, Brazil
 crime in, 38
 slums of, 15–16
Rio del Plata, Argentina, 169
robberies, 45, 46
rural-urban migration, 6–7, 8, 11
rural zone, 148

Salazar, Alonso, 193
San José, Costa Rica, 230, 235, 239, 243
Santiago de Chile, 9, 21–2
 ferias regulation in, 165–83
 income distribution in, 82
 low-income housing, 83
 mobility issues in, 80–98
 segregation in, 81–4
Santiago Segundo, Bolivia, 103–4, 109–18
São Paulo, Brazil, 21, 124
 building occupations, 156–60
 crime in, 38
 downtown areas, 148–50
 growth of, 160
 housing movements of, 145–62
 income inequalities, 146
 Master Plan for, 131–2
 participatory democracy in, 129–32
 peripheral areas, 146–52, 160
 population of, 146
 segregation in, 146–50
 slums, 148–9
 social mobilization in, 150–2
 urban policies, 153–6
secondary cities, 7–8
security
 citizen, 53, 261
 private, 42, 47, 50–1
security-industrial complex, 50–1
segregation, 9–10, 16, 20–1, 80–4, 97n3, 129, 130–1, 137, 146–50, 154, 166, 178–81
sensationalism, 41
'separate but equal' development, 124, 133–4
shantytowns, 10–16, 17
signalling, politics of, 194–6, 200
Slim, Carlos, 45, 58n4
slums, 10–16, 17, 148–9
social consequences, of violence-insecurity nexus, 40–3
social development index (SFO), 230
social exclusion/inclusion, 52–3, 86, 96–7, 154
social justice, 134–5
social mobilization, 21, 42–3, 53
social movements, 14–15, 21, 24n14, 145–62
social services, 8
social stigma, 150

socioeconomic segregation, 20–1
South Africa, 124, 133–4, 161
Spanish colonizers, 6
spatial segregation, 80–4, 129–31, 154
Special Zones of Interest (ZEIS), 132
squeegee men, 42
state margins, 114–17
street market regulation, 21–2, 165–83
street vendors, 42, 165–83
subaltern class, 106, 128
suburban infrastructure, 44
suburbanization, 51–2
supermarkets, 165–6, 178–80, 274–5
sustainable urban development, 23

taxation, 196–9
television, 194–5
Toscana, Alejandra Moreno, 58n4

UMM, *see* Uniao de Moradores Municipaes (UMM)
unemployment, 8, 37, 180–1
Uniao de Moradores Municipaes (UMM), 21, 152–62
United Kingdom, 169
United States, 169
Urban Audit system, 227, 228
urban culture, 3
urban development
  holistic approach to, 23
  key issues in, 10–17
  patterns of Latin American, 5–10
  policies, 17
  research agenda for, 259–64
  'separate but equal', 124, 133–4
  sustainable, 23
urban imagination, 4–5
urban inequality, 80–4
  see also inequality
urban infrastructure, 150, 205–24
urbanism, 43
urbanization, 3–5
  see also urban development
  costs-benefits of, 260
  drug trade and, 60–1
urban life, quality of life monitoring, 227–53
urban mobility, *see* mobility
urban planning, 169
urban policies
  Brazil, 130–1, 153–6
  innovation in, 188–90, 200–1
  on open-air markets, 166–83
  quality of life monitoring and, 250–1
  to reduce violence, 186–202
urban politics, 22, 24n8, 188–90, 263
urban poverty, 8
urban primacy, 7
urban renewal, 45–6, 51–2
urban-urban migration, 8
utopian representations, 4, 11, 17, 126–7

vecinos, 20, 103–21
Vespucci, Americo, 61–2
Vienna, Austria, 227
violence, 9, 15–16, 19, 22, 37–58, 129, 260
  reduction, in Colombia, 186–202
  responses to, 41–3
violence-insecurity nexus, 39–58
  economic consequences of, 46–7
  institutional framework for enabling progress on, 54–7
  political consequences of, 47–50
  spatial consequences of, 43–6
  urban social consequences of, 40–3

water supply, 44
water war, 120n12

youth gangs, 16, 186, 243

zero tolerance, 41–2
zona de mineros, 109–17
Zurich, Switzerland, 227